MONEY

GOING OUT OF

STYLE

The story of money
and the mystery of its demise

Zvi Schreiber

www.zvi.net/money

ZEDESS
publishing

ISBN:
978-0-9833968-5-7 (paperback)
978-0-9833968-6-4 (ePub)

Library of Congress Control Number: 2021910363

Cover design: Nabin Karna

ZEDESS PUBLISHING

First edition 2021-08-12

Also by the author:

A young woman time travels to meet Galileo, Newton, Einstein, and unravel the secrets of our universe.

CONTENTS

INTRODUCTION

Far out in the uncharted backwaters of the unfashionable end of the Western Spiral arm of the Galaxy lies... a little blue green planet whose ape-descended forms... were unhappy for pretty much of the time. Many solutions were suggested for this problem, most... concerned with the movements of small green pieces of paper, which is odd because... it wasn't the small green pieces of paper that were unhappy.

Douglas Adams, Hitchhiker's Guide to the Galaxy

WHAT ARE THOSE small pieces of paper? What does a $10 bill or the two-tone €2 coin actually represent? What does the statement emailed to me every month by my bank mean? And why do I attach such importance to the number on its bottom line?

I have long had a vague intuition that stuff is real, and money is not. "Stuff" is my shorthand term for goods and services, including, where context allows, assets such as land, homes, and tools; in other words, everything you can consume, utilize, or experience.

At most, I believed that money is a shorthand way of keeping track of stuff and who owes stuff to whom. If money is really a way of keeping track of stuff owed, and since there is a balance between those who owe and those who are owed stuff, shouldn't the total value of money be zero?

This book is my attempt to clarify my own thoughts about how the economy actually works, and the role of money in the economy. My original motivation for thinking about an island tribe, which gradually develops commerce and money, was a desire to gain a better understanding of the daily news, financial activities, such as using a bank, and periodic financial turmoil, such as the 2008 crisis and the recession triggered by Covid-19. I hope my readers will find this approach to understanding the economy as enlightening as I did.

As I recreated the fundamentals of economics by way of a simple story, I found that many of my intuitions were confirmed—that money is essentially a shorthand way of tracking stuff, and that, in some senses, the total value of money in the world is zero. But it all depends on exactly what you mean by "money," which turns out to be rather more complicated than I had expected.

This story of economics puts money in its rightful place: secondary to *stuff*. And the book is not expensive, which really means that you won't have to give up too much other stuff to own it!

Embarking on my journey to better understand money, the first thing I discovered, very much to my surprise, was that the modern concept of money is actually younger than me! I say this to emphasize how young modern money is.

When I was born in 1969, each U.S. dollar represented 1.1 grams (or 1/35 of a troy ounce) of physical gold, sitting in the basement of the Federal Reserve Bank in Manhattan, or in Fort Knox, Kentucky. I was born in England, and the British pound, like most major currencies, was at that time pegged to the U.S. dollar, at exactly $2.40.

As a two-year-old child, I could have taken a 50-pence coin (half a British pound), with its controversial seven-sided shape (*heptagonal*, apparently), and I could have exchanged it for exactly $1.20. If I could have somehow reached Manhattan, $0.30 would have bought me a ride on the subway to 33 Liberty Street, and I would still have had $0.90 left to exchange at the *Fed* for exactly 1 gram of pure bullion gold.

As a two-year-old, I might not have known what to do with a gram of gold, but at least I could have held it in my hand, felt the cold metal, and admired its yellowish gleam. And even as a toddler, this little exercise would have helped me understand what a 50-pence coin meant: it was a token that could be exchanged for one subway ride plus a tiny nugget of yellowish metal.

By my third birthday, everything had changed. One morning in August 1971, President Nixon decided that he didn't fancy exchanging dollars for gold anymore. This was called the "Nixon Shock" because Richard Nixon didn't consult me in advance of the announcement. Nor, for that matter, did he consult any of the world leaders whose currencies were pegged to the dollar.

Soon afterwards, the UK decided that if the dollar wasn't backed by gold, it no longer cared to link the pound to the dollar. Almost overnight, money became nebulous. True, there have been other times in history when the convertibility of money to gold has been suspended, but only as a temporary measure.

Would people still trust and desire money when it no longer had any guaranteed underlying value? President Nixon soon received positive confirmation that they would, when the Watergate burglars blackmailed him. This new type of money was clearly still desirable.

Although money retained its allure even without the backing of gold, its value did become less stable. The dollar price of that NYC subway ride has increased tenfold since Nixon's time, and the British pound is worth about half as many dollars as it was then. Then again, borders have been opening, and 50 pence, when exchanged for yuan, will still buy multiple rides on the subway in Beijing.

On a positive note, thanks to Nixon, money, and the economy it drives, has become a source of great confusion—and therefore an interesting subject for a short book published around the half-century anniversary of the Nixon Shock.

While researching money, I learned a lot of things which I aim to share by way of a story. Firstly, I learned that fiat (besides being an acronym for *Fabbrica Italiana di Automobili Torino*, the Italian car) also means a decree, and that modern money is actually "fiat money" because it has no intrinsic value other than by government decree and social convention. I learned that most money is created by commercial banks, not by governments, and I started to worry that bank money might not be a positive force in the world.

I learned that cash and checking account balances are two very different things; that economists often pretend that they understand money and the economy a lot better than they do; that the Fed and other central bankers seem to claim that they can control the economy rather better than they can. Even if they knew how the economy worked in the twentieth century, it's all changed in the last two decades. I learned that the U.S., Europe, and China have chosen three distinct solutions to the same central "trilemma" of international finance. I learned that trilemma is a word.

Every day on the news we hear politicians discuss interest rates, government deficits, government debt, and tax policy. Never has monetary policy been more confusing than during the Covid-19 pandemic, during which the Fed printed close to two trillion dollars of brand-new money.

By the time you reach the end of this book, I hope you will understand these issues at least as well as the politicians interviewed on the news. Fortunately, this is not a very high bar.

Author's note

I HAVE CHOSEN to introduce the basic concepts of money and *macroeconomics* (the overall behavior of an economy) through a story which takes place on a fictional island. The developments on this island vaguely mirror the historical development of economics and money, at a highly accelerated pace. But my emphasis is on building up the concepts in a logical way rather than recreating the correct historical chronology.

EACH SHORT CHAPTER ends with **notes** which are formatted like this. These offer a quick discussion of how the developments on the island relate to what we see in today's world or what happened historically. I will use the first person "I" in the notes, mainly in the later sections of the book, to indicate when I am sharing my own personal opinion or insight which may not be part of the consensus of economists. I am not a professional economist, which gives me the advantage of being able to take a fresh look at some issues, as well as the obvious disadvantages of less experience and expertise. But when I find myself feeling insecure about my status as an amateur, I remind myself how often professional economists get things wrong.

Once all the basics of economics have been covered, by following the development of our island economy, we skip a couple of centuries, and the book examines modern issues, tackling the erratic and worrisome behavior of money as it approaches the age of fifty and beyond. If you already know all about economics, you may wish to skip directly to sections VII and VIII which address modern-day issues.

I mostly use the U.S. economy as an example in the text. This does not reflect an American-centric worldview. Rather it's because the U.S. is the world's largest economy, has excellent public data, and is often a trendsetter. In most respects, the EU economy, in aggregate, has similar parameters to that of the US. Other developed economies also typically have similar characteristics, although they are proportionally smaller.

In footnotes, I unashamedly make extensive use of Wikipedia, as it is such a rich, accessible, and generally high-quality resource;[1] academics can always find the primary sources from the Wikipedia article references.

So here it is, the story of economics, with money taking a back seat to the real economy of *stuff.*

Acknowledgements

WRITING AND RESEARCHING this book has been a family effort. Many thanks to my wife Rina Frei Schreiber, son Daniel Schreiber, parents David Schreiber and Ruth Schreiber, sisters Tamar Daniel and Avital Schreiber Levy, brothers Arye Schreiber and Daniel Schreiber for their insightful feedback and encouragement. Also, thanks to my writing buddy Ben Dansker, friend Joshua Fox, and to other editors I consulted, Kelly Davis, Jeff Edwards, Joel Pierson, Brian Baker, and Jeremy Clift.

PROLOGUE

A TRIBE NUMBERING a few hundred people lives on a tropical island. The island has a river, some fruit trees, berries, nuts, and corn. The occasional gaggle of geese waddles by. The island is also endowed with natural resources such as iron deposits and traces of gold in the river.

For centuries, the islanders are hunter-gatherers, and they spend all their days, well, hunting and gathering. The opportunities for hunter-gatherer societies to break out of the poverty cycle, and accumulate some wealth, are incredibly slim. First, the tribe will have to develop agriculture, just as some societies started to do around 12,000 years ago in the first agricultural revolution, during the Stone Age.

We join our desert island tribe after they progress beyond hunting and gathering and develop farming. There are apple orchards and orange groves, and the islanders cultivate mushrooms and take care to replant some of the corn and berries that they pick. Over time, through selective breeding, their crops are domesticated, evolving to become larger and sweeter. And yet, as the food supply increases through farming, the island population grows, and they are always struggling to sustain themselves.

What will happen to the tribe in the long term? Will they continue living on the verge of starvation for generations? Will they battle over resources, killing each other and reducing their numbers until the remaining population can eat more comfortably? Or might they, in fact, grow richer over time?

All three scenarios are possible, and all three have played out at different times in human history. Up to around the year 1700 CE, strong economic growth was rare, and most countries changed little economically during most centuries.[2] In stark contrast, since around the year 1800, most of the world has experienced spectacular economic growth. This book focuses on how this more positive scenario plays out.

I. THE BASICS

PRIVATE OWNERSHIP

THE TRIBE SHARES all the food that they farm, gather, and hunt. There is a designated spot on the beach known fondly as the depot, where all food is stockpiled and then distributed daily. The depot also stores non-food commodities such as firewood and flint.

One day, Paula finds a nugget of gold in the river. She finds it aesthetically pleasing and notices with satisfaction that it shows no sign of rust. The metal is fairly firm but also pliable if subjected to sufficient force. She punctures a hole in it and wears it on a string around her neck. The sight of her necklace triggers an uproar amongst other members of the tribe. It is quickly decided that all gold nuggets, rare shells, and other ornaments shall also be pooled in the depot.

Over the next few decades, the island's population expands to over a thousand people, and not everyone is acquainted with everyone else anymore. Some people don't even know each other's names.

The air is hot, and Charlie is standing at the foot of a coconut tree at the end of a tiring day in the field. An agile teenager, Charlie can scale a coconut tree like no other islander. Panting, he gently rubs his aching thighs, while straining his neck to glance vertically upwards at the green spheres, imagining their sweet milk and white flaky fruit.

Will an exhausted Charlie make the extra effort to climb the tree and pick a couple more bunches of coconuts? He may be a decent enough young man, but he's only human. If he will feast on the coconuts by himself, he'll probably make that extra effort. If he has to share the coconuts with his immediate family, or a tight-knit group of close friends, he might still make the climb. But Charlie knows that each coconut has to be deposited in the depot, to be shared with a thousand other people, most of whom are strangers to him.

Eventually, Charlie does make the effort to ascend the tree; he throws down a dozen coconuts and descends a little clumsily. At one point Charlie maneuvers his tired left foot, and the branch stub supporting his right foot snaps right off; Charlie finds himself dangling precariously from one hand.

As he regains his composure and completes the descent, a squirrel runs past Charlie and stashes a nut in a small hole halfway up a nearby banyan tree trunk. Charlie stops and stares at the nut stash for a while. Completing his descent, he finds himself a discreet spot between some bushes, cracks a couple of coconuts open with some rocks, and starts to drink the milky coconut water.

By chance, Bella is within earshot as the first coconut explodes, and she follows the sound right to Charlie's hideout. "Erm, you're on the way to the depot, with those, are you Charlie?"

"Take a hike, Bell. I almost died on the climb."

"Oh, the climb was tough. Why didn't you say so? Don't worry about it, no need to share your coconuts. You enjoy them, Charlie. Just one thing. I will keep the berries I picked today for myself, thank you very much."

And although Charlie tries to explain to Bella that he deserves these particular coconuts for himself, she isn't convinced and turns him in. Pretty soon everyone is saying, "Well, if Charlie is hoarding coconuts and Bella isn't sharing berries, I'm not pooling my…"

Within days the island's sharing system is in tatters. Suddenly everything is "mine" or "yours." A committee is appointed to shut down the depot and distribute the remaining supplies equally to all islanders, who would now own them privately. A few weeks—and hundreds of arguments—later, the depot is empty.

As time goes by, private ownership motivates everyone to work harder. Now Charlie always climbs the extra tree. Bella keeps planting and picking berries, even in the failing light of dusk. Arthur wakes up 30 minutes earlier to start his fishing at the crack of dawn. And so, overall, the production of food on the island expands.

But Martha is elderly, and while she cultivates some mushrooms and picks berries near her home, she cannot possibly sustain herself. Under the sharing system, she ate well and honorably. Now she's dependent on charity.

And so, the evolution from a community built on sharing to one built on private ownership is a critical, though somewhat brutal, milestone on the island's journey to improved fortunes. Private ownership increases motivation to produce more, but it also increases inequality.

IN THE REAL WORLD, societal sharing, inspired by the ideas of Karl Marx, was one of the largest and most disastrous experiments of the twentieth century, with communist countries from Russia and China to Cuba and North Korea struggling with poverty and at times starvation, while countries with capitalist private ownership generally thrived.

One intriguing turning point was when the soon-to-be Russian president, Boris Yeltsin, visited a Texas supermarket in 1989 and was overwhelmed to discover that even unskilled laborers in the U.S. had access to a far greater variety of goods than anyone in the Soviet Union, even then president, Mikhail Gorbachev.[3] Two years later, Yeltsin left the Communist Party and began making reforms to bring back private ownership and private enterprise to Russia.

At the time of writing, every country in the world recognizes private ownership, although four countries still label themselves communist: China, Cuba, Laos, and Vietnam.

There is an ongoing and probably eternal debate about the right balance between private ownership and some elements of social sharing or social insurance, which we will return to later.

DIVISION OF LABOR

ONE MORNING MARTHA finds Charlie picking mushrooms.

"Good morning, young man. Say, why aren't you collecting coconuts? I can pick mushrooms."

"So, you can, Auntie Martha, but I can pick mushrooms faster than you."

Martha stares at the boy. "Yes, indeed. No doubt. But then again, you can climb a coconut tree like no one else. I do think I have some comparative advantage picking mushrooms."

"What comparative advantage? Watch me, I pick mushrooms faster than you."

"Yes, Charlie. But tell me this: what do you think will work better for the island, me cultivating mushrooms while you scale coconut trees? Or you cultivating mushrooms while I attempt to climb trees?"

Charlie leaves the mushrooms to Martha. Over time, more and more islanders specialize in the one activity at which they are the most skilled, or where they are at least relatively skilled. Martha becomes expert at germinating mushroom spores on rotten logs. Brody spends all his time growing apples, while Charlie spends much of his day up coconut trees.

Specialization becomes the second major milestone in increasing the island's production and improving the island's well-being.

ADAM SMITH, often called the Father of Modern Economics, opened *The Wealth of Nations*, his classic work on capitalism written in the 1700s, with a chapter on the division of labor. In this chapter he described visiting a pin factory where he witnessed the process of producing a pin divided into 18 subprocesses, with each laborer specializing in just one or two subprocesses.

Since the time of Adam Smith, specialization has continued apace. At the time of writing, CareerPlanner.com lists no fewer than 12,000 job titles.

The term *comparative advantage* is most often used to compare skills between countries,[4] which we will return to much later. But the same principle applies to individual skills. Martha does not have an absolute advantage over Charlie in picking mushrooms but there is a *comparative advantage* to her picking mushrooms. She picks mushrooms well enough, and this frees up Charlie to pick coconuts, which he can do far more efficiently than her.

BARTER

PRIVATE OWNERSHIP and the division of labor create a rather obvious problem on the island. Martha can't survive on a diet of mushrooms, and Charlie is growing sick of coconuts. With specialization comes the need to barter, with people swapping the goods they personally produce, for various foods they need or want. People barter for services as well, for example, Charlie offers Fred a coconut in exchange for a haircut.

As the people of the island start specializing, the tribe sets up a marketplace where people meet each Monday and Thursday to inspect each other's goods, and to trade.

Charlie often trades a coconut with Bella, in return for a cupful of berries. Brody trades two apples with Arthur, in exchange for a fish. Each islander trades the stuff they produce for the stuff they desire.

Unfortunately, the system is far from perfect. One day Charlie says, "No way, Bella. I couldn't eat another berry."

"You're kidding me." Bella glances up and down Charlie's neat pyramid of coconuts. "How can you possibly resist these sweet berries? OK, if you don't want berries, what do you fancy?"

"I was counting on having fish for dinner. But Arthur doesn't want a coconut."

Bella strides over to Arthur and trades some berries for a fish. Coming back to Charlie, she slaps the fish on the counter of his market stall and helps herself to two big coconuts from the top of the pyramid.

"You're welcome," she says.

So now all three of them have what they desire. Effectively, the two trades were equivalent to a three-way trade, where Bella gave Arthur berries, Arthur gave Charlie a fish, and Charlie gave Bella a coconut. But for just a few minutes Bella was stuck with a fish she didn't want, trusting she could trade it for the coconuts.

A couple of weeks later, Bella is faced with a situation where neither Charlie nor Arthur want berries. Bella glances round the market. She could keep trading berries for other products until she obtains something that Charlie would accept. But this would be a time-consuming and risky strategy. It's also quite difficult to keep track of the relative value of dozens of products. "How many mushrooms are a cupful of berries worth? How many apples for a fish?"

Bella ends up eating her own berries for dinner that evening. Again.

Practically everyone on the island is now producing one specialized product and wants to trade most of that product for other goods and services. Barter is providing an imperfect solution.

IN THIS CHAPTER we introduced barter—that is, trading goods and services for other goods and services. We encountered the limitation of the barter system, namely there isn't always a *coincidence of wants*; most people want to trade stuff, but any given pair of people may not want each other's stuff at the same time. We will come back to the solution to this problem, which—as you may have guessed—is money. But first, let's explore some of the other, rather important, economic concepts that can develop, even in a moneyless society.

Bartering is deeply ingrained in human nature. Every relationship is based on explicit or implicit *give and take*. I do the dishes while you take out the trash. I give you support when you're feeling down today, you support me tomorrow, and so on.

More formal bartering still exists as a secondary way of conducting business even in developed, money-based economies. Several organizations promote bartering, including the International Reciprocal Trade Association and the U.S.-based National Association of Trade Exchanges.

The aim of this chapter is to introduce the concept of trade, before introducing the concept of money, without necessarily implying that this was indeed the historical progression. Although textbooks generally teach that barter gave way to money, as in our story, David Graeber has argued that historically money appeared *before* barter, and debt and credit preceded money.[5]

CAPITAL AND INVESTMENT

PAULA'S ORANGE TREES are flourishing. In fact, they are growing a little too well, as Paula can no longer reach the fruit. Paula tries to climb the trees; she shakes the tree trunks; she balances herself on piles of rocks; and she tries hitting the branches with a thick stick. All the time, Paula is imagining what life would be like if she had a ladder, enabling her to zip up and down orange trees, one after another.

Slowly Paula constructs the ladder in her mind. She imagines two long logs with a series of ten holes in each, and branches of medium thickness threaded through the parallel holes to form rungs. She reckons each hole would take at least a day to drill with available stone tools. And she would have to find or cut the right logs and branches. Paula estimates that the whole project would take a month of hard full-time labor.

What would she eat for that month?

Paula goes to the market. "Charlie, would you lend me thirty coconuts?"

"What?" Charlie says.

"I need a stash of food to live on while I build a ladder."

"And what's in it for me?"

"Well, the ladder will be a valuable asset, a tool that will help me to pick more oranges. What if I let you borrow the ladder from time to time?"

"Your ladder is going to be as high as a coconut palm?" Charlie looks upward.

"Well, no. But it will help us to have more oranges on the island."

"Your oranges."

"Yeah, OK, Charlie. Look, I'll reward you. When I repay the loan, I'll give you ten percent more oranges than the usual trade for coconuts. Think of it as saving. You give up some food now, but you have even more food in a few weeks' time. Ten percent for just a few weeks."

Paula also borrows some corn, berries, and mushrooms, and then she sets to work. The island is poor, and she has to pay exorbitant interest rates of around ten percent, to persuade anyone to give up some food for just a few weeks. But she eventually scrapes together four weeks' worth of survival rations.

A month later, a hungry and tired Paula is the proud owner of a ladder. Soon she is picking oranges at twice her previous rate, which adds to the food production of the island. And over the next few weeks, Paula has little trouble repaying her loans plus the agreed interest.

With the newly abundant supply, oranges start getting a bit cheaper in the market. So Paula does pretty well, but she's disappointed to find that she isn't quite as rich as she anticipated. And every other islander also enjoys a slight benefit from Paula's ladder. For example, Charlie can now get three oranges for each of his coconuts instead of two. "Hmm. You see, Charlie, you are getting some benefit from my ladder," Paula says as she begrudgingly hands over three oranges.

Paula is already thinking about her next investment, weaving a large basket for transporting oranges. And her entrepreneurship doesn't go unnoticed by others. Arthur starts making plans to invest in producing a wooden cart with wheels for transporting his fish. Paula and Arthur will have to take loans, which means they too will have to persuade other people to delay gratification and save, by granting them an interest-bearing loan to finance their investment.

As tools slowly accumulate on the island, production increases: there is more food being harvested, as well as other new products and services. The owners of the tools benefit most from this trend, but the entire island is better off as a result of the increased production, with various products becoming cheaper and more abundant.

In every case, the people producing the tools have to take a break from producing other goods. This means that they, and the people providing them with loans, must put up with delayed gratification, in the expectation of accelerated production later. If they are patient, their loans will be repaid with interest, to compensate them for the delay.

Over months and years, as tools accumulate and production increases, the island gradually gets richer. Delaying gratification becomes slightly easier, and interest rates ease downward.

A TOOL, such as a ladder or basket, that aids production is called *capital*. Creating the first capital is a huge strain for the island, as poor islanders have to postpone critical food production in order to invest their time and skills in capital creation. But it's worth the effort, as capital is a major engine of growth. Accumulation of capital is a virtuous cycle: the more capital the islanders create, the more productive the economy achieves, and the easier it becomes to spare some resources to invest in further capital creation.

Capital accumulation is central to societies getting richer over time.

In common contemporary language, *capital* may not only refer to tools, but also to the money which finances their creation, as in *venture capital*.

And as we have seen, capital creation is closely tied to the availability of such credit. But in strict economics parlance, *capital* refers to the actual tools. And in this book, *capital* is always used in the strict sense of assets which are used to accelerate or enhance production.

While introducing the term *capital*, it's worth mentioning that in line with the U.N. system for national accounts, in this book the term *capital* includes homes. This keeps things simple. You may argue that homes are something else again, a consumer asset, not a capital tool for business. But in fact, many homes are owned by landlords who are in the business of renting out homes, and these are clearly business capital. Even people buying homes for their own use are, in fact, making an investment in an asset which will provide them with dwelling services over time.

In the United States, businesses now own $18.5 trillion worth of capital,[6] including factories, vehicles, machinery, tools, software, office furniture, staplers, and paperclips, all of which help those businesses to produce a record quantity and variety of goods and services. The accumulated stock of capital is a major distinction between developed and developing countries, allowing developed countries to produce far more goods and services per worker.

LABOR AND BUSINESS

THANKS TO AGRICULTURE, specialization, and now the accumulation of some capital tools, such as ladders, nets, baskets, and hand tools, the island is finally producing more food than its people need to survive. Bella sees an opportunity to start a business producing and selling the island's first luxury goods, some simple jewelry. However, crafting jewelry is not something she can undertake on her own—it involves a combination of several skills, including design, collecting shells, mining and smelting metal, and workmanship.

At this point, Arthur is completing his fishing in half a day, assisted by the capital assets of nets and trolleys; and Brody is only busy part-time tending to his apples. So Bella employs Brody part-time to collect shells, and

Arthur to prospect for iron. She pays them in berries, which they either eat or trade for other goods in the market. Arthur and Brody become the island's first laborers. They are bartering their labor in exchange for some of the goods that they help produce.

And Bella now owns the island's first business with employees, a jewelry production and retail business. Over time, Bella invests in premises, a large hut on her patch of land, and an assortment of pliers and other capital tools. She promotes her brand as "Bella's Jewelry" with each piece of jewelry embellished with a distinctive ℬ.

Bella's Jewelry is bartering jewelry for all kinds of other goods and services, which she calls her *revenue*, borrowing the old French word for "return". It works out that approximately two-thirds of the revenue is distributed to the employees, in exchange for their labor.

Brody protests. "Bella, you're not doing anything like one-third of the work, so why are you pocketing a third of the revenue?"

"There's more to this business than labor, Brody. I'm providing the tools, which I invested in, at some personal risk. I'm providing land for our workshop, and I'm the entrepreneur who is organizing the business. Whatever revenue remains after paying fair wages, is mine. It's my profit. If you can't accept that, no one is forcing you to work here."

Over time, as the island grows wealthier and more sophisticated, more goods and products are produced by businesses—teams who come together to build sophisticated products. And the revenue of each business is split between the employee wages, and profit for the people who own the business and its capital tools.

TODAY, almost all work is organized into businesses. In the US, 94 percent of people are employed by multi-person businesses or other organizations, while only six percent of those in work are self-employed, the lowest proportion of any country.[7]

In classic economics textbooks there are three *factors of production*, that is inputs to the production process. They are *land, labor*, and *capital*. Interestingly, land was traditionally listed first, reflecting the agricultural societies of yesteryear. In the twentieth century, many authors added a fourth factor, *organization,* or *entrepreneurship*. There have been proposals to add a fifth factor of production, *human capital* (knowledge, which some like to separate from labor), or *natural resources* (which others would include in land).

For the sake of conciseness, in this book the factors of production are grouped into just the two factors of *labor* and *capital*, including entrepreneurship in labor, and land in capital.

Economists used to consider that the *wage share*[8] was fairly stable, with about 60–75 percent of all production in the economy being paid out as salaries to employees. The 66 percent wage share in the story reflects this. This empirical observation of a stable wage share even earned the name of Bowley's Law.[9] However, since the 1980s the wage share has declined to about 56 percent, with almost half of income being paid to the capital owners. This has contributed to increased inequality between the income of laborers and those with significant ownership of capital. We will return to this modern trend later.

In summary, there are two main factors of, or inputs to, production: *labor* and *capital*. And all the production in an economy is distributed in the form of *wages* to the laborers and *profits* to the capital owners.

THE ECONOMY

PRETTY SOON MOST stuff on the island is being traded. Admittedly, Charlie occasionally eats one of his own coconuts, but the vast majority of products are now traded between producers and consumers. Each business produces what it is best at producing. The laborers and owners of that business receive the output of their business as wages and profit, and then trade their wages and profits in the market, in exchange for a variety of goods and services.

John is a thoughtful guy, and often observes the market from the vantage point of a nearby hill. He sits on a rock there and watches goods changing hands. He sees Arthur dragging a cart full of fish to market. Arthur trades a fish for a couple of Paula's oranges. Then he trades another fish for a punnet of Martha's mushrooms. John watches Arthur from afar as he does the rounds, and finally heads home with a cart filled with a dozen different ingredients for dinner.

Over the years, John observes a greater quantity of goods in the market, as well as increasing variety, with new products and services being introduced periodically. Aided by a raft and a net, Arthur comes to market with a bigger cart of fish and goes home with a greater quantity and variety of goods.

John is witnessing the island's economy slowly expanding. Production is increasing, and with it, consumption is also increasing. To be sure, the population is also growing, but production is increasing even faster than the population, so there is more stuff per person. The result is that many people eat a little better and can afford the occasional treat.

John wants to measure the growth of the island's economy, but it is too complex. He tries to etch on some bark all the products changing hands in one week: 100 coconuts, 50 cups of berries, 20 necklaces, 100 apples, 200 oranges. He would like to add it all up, but it is, well, apples and oranges. He tosses the bark aside.

The island already has a growing economy, but John will have to wait for the island to invent money before he can measure economic growth accurately. For now, he just listens to the buzz of traders negotiating, and uses the volume of the haggling as a rough indicator of economic activity.

THE ISLAND IS PROGRESSING. Conceptually, we can start thinking about the total production of all goods and services as the island's *domestic product*. John observes that the island's total domestic product is increasing over time, and the domestic product per person is also increasing. In other words, the average islander is becoming wealthier, consuming more food and other goods and services. John will return to this concept once money is introduced, making it easier to measure domestic product.

Now that the island has capital and businesses, can it be called a modern economy? Far from it. Firstly, the island does not have money, and has only an informal credit system. But also, as a matter of degree, the island is producing only very simple products that can be manufactured by a single small team using basic tools.

How far is our island from a modern economy? And why will it take the island many generations to develop what we might recognize as a modern economy?

A charming illustration of the complexities of modern economies may be found in Leonard Read's essay *I, pencil*, published in 1958.[10] Here, a pencil tells the story of its own creation, listing all its components—cedar wood, lacquer, graphite, ferrule, factice, pumice, wax, and glue—and the numerous people and factories involved in producing and transporting them, right down to the cleaner in the factory and the lighthouse keeper guiding shipments into port. The pencil also notes the pieces of equipment needed at each stage of production, and each of these items in turn has a story of its own. The conclusion is that no one person knows how to produce a pencil from start to finish, neither is any one person coordinating this entire *supply chain*. Instead, many different businesses with different know how, some of which don't even know each other, are all collaborating to produce pencils.

Read intentionally chose to illustrate the complexity of the economy using one of the simplest products around, a pencil. I shudder to think what an essay entitled *I, laptop* might look like. A laptop has thousands of components, many of which require highly specialized semiconductors, fabricated in extremely complex factories, with each piece of equipment having its own story, involving many thousands of substories and sub-substories branching like a fractal.

Anyway, we're getting way ahead of ourselves. Our island has a long way to go before we need to start worrying about such sophisticated manufacturing. Meanwhile, the islanders are just starting to invest in basic types of capital equipment and production. And in order to take the next steps along this road, the entrepreneurs will need more credit.

CREDIT

PAULA IS LONGING to purchase John's beachside hut.

"I'll sell it to you for 5,000 oranges, Paula."

"You what? How can I possibly pull together 5,000 oranges at one time? What would you even do with 5,000 oranges, John? Even if I bartered those and gave you a mix of oranges and apples and berries, most stuff is perishable, and you won't be able to consume it all."

"That's exactly why I don't want the payment at one time. Give me 50 oranges a week for two years. Then I'll give you the hut."

"Well now we're talking. But what if you don't give me the hut? Tell you what John, how about you give me the hut first, and then I give you 50 oranges a week for the next two years."

"OK Paula, you save up for one year. Then pay me half, and take possession of the hut. Oranges won't keep for a year so trade them for something valuable that will keep. Let's say goose feathers. Then I'll accept the other half in oranges, spread over the following year. That way we are both trusting each other."

Sure enough, a year later Paula turns up on the doorstep of the beach hut with a couple of sacks full of high-quality goose feathers and makes her, ahem, down payment on the seaside home.

MEANWHILE, more islanders are taking loans to finance the creation of tools. As the island gets richer, there are more people who can afford to delay gratification and make a loan, in return for interest. Credit becomes a new function of the twice-weekly market, matching people who want to borrow food to finance their investment in capital with people who might be willing to save by lending food for interest.

Credit is not limited to financing the creation of capital. A nice crop of apples is just ripening, and Brody can't pick them fast enough before they start rotting.

"Can I borrow your ladder, Paula?"

"Seriously, Brody? You know the sacrifices I made to produce that ladder. I need it for picking my oranges."

"Have you seen my trees lately? This week I need that ladder more than you."

"Hmm. Then you should be able to make it worth my while."

So, Brody rents the ladder from Paula for a week, in return for 30 apples. The loan of the ladder is also a form of credit. Since Brody has a greater need for the ladder at this point in time, Paula lending Brody the ladder helps to increase the island's overall production this week.

In the meantime, Arthur wants to build himself a mud hut and asks Bob if he can borrow some of his corn each month, for a year. Arthur will use this corn to sustain himself while he is building his new house.

"A house? How will you repay me, Arthur? Having a house isn't going to help you catch more fish and pay me back".

"I'm already catching more than I need to survive. This loan is for my personal lifestyle. I'll pay you back gradually, Bob. Each month I'll give you a few fish which you can eat or trade, till I pay off the loan and the interest."

"Aha. And what if you don't catch enough fish to pay me back?"

Arthur offers the home itself as security for the loan, and thus he draws the island's first mortgage.

THE WORD *credit* comes from the Latin *creditum*, which means "believing". It is trust that allows one party to provide stuff to another party, based on the promise of later compensation. Credit depends on either a high level of trust, or on a social or legal system that enforces people's contracts.

Without credit, the island's weekly production would always be distributed in a fairly inflexible way between each business's laborers and capitalists. But with credit, the entire economy has what you might call elasticity. A borrower can temporarily receive *more* than their fair share; and a lender can temporarily receive *less* than their fair share, knowing that it will be repaid later, and generally it will be repaid with extra interest. This is perhaps reminiscent of an elastic band that can be pulled to one direction and will later bounce back to its original position, and even overshoot.

Discussing credit before the invention of money enables us to see various uses of credit, which may blur together later once money comes into play. We think of credit as allowing us to buy something now and pay for it later. But in fact, the most basic use of credit is even simpler. Paula wants to buy a valuable asset from John and the price is way more stuff than John can consume at one time. So they agree to transfer some of the island's production between them over two years. Paula has to trust John for the first year, and John has to trust Paula during the second year after the house is transferred. Because they trust each other, they can trade a valuable asset for a two-year long production stream.

Meanwhile, Arthur wants to construct a capital asset himself, in the form of a house. He therefore borrows some of the island's production every month from Bob to sustain himself and finance the construction. He will repay this over the subsequent years.

Finally, yet another form of credit is the loan of a capital asset, such as a ladder, in return for rent. This may be a rental, but it still involves credit—the promise to return the ladder at a later date. Economists usually use the term *capital mobility* for cross-border investments, but the mobility of capital can start with the simple rental of a tool. A ladder, as we have seen, can boost production if it has the mobility to be rented by the business that most needs it in any given week.

Without credit, valuable assets like homes, worth many months of income, would never change hands. And no one would be able to invest in creating a new capital asset, which requires many months of labor.

With credit, all these things become possible. People can give up some of their consumption over a number of years, to save up for a home or for a future business investment, or to pay off a mortgage for a home they already possess, or a business loan for an investment they made in the past. So credit is crucial to capital creation and to our ability to rent and sell capital assets, so that capital can be deployed where it best helps production. And, as we saw, the creation and accumulation of capital is the key engine that enables the economy to grow over time.

Of course, credit can go wrong as well, a point we return to later.

At the time of writing, in 2021, U.S. nonfinancial corporations in the U.S. are approximately $16 trillion in debt, mostly due to financing capital such as equipment, research and development of future products, and working capital, that is inventory (stock). Households are about $14 trillion in debt,[11] mostly due to mortgage credit allowing people to live in homes that they will pay for in the future.

AS WE COME to the end of this first section of the book, it is worth reflecting that even without money, the island was able to develop specialization, trade, businesses, capital, and credit. Remember that no money has been used so far, only real goods and services. This underlines a central theme of this book: that money is secondary to actual stuff, and the financial economy is secondary to the *real economy*.

We can summarize the basic functioning of a moneyless economy in a surprisingly simple diagram. First, consider the two factors of production.

People can provide labor, and they may own capital (tools, land etc.); and businesses organize the labor and capital to produce stuff.

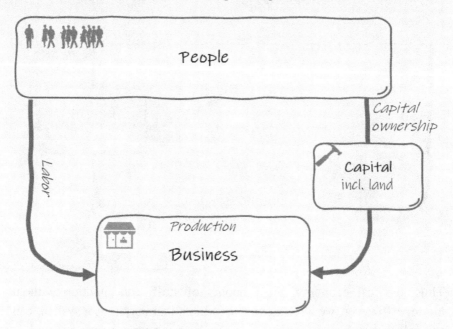

The businesses produce goods and services for consumption, but they may also invest some of their efforts in producing further capital. The production of each business is awarded to the business' laborers in the form of wages, and to the capital owners as profits. The laborers and owners will in turn barter their wages and profits with others, to obtain a variety of goods and services.

Finally, credit will provide flexibility as to whom receives the production each month, allowing people to invest resources in capital creation or asset purchase and pay for it over time, either before or after the purchase. Credit is therefore critical for capital creation and capital mobility.

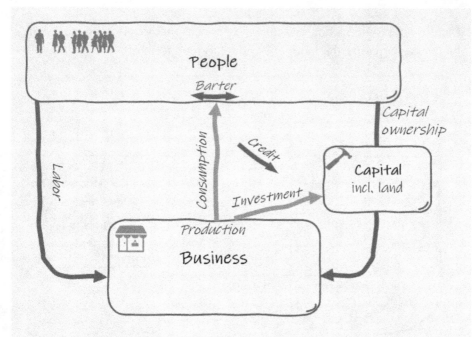

Thus, the real economy, the economy of stuff, can function without money. However, we have already seen hints that barter, as a system, can struggle to match all the producers with all the consumers, especially when there are many types of goods and services. Undoubtedly, money makes both trade and credit a lot easier and more efficient. It is now time to introduce money, starting with commodity money, which was the dominant form of currency throughout economic history, until 1971.

II. MONEY AND BANKS

MONEY

OVER TIME, capital tools accumulate on our island. People organize themselves into business teams which produce stuff ever more efficiently, and new manufacturing techniques are invented from time to time. As a result, the total production of goods and services is gradually accelerating; the island is becoming wealthier.

Not only does the quantity of goods and services increase, but also their quality, variety, and complexity. There are now artificial materials such as paper and fabrics; simple assembled products such as toys and garments; complex foods such as pastas and cakes and pies, and services including pedicures and massages. And as more resources become available, the population grows.

John, as per his habit, observes the market in quiet amazement. Thousands of people produce many hundreds of different products and services. And, of course, the same thousands of people consume hundreds of products and services. The products and services have to route themselves from producers to consumers, sometimes through multiple barters. John imagines a tangled mound of seaweed, where each green strand represents the path of one product from its producers to its consumers.

It doesn't always work well. Often people simply don't want each other's stuff, there isn't a coincidence of wants. For example, Bella can't easily sell jewelry to Paula because Bella doesn't like Paula's oranges. People can only barter if they want each other's stuff.

One day, Bella wants Charlie's coconuts, Charlie wants Arthur's fish, but Arthur doesn't want any of Bella's berries.

"Charlie, these berries won't kill you. Go on, trade some for a coconut."

"Sorry, Bella, if I eat anything this evening, it's going to be fish."

"So, what should I do?"

"If you really want one of my coconuts, find someone who wants your berries and trade. Then trade whatever you get. Keep trading till you get hold of something that Arthur wants. Then go bring me a fish."

"Oh yeah, that's a really terrific idea, Charlie. I'll probably go home with a snail or something—if I don't get confused first with all the exchange rates. Remind me, how many mushrooms are an orange worth? How many cups-full of corn for a fish?" She sighs. "You know I might just slow down with my berry cultivation if they are so hard to trade."

She turns to go, then changes her mind.

"Wait a second, Charlie," Bella says. She pulls out of her pocket a seashell which she was saving for a necklace.

"Nah, I don't need a shell."

"Take the shell, Charlie. Beautiful, rare shells like this are always in demand. Everyone recognizes their value. They don't go bad. You can always trade the shell later for something that you want."

Charlie studies the shell. "I don't know, Bella. A shell isn't the most convenient thing. Each one is worth quite a bit. What if I want to make a small purchase? I can't split it. And it's a bit bulky and delicate to keep in my pocket."

"Hmm. OK, hold on. I may have a better idea." She reaches into her other pocket for a tiny nugget of gold. "How about this, Charlie? Gold is rare and desirable, and it's not perishable. And it's certainly more compact than a shell, and easier to divide." She smiles at him.

And so Charlie takes the little nugget of gold. He approaches Arthur and repeats the argument about gold being a convenient way to carry value around. Arthur has a vague idea of the value of gold, relative to the value of fish, and he's reasonably confident that he will be able to trade the gold later. Sure enough, Charlie comes back with a fish.

Next, Arthur uses the same gold nugget to buy mushrooms. And the following market day, Martha approaches Bella and uses the gold nugget to buy some of her berries.

Bella smiles and puts her gold nugget back in her pocket. The nugget has circulated all the way back to Bella and everyone is happy. The gold nugget navigated the multi-party trade all on its own. By passing through four people in a circle, it helped each one of them to trade, even though no two of them wanted each other's stuff.

Bella now decides she will save the gold for some future shopping and stashes it in the ceiling of her hut.

John still likes to sit on his hill, watching all the comings and goings on market days. Over time, he notices that more and more trades in the market involve gold. He realizes that this makes trading much simpler, as every product only needs one price—its value as a weight of gold. Trades no longer require a coincidence of wants. Now people sell their stuff for gold, and they keep the gold and use it later to buy the stuff they want. Soon laborers are paid their wages in gold too. Gold has become money. John has purchased a pad of paper and he sketches these diagrams.

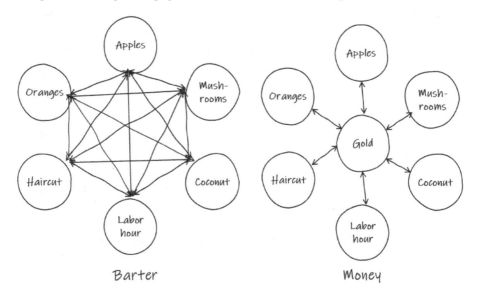

Barter   Money

There is nothing very special about gold, John thinks. The islanders are still trading one commodity for another. But most trade now pivots around one specific commodity, gold. If someone has coconuts and wants oranges, they no longer trade coconuts for oranges. They now typically trade coconuts for gold, and then trade gold for oranges. This way, they don't need to worry about the coincidence of wants. For instance, Charlie can trade some of his coconuts for Paula's oranges, even if Paula doesn't actually want any coconuts.

As gold takes on this special role in trade, John notices how the island's language evolves. Trading coconuts for gold is now called *selling*; and trading gold for oranges is *buying*. Even though both are just trades, trading to gold and trading from gold earn different designations.

Of course, gold is not functioning exclusively as money; it still has other uses. For instance, Bella uses gold to make her jewelry. But soon gold's primary purpose on the island is to mediate the exchange of goods and services, and that earns gold the title of *money*.

Gold money is not only used for trading but also for storing value—like the nugget stashed in Bella's ceiling. Soon enough, money is playing a third, conceptual role: gold is also used for accounting. Prices are set in grams of gold; and debts are measured in grams of gold. Bella will measure the revenue of her jewelry business in terms of gold. The value of all goods, services, and assets is soon being expressed in grams of gold.

COMMODITY MONEY—money comprising objects or materials with an intrinsic value or use, like gold, salt, or tea—was adopted at least as early as 3,000 BCE.

Economists give fancy names to the properties a commodity should possess in order to function as money:

- *Fungibility:* interchangeability—one gold nugget is as good as the next

- *Durability:* ability to withstand repeated use

- *Divisibility:* ability to be split into smaller units for making smaller purchases

- *Portability:* ability to be easily carried and transported

- *Cognizability:* ability to have its value easily identified

- *Stability of value:* sufficient rarity to maintain its value; we will return to this in detail in Section III, when we discuss money supply and inflation.

As the story hints, even fairly recently, shells have often functioned as money,[12] despite having the disadvantages that Charlie mentioned. Shells are not perfectly fungible, as one shell may be slightly more attractive than another; shells may be delicate rather than durable; they are not particularly portable; and shells are not divisible.

Other commodities that have functioned as money include: copper, rice, wampum beads (which are beads made of shells, apparently), peppercorns, large stones, decorated belts, alcohol, cigarettes, cannabis, candy, and salt. Salt, in particular, features in the English expression "worth one's salt" and the word "salary" which comes from the Latin *salarium*, meaning "salt money".

Rare metals, such as gold and silver, make better money than shells because metals are fungible. Once melted down, one ounce of gold is just like another. They are also easily divisible.

The specific choice of money can be controversial. Apparently, the U.S. election of 1896 was largely fought between *gold bugs* who wanted the dollar backed by gold, versus *silverites* who favored *bimetallism*, with the dollar backed by both gold and silver.

Historically, gold and sometimes silver have been very popular as money. Even in the era of government banknotes, paper money used to function as a receipt for gold. Before 1934, $20.67 could be traded for one troy ounce of gold; and then, from 1934 to 1971, it was $35. A gram is 1/31 of a troy ounce, or 1/28 of a normal ounce, and so 1 U.S. dollar was actually a receipt for approximately 1 gram of gold. Until 50 years ago, in 1971, money almost always comprised a valuable and convenient commodity, which came to function as money by way of social convention or law.

The final desirable property of commodity money is that it should have a stable value. This means the commodity needs to be in limited and stable supply. Gold and silver fit this profile because they tend to be rare. However, in the 1500s the Spanish discovered and looted large deposits of gold and silver from the Incas in South America. This didn't make the Spanish conquerors as rich as they expected, because the sudden influx of gold and silver into Europe caused the value of the metals to drop. Or, to put it another way, the prices of all other products, measured in terms of gold and silver, increased. This process later became known as *inflation*. Money, just like Paula's oranges, loses value when it's more abundant.

Once an economy adopts a commodity as money, it tends to serve the following main functions, all of which were mentioned in the story:

- *Medium of exchange:* the islanders are trading stuff for gold and gold for stuff rather than bartering.

- *Store of value:* Bella is using gold to store her purchasing power for the future.

- *Unit of account:* prices and debts are denominated in terms of gold, and the total economic activity will be measured in terms of gold.

THE SIZE OF THE ECONOMY

GEORGINA HAS STARTED a campaign to become governor of the island. She finds John on his favorite hill, observing the market.

"You're influential, John. Will you endorse me as governor?"

"Governor? Why do we even require a governor?"

"We need a bridge over the river. It won't build itself. We need laws to regulate trade and credit disputes. We need a safety net to help the elderly and poor."

"Well, Georgina, I think most of all we need growth. No single project can help our people as much as the overall expansion of our production capacity. If you are going to help our economy grow, you have my vote."

"Sure, John, you bet. But, um, what does that mean?" She thinks for a minute. "Things grow if they have a size. Does our economy have a size?"

"Absolutely, it has a size. Look, watch the market." John points at the market below. "Charlie just sold a coconut for half a gram of gold. Bella sold a necklace for 10 grams of gold. Martha sold a punnet of mushrooms for half a gram. So that's 11 grams of gold's worth of production of consumer goods. The total production of goods is our economy. Now, Fred gave a haircut for two grams. That's a consumer service. And Brody sold a chisel to Paula for her business. That's a capital tool. Services and tools are also part of our economy."

"So?"

"Well, you asked if our economy has a size. Sum up all the transactions over a year, and that gives you the total production of our island's economy, including goods, services, and investment in capital. We can call the total of all of those the domestic product. The domestic product is the size of our economy and what it's producing. And since virtually all trades are now carried out using gold, we can measure our domestic product in grams of gold per year. And if you want my vote and my endorsement, Georgina, that domestic product total had better carry on increasing."

Georgina surveys the market for a minute. "Hmm, the thing is, John, you can't really see every single thing produced from your little perch up here. Charlie probably ate some of his own coconuts. A few people are still bartering. Not every single good or service or tool that is produced is sold for money in the market. And vice versa. For example, some goods are sold second-hand—not every money transaction in the market actually represents new production."

"Yes, that is quite perceptive. Perhaps you do deserve my vote. But, Georgina, those are fringe activities. Most goods and services, and most capital tools, that are produced on the island, are sold in the market for gold. And most are sold just once. So adding up the quantity of gold changing hands in all transactions in the market provides a pretty good measure of the production of our economy."

Georgina looks thoughtful for a moment. "OK, that's all well and good. But we don't only produce things. We're good at breaking things too. Bella's old chisel broke. Look at the state of Arthur's fish net over there— it's ripped and just about useless."

John nods. "Correct, Georgina. So to be accurate, we can call what I'm measuring *gross domestic product*. If you're very pedantic you can deduct from that figure all the capital equipment that has depreciated. We can call the new production, minus the reduced capital, net domestic product. But honestly, I do not think there is a huge difference. If you become governor and you want to get a feel for the economy, it is probably easier and just as valid to track gross domestic product."

"OK then, John. As your governor, I pledge to increase gross domestic product. I'll call it GDP. And Governor Georgina will put the G in GDP! But then you have to do your job, John, and track my GDP growth achievements, so that I can take full credit and win a second term. How will you measure GDP anyway?" She stared at the market where hundreds of people were buzzing around, trading with each other. "Look at them. Surely there are far too many transactions going on for you to sit here tracking them all and adding them all up?"

"Funny you should ask, I have been thinking about that. I have two ideas. My first idea is to estimate the average amount of gold that changes hands in each transaction: in other words, the average price level of a transaction. Then I will estimate the number of transactions per market day. And finally I will multiply that total by the number of market days, to estimate the number of transactions that take place per year."

"OK, I guess I'd better get a feel for this stuff. Hit me with the numbers, John."

"All right. There are all kinds of transactions taking place in the market, but I have estimated that the overall average price of a transaction is 10 grams of gold. That is the price level. Now, there are about 1,000 adults on the island. Each market day, each person buys an average of five items—that makes about 5,000 transactions per market day. That's 50,000 grams of gold's worth of production changing hands each market day. And there are two market days a week, which makes about a hundred market days per year.

"Therefore, the island's gross domestic product is approximately 50,000 times 100, amounting to 5 million grams of gold. That is the value of our total goods and services and capital production per year; our GDP, as you called it earlier. It is a simple enough calculation really—the average price of a transaction, multiplied by the total number of transactions per year."

"Well, OK then. That's good to know, I guess. Especially if I am on the hook for increasing this GDP. Good talking, John."

"Hold on a minute, Georgina. You are going to need to know the other method. It is more subtle, but equally important. I call it "follow the money". Instead of adding up all the transactions, I follow the gold. Remember, although islanders spend 5 million grams of gold per year, we don't have anything like 5 million grams of gold on the island. Instead, I reckon that each specific nugget of gold circulates at a velocity of once per week. This means that businesses pay salaries and distribute profits in gold once a week, and then people go shopping and spend that gold and it is paid back to the businesses each week. The same physical nugget is used again for salary and shopping the next week. Gold nuggets go around in circles."

"Rather like the days of the week themselves," says Georgina. "So?"

"I estimate that the average islander has about 100 grams of gold in their home or business. There's plenty of variation but, based on my survey, that's the average. So there's about 100,000 grams of physical gold functioning as money on the island. Now, 100,000 grams of gold, circulating with a velocity of about once per week, or about 50 times a year, gives me once again 5,000,000 grams of gold. Again, our GDP comprises 5 million grams' worth of goods and services and capital creation per year."

"Same number, so what's the difference?"

"Well, Georgina, you are correct, it is the same GDP either way. It's just two ways of calculating the same thing. The first time, I added up all the transactions—the average transaction price, times the number of transactions in a year. The second time, I followed the money instead—the number of physical gold nuggets in existence as money, multiplied by the velocity of how often each nugget is used in a purchase."

Georgina frowns. "Hmm. I guess it's like a cart. If I want to know how many miles it's traveled, I can multiply the number of trips by the length of the trip. Or I can multiply the circumference of the wheels by the number of rotations of the wheels."

John raises an eyebrow. "As analogies go, Georgina, that works well enough. But the important thing to remember is that it is an equation, and both methods give the same estimate of GDP."

"OK, John, vote for me and I bet I can increase our GDP to 6 million grams of gold per year before you can blink—no matter which way you measure it!"

WE WILL COME back to these two equivalent ways of measuring the GDP of the economy in Section III. This equivalence is better known as the *equation of money*; it is an antique equation which lies at the heart of the modern understanding of the economy. But first, we need to explore some types of money other than cash.

The introduction of money gives us an opportunity to update our diagram of the economy to show that money provides tokens to track the exchange of labor for goods and services, or for investment in capital. As before, the factors of production are labor and capital. But now the laborers and capital owners receive money as wages and profits. They then use that money to purchase the products they want to consume. In the following diagram, the dotted lines show money paid by businesses to laborers and capital owners; and then returning to businesses as payment for the goods and services that are consumed.

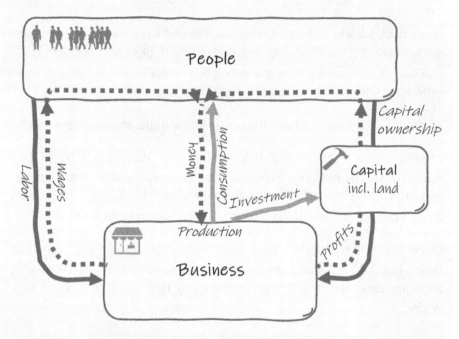

As well as producing goods and services, businesses can use some of their resources to invest in creating new capital, or in buying capital assets secondhand. However, we saw that capital investments usually require credit, and we will see how credit works in a money economy a little later starting in the chapter on Simple Bank Loans.

DEBT MONEY

BELLA WANTS TO buy coconuts from Charlie again, but she doesn't have a gold nugget to spare.

"Charlie, do me a favor, give me a couple of coconuts; I'll owe you a gram of gold. Please."

"Write it down."

So Bella writes on a sheet of paper: "IOU a gram of gold. Signed: Bella," and exchanges the written I-owe-you for two coconuts.

A bit later, Charlie catches a whiff of fish and his stomach rumbles. He doesn't have a gram of gold to spare either. He thinks about going to Bella and calling in his IOU, but obviously Bella doesn't have the gold at hand right now, and it might take her a day or two to get it.

"Arthur, I'll pay you with this IOU. You know Bella, she keeps her word."

Charlie comes back with a fish. Arthur uses the same IOU to buy mushrooms. The next day, Martha approaches Bella and buys a couple of cups full of berries. Much to Bella's surprise, Martha pays Bella with Bella's own IOU. Now Bella has her IOU back—and rips it up.

Once again, everyone has what they want. Amongst people who trust Bella, her IOU is literally as good as gold, circulating between people, allowing each one to sell their product and later buy the product they desire.

However, there is an obvious problem. Bella's IOU can only function as money for trades between people who trust Bella implicitly. This rather limits the use of Bella's IOU as currency. But, as far as Bella's circle of friends goes, it establishes the principle that an IOU can function as money, provided people trust the person who signed the IOU.

BANK DEPOSITS AND BANK MONEY

BELLA'S JEWELRY BUSINESS is taking off, and she is now saving up gold to purchase a better home eventually. She feels nervous about stashing the gold in her current mud hut, where it may be vulnerable to theft. Bob has a relatively secure brick home, with a big dog tied up outside. Bella asks Bob to store her 10 grams of gold for safekeeping. She pays him a small fee for the service. Bob gives Bella ten deposit receipts for the gold, each receipt reading simply "IOU one gram of gold. Signed, Bob."

Soon other people start paying Bob for the same safe deposit services; and Bob earns a reputation for providing a secure place to store gold, in exchange for a small custodial fee.

ONE DAY, a chair in the market catches Bella's eye. It's on sale for 2 grams of gold. "Milton, save that chair for me. I'm going to withdraw a couple of grams of gold from Bob. I'll be right back." She waves her deposit receipts to prove that Bob owes her gold.

"Don't bother Bella, I'll only deposit the gold back with Bob myself. Just give me the IOUs."

"Hah." So Bella gives Milton two notes which each read "IOU one gram of gold. Signed, Bob," and she heads back home carrying a brand-new chair. At the end of the day, Milton uses one of the IOUs to buy Charlie's newest product, a piña colada cocktail, and saves the other in his pocket.

And just like that, without anyone planning it, paper bank money is born. People find it more convenient to count Bob's IOUs, rather than weigh gold. And soon a considerable volume of trade involves Bob's IOUs, which become affectionately known as *bob*, as in "that chair will cost you two bob." Bob adopts a more flamboyant signature to stymie potential counterfeiters.

Each bob is an IOU from Bob, and these IOUs are trusted by more or less everyone. This is not only because Bob is well known in the community, but also because of his promise that each bob is backed by physical gold in his vault, and Bob has never failed to cash in his bob.

IN THE REAL WORLD, banknotes emerged in the same way when people deposited their gold with goldsmiths in London in the 1600s, and it then became common to use the receipts as money.[13] Mind you, in this situation the receipts became as valuable as the gold itself, so one wonders why they didn't need to keep the receipts in safety deposit boxes. Presumably, over time it stopped being merely a matter of security; people appreciated the convenience of storing and counting paper money.

In the story, the name given to the currency, *bob*, is a nod to the British shilling, which was often known as *bob* until it was retired in 1971. The plural is also bob. Some former British colonies, such as Kenya, still use shillings and refer to them as bob.

Note that while Bob's Bank is issuing receipts which may function as money, this is not yet what we will call *bank money*, as these receipts are simply substitutes for physical gold in his bank vault.

SIMPLE BANK LOANS

"GOOD DAY, Bella. Tell me, might you know when you will withdraw your gold?" Bob is passing Bella's marketplace stall, as if by accident.

Bella squints slightly at Bob. "Whenever I like."

"Of course, Bella, certainly. Whenever you like. But if you choose to commit to leave that gold deposited for a bit longer, I will waive your safe-keeping fees. I will even pay you interest. If you don't need that gold for a year, say, I can pay you 5 percent interest."

"I'm listening. What's the catch? What are you going to do with my gold?"

"I'm going to loan it to Arth—" Bob paused. "Well let's say that Bob's Bank is going to loan the gold to someone who wants to buy a net for his fishing business."

"And I guess he's paying you more than 5 percent?"

"Well, yes, it's not a secret, 7 percent actually. The bank has to make a living."

"So, Bob, what's to stop me loaning my gold directly to Arth— I mean, I can also find someone who wants a loan to finance some capital for their business. What's to stop me lending to them directly? Then I can pocket the whole 7 percent interest."

"If you can find a borrower on your own, then certainly, you can extend a loan directly. But you will be risking your money. My bank is expert at ensuring that the borrower has a solid business plan to repay the loan. The net itself will be security—if he doesn't repay, the bank has security; it will repossess and sell the net. And even if that fails, I will use my other profits to repay you in whole. You are simply far safer making the loan through my bank."

Bella gives Bob back her remaining eight "bob" IOUs, which were payable on demand. In exchange, Bob gives her a special IOU: "IOU 8 grams of gold plus 5 percent interest. Only claimable in one year—Bob."

Now Bob lends Bella's 8 grams of gold to Arthur, and Arthur writes Bob's Bank an IOU for 8 grams of gold plus 7 percent interest, payable in one year.

And thus, Bella delays gratification and saves for one year in the future, while Arthur is able to advance gratification and purchase a net today, which he will only pay for in a year. Later, Arthur will have to reduce his consumption to repay the loan; and Bella will be able to enjoy consuming more in a year's time.

With this capital tool, Arthur catches more fish, and fish become more plentiful and affordable for everyone on the island.

BOB'S LONG-TERM IOU to Bella is the island's first *bank savings account*. Arthur's IOU to the bank is the first *bank loan agreement*.

The bank is making it easier and safer to make loans by matching savers and borrowers, by vetting the borrowers and their security collateral, and by guaranteeing the savings—even if borrowers default on their loans.

This function of the bank in turn increases the availability of credit on the island. And as we have seen, credit is key to enabling capital creation. In general, the businesses which have the best use for capital will pay the highest interest rates to borrow. In this way, resources will flow to where they can contribute to financing the most worthwhile capital, which will most improve future production.

Of course, not every business investment works out as intended, but at least the banking system allows resources to flow into investments that are most likely to pay off with increased future production.

Credit also gives people the flexibility to advance gratification and buy homes, or other large assets, and pay for them later. In the meantime, it allows other people to save up for future purchases or for their pension.

Let's take a moment to understand the importance of bank loans. Suppose Bella and various other islanders all decide to start saving up. That means they are spending less gold and consuming fewer goods and services today. Without the bank loan, some businesses will have to start downsizing and firing staff because fewer goods and services are being consumed.

The bank loan puts Bella's gold back into circulation in the market. Arthur spends the gold, paying a laborer to construct a net, and the laborer in turn goes shopping in the market. The gold is back in action, as money circulating, instead of sitting in Bob's vault. Somebody somewhere isn't producing goods for Bella's consumption but instead they may be working on producing a net for Arthur. When the bank matches delayed gratification with advanced gratification, it is helping to maintain full employment.

We will talk later about the importance of the quantity of money in circulation and how banks can influence that. So far, we have seen *simple bank loans* where the bank matches long-term savers, who are willing to give up the liquidity of their money for a fixed period of time, with long-term borrowers. The bank then makes money on the interest differential. In real terms the saver promises to delay some of their consumption of goods and services to a future date, allowing the borrower to invest in procuring or producing capital tools today.

Simple and appealing as this may sound, most modern banking actually doesn't work this way.

FRACTIONAL RESERVE BANKING

ARTHUR'S FISHING BUSINESS is thriving, and he approaches Bob for another loan to finance another net.

"Another net, Arthur?"

"There are a lot of fish in the sea."

"Sorry, Arthur, no can do. All the gold I have on long-term deposit is already loaned out at the moment. Next customer!"

"Wait, hold on Bob. Just lend me some of that gold over there. It's not doing any good in your vault." Arthur waves his hand at the strong wooden boxes where Bob stores his customers' yellowish shiny nuggets. "I'll pay you the usual interest and repay the loan over the course of a year."

Bob raises an eyebrow. "Arthur, those are demand deposits of the bank's customers. They are covering my bob IOUs. You know that my customers trust me to keep their gold safe; and they also expect that it will be available, on demand, at any moment. No, sir, Bob's Bank cannot lend gold to you unless someone commits to a long-term deposit."

"Come on, Bob. It's not as if your customers are going to waltz in here and all withdraw their gold at the same time. That won't happen, will it? Go on. Wouldn't you rather be earning my 7 percent interest?"

"Hmm. You know what, please come back tomorrow afternoon, Arthur."

The next morning, Bob strolls round the market and has a chat with a few of his regular depositors, explaining his new proposal.

"What's the incentive for me?" asks Milton.

"Well, Milton, I will waive your safekeeping fees. If I can make money by lending out your demand deposits for interest, I don't need to charge you custodial fees."

"Bob," says Milton, "if you start lending out my gold, what assurance do I have that you'll have gold available when I need it?"

"Well, that's a fair question and I've come up with a solution. I will always ensure that I hold a reserve of at least 10 percent of the deposited gold in my vault. That should cover it—I never have more than 10 percent of my customers wanting to withdraw their gold at one time."

"Bob, you're playing with fire here. What if people *do* decide to withdraw more than 10 percent? It only takes a one-time event," Milton looks worried and raises an index finger. "Even if someone tries to cash in their bob just once, and finds there's no gold in your vault, the whole system will collapse. All your bob will become worthless, and your bank will implode."

"Isn't that a bit far-fetched?"

"Not necessarily. Look, I will agree to your scheme if you implement it gradually. For now, keep 50 percent of deposited gold in your vault, and then gradually reduce it to 10 percent over time, as confidence grows. Gradually."

"OK, Milton. That's agreed. For now, all the on-demand IOUs will be backed, at least 50 percent, by gold in the vault. Over time, I'll reduce the reserves toward 10 percent."

And just like that, Bob can lend out a proportion of his short-term deposits, and Arthur receives his loan. Suddenly, more bank loans are available on the island, more people can finance capital tools and homes, and even more gold is back circulating as money. Eventually, as confidence grows over some years, Bob loans out up to 90 percent of his demand deposits, as well as up to 100 percent of long-term deposits.

BOB BUYS A FISH from Arthur in the market. "Honestly, Bob, business is going so well now. If it weren't for your loan, this fish would still be swimming in the ocean. But I'm a bit confused. Who actually loaned the money for the net?"

"Well, Arthur, obviously production on the island didn't suddenly increase to produce a net for you. So you are correct that if you purchase an item you can't afford today, someone else has to delay their gratification and not buy something that they can afford today. But in this case, it's not a particular person or people. There are always many people who are putting aside a bit of money for a few days or weeks and leaving it in the bank. And the bank is aggregating all those small, casual delays of gratification and utilizing them to advance you a loan. In other words, my bank is matching many short-term delays of gratification with one long-term advancement."

MILTON DEPOSITS ANOTHER 100 grams of gold in Bob's Bank. Bob lends out 90 grams to Arthur to finance the construction of a raft. Arthur spends the 90 grams on wood in the market, and he hires Brody to construct the makeshift seacraft. And now something interesting happens; at the end of the week, Brody deposits his wages in Bob's Bank. Charlie, who supplied Arthur with coconut timber, does the same. Bob actually recognizes the shapes of some of the individual nuggets of gold, and realizes that some of the 90 grams being deposited are the very same nuggets that he lent out to Arthur just a few days earlier.

Bob smiles, ever so slightly.

Milton still has a balance of 100 grams at the bank but now Bob has lent out 90 grams of it, a lot of which has come right back to him like a boomerang, this time as deposits in Brody and Charlie's accounts. With a fresh 90 grams on short-term deposit in the bank, Bob starts to look out for someone to borrow 90 percent of that 90 percent, or 81 grams. If he's really lucky, those 81 grams will be spent, and they too may be redeposited in the bank. Bob draws himself a chart:

	Deposited	*Bank loans*	*Spent by borrower*
Milton	100	90→Arthur	90→Brody, Charlie
Brody, Charlie	90	81→others	Up to 81 in market
Other vendors	Up to 81	Up to 73	

...

In fact, Bob reflects, if all the amounts get spent and redeposited in the bank, he might actually go through several cycles of lending out 90 percent of the original deposit, and then 90 percent of the 90 percent, and then perhaps 90 percent of 90 percent of 90 percent, and so on, or 90+81+73+...

Bob rubs his hands together gently. Provided the loans he advances are spent and then redeposited in the bank, at least in part, he won't be limited to lending out 90 percent of the demand deposits. Instead, there may be several cycles of lending, each followed by spending and new deposits, and Bob may end up lending a multiple of the original demand deposit.

Bob is excited to realize that he may be able to lend out the same money multiple times for interest. But now he is wondering whether there is any short cut, rather than waiting and hoping that the money he lends out will make its way back to him.

IN THE PREVIOUS CHAPTER we saw that in simple banking, or *full reserve banking*, the bank matches long-term lenders with long-term borrowers but does not lend out the short-term *demand deposits*. In fractional reserve banking, the bank can also take all the short-term deposits—all the pockets of money in people's *checking accounts* (aka *current accounts*), each of which might be parked there for just a few days, and lend a significant proportion of those funds to long-term borrowers.

Without fractional reserve banking, there would always be people saving bits of money for just a few days or weeks, but no one else would be able to use that money to create capital. With fractional reserve banking, the bank is taking all these small ad hoc savings in checking accounts, aggregating them, and making them available as longer-term bank loans which can be used for capital creation. Once the loan is made, the money is spent, and the money goes back into circulation.

Typically, entrepreneurs will invest this bank credit to build or purchase capital, which will increase the overall productive capacity of the economy over time. In fact, banks will often only agree to make loans for the purchase or creation of capital assets, such as business plant and equipment, or homes and cars, because the banks need an asset as security for their loan.

Fractional reserve banking is a windfall for banks. Bob is lending out gold at 7 percent, but he is not paying interest on those checking accounts. His potential profit is the entire 7 percent, and not just the couple of percent gap between borrowing and lending. Fractional reserve banking greatly increases the credit available in a society, which in turn can finance the creation of capital, which will grow the economy. But it may have significant downsides too, which we will discuss later.

As we saw in the story, fractional reserve banking can actually generate loans way above 90 percent of the deposited cash. If the bank lends out 90 percent of the cash in a checking account and the borrower spends it on wages or purchases, and then the laborer or vendor deposits it in the bank, you may get a second-generation loan of up to 90 percent of 90 percent, and then 90 percent of 90 percent of 90 percent etc. Mathematically, this cycle adds up to a theoretical maximum of 900 percent of the cash, if every loan is fully reinvested and then a full 90 percent is loaned out again and again. We will see, in the next chapter, that there is actually a more direct way for the bank to lend out 900 percent of cash deposits.

Of course, in today's world there are many banks, and the second and third cycles of loans are not necessarily in the same bank, but the principle remains the same: $100 cash deposited in a checking account can ultimately back up to $900 in new loans and new checking account balances, in addition to the original $100 balance. The math works out nicely. The $900 in new loans is consistent with the 10 percent reserve requirement—since the total checking balances, the $900 in loans plus the original $100, is $1,000, backed by $100 in cash in the bank's vault. So, overall, in optimal conditions, with a 10 percent reserve requirement, banks can lend out not 90 percent, but 900 percent, of demand deposits.

Fractional reserve banking dates back at least to the 1400s, when the London branch of the Medici Bank lent out some 50 percent of demand deposits.[14] And the practice was seemingly commonplace with goldsmiths in the 1600s.[15]

The 10 percent in the story was the real reserve requirement in the United States from 1992 to 2020, which meant that for every $10 of checking account balances, banks only had to have $1 of physical cash in their vaults, or on deposit with the Federal Reserve. Reserve requirements for national U.S. banks used to be higher, at 25 percent,[16] but this rule was relaxed over time. In March 2020, when Covid-19 hit, the Fed reduced its reserve requirement to zero! This is largely theoretical, as banks have not been loaning out much money in 2020; and with zero interest rates, they have less incentive to do so. In our island story, we have stuck with the 10 percent reserve requirement, reflecting the previous 28 years. This is also because the recent move to zero may turn out to be a temporary measure implemented during the pandemic. It is also rather academic, as most banks have significant reserves in practice.

Other countries have different requirements, ranging from zero percent in the U.K., New Zealand, Australia, Sweden, and Hong Kong, to 30 percent in Lebanon.[17] Banks are always subject to various complex *solvency requirements*, and *stress tests*, so even if there isn't a specific reserve requirement, there is always a limit on how much money a bank can lend out.

Fractional reserve banking is profitable for banks, and increases available credit, but is it good for society? We will return to this intriguing question soon. But first, you may be wondering whether it is realistic for loaned money to circulate in the way described earlier. Can banks really rely on money cycling back to them, thus enabling them to lend out a multiple of cash deposits? This is a moot point, as long ago banks discovered a short cut to loaning out a multiple—rather than a fraction—of checking account demand deposits...

FRACTIONAL RESERVE BANKING AND BANK MONEY

A FEW MONTHS LATER, Paula visits the bank to ask for a loan to purchase another ladder; this time she is buying a second-hand ladder from Brody. "Lend me 200 grams please, Bob."

Bob has a total of 10,000 grams of gold on deposit, of which 4,000 are physically in his vault and 6,000 have been lent out. He is now working with a 10 percent minimum reserve requirement, so he is free to lend more. He walks over to his wooden safe and starts weighing the first nugget.

"I don't want to walk around with a fistful of gold, Bob. Give it to me in bob."

"You wish to borrow bob?"

"Sure. If you lend me gold, I'll just deposit it for bob anyway."

"Well, that is an intriguing idea. Give me a minute to consider."

Bob paces around for a minute, trying to hide his excitement with a frown. Up to now, he has only ever written out a bob IOU as a receipt for an actual gold deposit. Paula isn't depositing gold, so he cannot issue her bob. Or can he?

There is no actual rule that says he can only write out bob when receiving gold. His only rule, up to now, has been to back bob with fractional reserves of at least 10 percent physical gold in the vault.

Perhaps he can turn the whole thing on its head? Bob tries not to smile. After years of hard work, most people consider his bob to be as good as gold. Bob are accepted as money at almost every market stall—so now he can lend out bob. By writing bob, he could mint his own money!

This is quite a game-changer, he thinks.

Bob plays out a scenario in his mind. Previously, someone deposited 10 grams of gold and received 10 bob IOUs. Bob had to keep at least 1 gram in his vault to back the bob, and was free to lend out 9 grams of gold. If he was lucky, some of that might be redeposited and he might get a second and third bite of the cherry.

But what if he lends out bob, not gold? What if he keeps all 10 grams of gold in his safe? A deposit of 10 grams of gold can back 100 bob. That would mean that, after issuing 10 bob to the depositor, Bob would still be in a position to write out 90 more bob. Lending out bob, instead of gold, would allow him to use the 10 grams of gold to lend out 90 bob, instead of just 9 grams of gold. He could lend out 900 percent, not 90 percent, and he could do it immediately.

Bob resolves to leverage his new flexible business model of fractional reserve banking, along with the trust that has been established in his IOUs, to write and lend out bob, rather than physical gold. He sits down and writes out for Paula 200 bob, split into 50s, 20s, 5s and 1s. Bob asks Paula to sign a loan agreement, "I owe Bob 200 grams of gold plus 7 percent interest—signed, Paula". Paula hands Bob her single, signed IOU—the loan agreement—and Bob gives her the individual IOUs amounting to 200 bob.

Paula fans out the 200 bob. "Wait a second, Bob. You just wrote out this stack of new bob. You didn't swap them for any gold."

"Yes, impressive, right? Bob's Bank just minted money."

"You did. But, I mean, who authorized you to create money?"

"Well… I believe I earned that authority, did I not? Firstly, the island has come to trust that when Bob's Bank owes money, it is as good as gold. So my IOUs have become accepted as money in the market. And secondly, the island has now accepted that my IOUs are good as gold even when they are only partially backed by gold in my vault. Honestly, I just now fully understood that this enables me to write out new IOUs even without receiving a new gold deposit. Provided, of course, that I have 10 percent cover. And those IOUs in your hand, even though I just wrote them out now, and even though they are only partially backed by gold, will be accepted virtually everywhere as money. So it's true that I just wrote them out and it's also true that they are indeed money."

"But Bob, how can you create new wealth by scribbling some IOUs? How does that even make sense?"

Bob scratches his nose for a moment. "I created new money, yes. New wealth—no. There is no more stuff on the island now than there was 10 minutes ago."

"Hmm. But what about this money in my hand? Surely new money is new wealth?"

"It is not. The IOUs I've just issued to you were swapped with the IOU that you gave me. So we have just swapped debt; you owe me, and I owe you. There is no new stuff, and no actual new wealth. Just a debt swap. But... there is new credit and new money. That's because your IOUs are not useful for trade; so they are not money. But mine are honored at virtually every market stall, so my bob are money. By swapping your debt for my debt, we've created money without creating wealth."

"But swapping debt—what does that even mean? If I owe you and you owe me, don't the debts cancel each other out?"

"Yes and no. Sure, if we owe each other, that cancels out. But by making the swap, I am effectively guaranteeing your debt. And now you can take my debt—my bob—and spend it; and then I will owe someone else. Just think of this IOU swap as me guaranteeing your loan, which effectively turns it into money, since sellers in the market trust my debt more than yours. You and I just swapped IOUs but now you have IOUs which are trusted and can be passed around."

BOB'S BANKING BUSINESS is taking off. Before this, he could only perform simple banking, borrowing grams of gold long-term from savers for 5 percent interest per year and lending them out for 7 percent. He made 2 percent to cover his credit risk and profit.

But now Bob can lend out far more money, far more profitably. For every gram of actual gold on short-term deposit, for which Bob pays zero interest, he can now give one bob to the depositor and write out another nine bob which he can lend out at 7 percent interest—without paying anyone 5 percent. He makes 7 percent instead of 2 percent!

Bob's main business is no longer borrowing for low interest and lending out for high interest. He is now primarily in the business of minting money for free, and lending out his minted money for interest.

PEOPLE OFTEN THINK, wrongly, that banks are in the business of borrowing at a low interest rate and lending at a higher interest rate. Such simple loans are a part of the business of banks, but this is not their main business. Modern banks' main business is creating new money by guaranteeing people's debt, and then lending that new money out for interest. This is much more profitable.

It seems confusing that a bank can create money. However, as mentioned in the story, Bob is not actually producing new stuff, and there is no new wealth directly created by the bank money. Every IOU that Bob issues is in exchange for an IOU to the bank.

So Bob is really in the business of guaranteeing debt. He exchanges Paula's IOU, which nobody trusts, for his bank IOU, which everyone trusts. And once he adds his guarantee, Paula can spend her loan as money.

In fact, Bob could just as well offer to sign his guarantee at the bottom of Paula's own IOU. Then Paula's IOU would probably be accepted in the market. But Bob is smart. He knows that Paula would find it hard, psychologically, to pay 7 percent interest just for a guarantee. By swapping IOUs, Bob makes it look as if he is lending money, for which Paula finds it easier to pay him 7 percent interest, even though swapping Paula's IOUs for freshly minted bob is conceptually identical to guaranteeing Paula's IOUs.

Every time someone takes a bank loan in the real world, the bank is performing the exact same trick. If you take a bank loan of $10,000 to buy a car, you sign a document saying that you owe $10,000 to the bank, and the bank emails you a statement that you "have" $10,000 in your checking account. That statement is actually just an IOU—the bank owes you $10,000. The $10,000 in your checking account is not cash—it is money which the bank willed into existence at the instant they gave you a bank statement with that "balance." The bank swaps your IOU (bank loan) with a bank IOU (checking balance), that is trusted and therefore widely accepted as money. The checking account balance is conceptually equivalent to the bob. And because people trust bank IOUs, you can spend the balance of your checking account using checks or credit cards.

The bank charges you just as much interest for guaranteeing your debt as it would for lending you actual cash from the vault, which the bank received from some saver to whom the bank is paying interest. Clearly, guaranteeing your debt costs the bank much less, as they are not paying any depositor for the money they have just created.

Fractional reserve banking makes more credit available and can therefore reduce the cost of credit for everyone—by reducing interest rates. People think of interest rates as being the price determined by the supply and demand of savings versus loans. But in fact, many bank loans are not backed by any savings.

Bank money is now so successful that people often don't realize there is a difference between bank money and cash. People say, "I have $100 in my checking account," but in fact what they have is a statement that the bank owes them $100. Of this, the bank may actually be holding as little as $10 in cash. But banks are so trusted that people will typically accept a bank check or credit card as readily as cash, forgetting the theoretical possibility that the bank may fail to honor its IOU.

ALTHOUGH THE WORLD'S developed economies have used fractional reserve banking for a long time, the system has its critics. In 2018 there was a referendum in Switzerland on the "Sovereign-money initiative", proposed by the Modernising Money Association,[18] to abolish fractional reserve banking and allow only the government to create money. However, this initiative was solidly defeated by the Swiss population.[19]

What are the arguments for and against fractional reserve banking? As usual we should consider this from the perspective of the real economy. In a simple bank loan, one person decides to delay gratification, perhaps because they want to save for a pension, and another wishes to advance gratification, perhaps by investing in a factory or a home. The bank allows the saving and borrowing to occur efficiently and relatively safely. In general, simple bank loans are a clear win-win.

Contrast that with a bank loan which leverages fractional reserve banking. No one is delaying gratification; they are just keeping their cash in a checking account for a few days or weeks between transactions. Suddenly the bank is creating new money, up to nine times the amount of the checking account balances. But in the short term, production has not increased, and no one else is delaying gratification more than usual. So there is an increase in money, with no new production. The borrowers are going out shopping with this new money—and competing to buy the same quantity of goods and services. As we will see later, this means they will bid up prices. There is new money, but there is also new debt, and there is no clear advantage to the real economy.

While I personally find the idea of banks creating money intriguing, I have failed to find any convincing argument that this system is actually beneficial for the real economy. And we will see that it comes with risks.

A FINAL WORD on the subject. Debates about fractional reserve banking often miss the fact that there are two separate phenomena at play here: *fractional reserve banking* and *bank money*. The two actually don't have to come together.

Imagine the Nocheck Bank Inc. which offers a demand deposit account, like a checking account, but without any checkbook or debit card. To spend money, clients have to withdraw cash from their account. Nocheck Bank has demand deposit accounts, backed by fractional reserves, and does not allow payments to be made directly.[20]

Nocheck Bank can practice fractional reserve banking for the demand deposit accounts and lend out money that isn't being spent. In this way, it can perform the social function of aggregating short-term delays of gratification and making them available as loans to businesses or mortgages. Just like Bob's Bank, Nocheck Bank can have $1,000 in checking account balances for every $100 in its vault, of which $900 are new loans.

While Nocheck Bank is creating new credit, it is not creating new money. Only cash can be used for shopping; the other $900 in the demand deposit accounts are not circulating in the market. Nocheck Bank is probably less profitable than a normal modern bank, but it may actually be better for the economy, because it doesn't destabilize the money supply by producing and destroying cash. This is a topic we will return to later.

It's interesting to consider what might have happened if someone had crafted such a compromise for the Swiss populace to vote on, rather than the more dramatic proposal of eliminating fractional reserves altogether. Perhaps the outcome of the referendum would have been different. We will return to fractional reserve banking briefly again after discussing the money supply, and again when discussing recessions.

NEAR MONEY

CHARLIE DEPOSITS A 10-gram ingot of gold in Bob's Bank. Bob rolls it in his hand thoughtfully. He could give Charlie 10 bob as usual, and he would then be free to mint 90 more bob to other people as interest-bearing loans.

But perhaps he could do even better. "Charlie, care to save this for a year?" Bob says, hoping to be able to loan out 100 bob and not just 90.

"A year? No thanks. Mind you, I won't need that money for the next month. Can you pay me interest on a monthly deposit?"

Instead of giving Charlie 10 bob as he normally would, Bob gives Charlie a slightly modified IOU: "IOU 10 grams of gold plus 3 percent per year interest; 30 days' notice required before collecting this debt—Bob's Bank". Bob thinks for a moment and then pens the title "Savings Account" on the IOU. He looks at the new banking product he has just created, before handing it over, and hides a smile.

Charlie takes the IOU to the market. He tries to spend it on some fish, but Arthur refuses it. "If I can't exchange that for gold whenever I want, I won't accept it as payment."

I can't make purchases with it, so it's not money, Charlie thinks. Even so, the IOU can be converted into bob or gold by simply giving 30 days' notice. That's pretty close to being money.

WHILE BOB USED the name *savings account*, this kind of *term deposit*, which can only be withdrawn after a fixed time period, is nowadays often known as a *certificate of deposit*, or *CD*. In some countries, savings accounts do require 30 days' notice to withdraw money, like in Bob's Bank. In the U.S., the current practice is that savings accounts allow withdrawals without notice, but no more than six withdrawals per month. What's important is that there are various flavors of bank accounts where the bank owes you money but imposes restrictions on how quickly, or how often, you can claim that debt and "withdraw" money. Banks usually have even lower reserve requirements for backing this kind of debt to their customers than they do for a checking account, which is a demand deposit.

We have now met several types of money. There is a convention central banks use to measure the types and quantity of money. These different types are typically called M0, M1, M2, or some slight variation of this nomenclature, depending on the country:

M0: Cash in circulation. On our island, this is actual gold, but in the modern world M0 typically means government-issued notes and coins, or central bank-held electronic balances. This type of money is also called *Monetary Base* (*MB*).

M1: M0 plus bank money. On our island, M1 comprises gold plus bob—the bank's unrestricted IOUs. In today's world, M1 is government-issued cash plus bank checking account balances, which are not backed by cash; in other words, bank money.

M2: M1 plus *near money.* This is M1 plus savings accounts which may be converted to money at relatively short notice or with restrictions on the frequency of conversion.

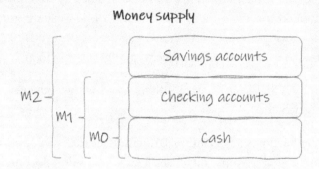

As we saw in the story, the quantity of bank money included in M1 can be rather more than the actual M0 cash. Indeed, in the real world, most of the money used for transactions is typically bank money, not government money.

CREDIT CRISIS, BANK RUN, FINANCIAL REGULATION

BELLA HAS NOW drawn loans from Bob's Bank to finance pickaxes and pliers for her business.

And as her jewelry business is booming, Bella is feeling wealthy, so she purchases a brick bungalow for her workshop and storefront. She pays 20 percent of the price with money she has been saving in Bob's Bank for the last year; the other 80 percent of the value is financed by a mortgage, to be repaid over the next four years.

In real terms, Bob has helped Bella both to delay and advance gratification. With his assistance, she can arrange a large payment for her new premises, all at one time. This is paid for by reducing her consumption, below the level of her income. She needs to do this for a year in the past and four years in the future. In the meantime, someone else will be consuming more. In the year before the purchase, that person would be whoever borrowed Bella's savings from the bank. In the years after, it may be the seller of the asset, who is now cash rich.

Bob is a little concerned about this loan. The value of the loan is a high proportion of the value of the house, and Bella's ability to repay it depends on the continued success of her business. But Bob has spare gold deposits that are not earning him any interest. He agrees to charge Bella 8 percent interest, instead of the normal 7 percent, and grants the loan.

Arthur, Brody, Charlie, and many others are drawing business loans and home mortgages too.

As the island becomes a little more affluent, Paula sees an opportunity and opens a competing jewelry business. Paula's jewelry becomes trendier, and Bella's business runs into trouble and eventually shuts down.

Bella can't afford her interest payments to Bob.

After she has defaulted for three months, Bob repossesses Bella's property. Unfortunately, Bella paid a rather high price for her house, and Bob sells the property for less than the value of the loan. The bank has taken a loss, and on a small island, everyone knows about it. A couple of other bank losses follow.

Bob reacts by tightening up credit. He refuses Brody's mortgage application.

The next day, Brody is selling apples in the market.

"Keep your bob, Charlie. If you want apples, pay me in gold cash. Between us, I don't think Bob is good for those IOUs. Did you know he couldn't afford to grant me a mortgage? Did you know only 10 percent of those bob are backed by gold in Bob's vaults? After his losses, I wonder if he even has 10 percent reserves."

Charlie frowns, reaches into his pocket, and slaps a gold nugget down on Brody's stall. Then he rushes back to his own coconut stand and hangs up a sign saying: "Gold cash only."

Paula and Arthur stare at the sign and look at each other. They go running to Bob's Bank to cash in their bob for gold. Soon there's a line of people outside Bob's bank.

Bob does, in fact, have well over 10 percent reserves for all the bob, even after his losses, but now 20 percent of his depositors are forming a line outside his bank, and they are becoming increasingly irate. He looks up and down the line in dismay. He simply cannot pay them all from his vaults. With a shaking hand, he hangs up the "Closed" sign and locks himself inside, as the crowds outside start shouting.

Georgina has been appointed governor of the island. The next day, with Bob's Bank still shuttered, she hurriedly pulls together an economic council to assess the crisis. She holds an emergency meeting of her new council, comprising John, Milton, Fred, Arthur, and Bob the banker.

The council decides that Bob is too big to fail and the government should guarantee the bob IOUs. Since the government can tax people as needed, the council hopes that people will trust the government's credit even when they have lost confidence in Bob's bank.

Sure enough, after the government announces its policy, and the run on the bank abates.

SOME PEOPLE HAVE now reverted to spending gold. But they rediscover how fiddly it is to weigh gold and test its purity. After consulting her council again, Georgina decides to introduce a government currency, the *buck*. She appoints Fred to set up a system which weighs and inspects gold nuggets, stores them on behalf of the government, and issues a buck bill for every gram of gold. Each buck bill bears the words "the government owes you 1 gram of gold". Fred calls the government's store of gold "the Fisc," borrowing some old Latin word he knows.

Bob now changes his bob IOUs to say, "I owe you 1 buck—Bob". However, with convenient paper money available from the government, people are seeing less advantage in carrying bob around.

So Bob changes the system. Instead of handing over piles of IOUs, he simply keeps a record of everyone's balance. Bob sends each customer a statement of their account balance each month. The account balance shows how many bucks they "have" in the bank; that is, how many bucks Bob's Bank owes the customer. With this innovation, bank money is even more convenient and secure than government-issued cash, as it doesn't need to be carried around at all.

And now Bob keeps his 10 percent reserves in government-issued buck banknotes rather than gold, so he requires less storage space for his bank vault. Meanwhile, Fred is storing physical gold in the government Fisc; and Bob in turn can store bucks, which are government receipts for gold.

ARTHUR WANTS TO BUY coconuts from Charlie, but realizes he has no bucks in his pocket, and under the new system, he no longer carries bob around.

So he writes a little note, "Bob, please transfer 1 buck from my account to Charlie's," and hands it to Charlie. Others start to make market payments in the same way. And at the end of the day Charlie, like other merchants, takes a pile of transfer instructions to Bob, who checks them and then adjusts the balances. Sure enough, before long, these transfer instructions become known as "checks" and the demand deposit accounts become "checking accounts."

The checking account balances are established as the new form of bank money, equivalent to the old bob IOUs. When people want a loan, Bob simply adds a number to their checking balance, creating the money; and people then spend it by writing checks, or withdraw part of it in government-issued bucks.

THE NEW BUCK currency has taken over from physical gold, and Bob's Bank has stabilized, and modernized by replacing IOU notes with a ledger of checking account balances. A couple of people are even contemplating opening competing banks. However, the island is not without challenges. The recent mortgage defaults and bank run have led to a credit crisis. Bob is granting fewer loans and is requiring more collateral. With fewer loans available, people start spending less.

Prices in the market start dropping. Piña colada sales plummet and Charlie has unsold coconuts which are at risk of rotting. He drops the price of a coconut from 0.50 bucks to 0.45 bucks. Paula drops the price of a necklace from 10 bucks to 9.50. This creates a vicious cycle. Customers notice the prices dropping and start to postpone their purchases, hoping for further price drops. Merchants are desperate to sell their goods and reduce their prices further.

Milton demands an urgent meeting of the economic council.

THIS CHAPTER EXPLORES the downside of fractional reserve banking, where the bank doesn't keep full reserves in its vaults to cover checking account balances.

Admittedly, even with full reserve banking, there are loans and credit which carry the risk that borrowers will default, causing losses to banks who could in theory go bankrupt and fail to repay savings. But with full reserve banking, only long-term savings are loaned out. The bank knows exactly when savings will mature, and a well-run bank which gives out sensible loans with adequate security, can plan accordingly. A responsible bank with full reserves is unlikely to fail.

Fractional reserve banking, on the other hand, amplifies the risk of a credit crisis. The bank owes the checking balances, which may be withdrawn at any time. The bank also knowingly takes the risk of assuming that not more than, say, 10 percent, will be withdrawn in any short period of time.

Suppose a bank has 20 percent cash cover for checking accounts. Even if no borrowers default, the bank will be in a deep crisis if one morning a number of customers make withdrawals totaling 21 percent of checking account balances. So, with fractional reserve banking, a psychological loss of confidence can rapidly turn into a real crisis and lead to the collapse of the bank. And a collapse of the bank means that all the bank money in checking accounts suddenly disappears.

We can conclude that a bank with full reserves will only fail if it makes bad decisions, leading to the loss of many loans without sufficient collateral. However, a bank with partial reserves may fail if there is a loss of public confidence, even if the loss of confidence is unfounded.

There have been many bank runs in history, including several in the U.S. during the great depression, from 1929 to 1933. In 1933, Franklin D. Roosevelt closed the banks for a forced bank holiday during which Congress introduced insurance for bank account balances.[21] In 2007–2008, there was a massive credit crisis that shook the world economy and triggered a bank run on the Northern Rock bank in the U.K. There were lines of depositors outside the branches, until the government underwrote the bank's debts, rather like Georgina did in our island story. There was also something of a run on IndyMac that year in the U.S.

These exceptions notwithstanding, bank runs in developed economies have been extremely rare since 1933. Banks and governments seem to have created pretty good safeguards to allow fractional reserve banking and bank money creation, while maintaining stability. The public don't always love banks, but they certainly trust them, and generally honor checking account balances as if they were cash.

Our island now has government-issued banknotes. In the real world, the use of paper government money dates back to seventh-century China. Just like on the island, throughout most of history, government paper money has been backed by commodities such as gold. For certain periods, convertibility was suspended, for example during the First World War,[22] but people generally trusted that the currency was backed by gold and that convertibility would return, as it did.

Our island also now has a sophisticated banking system, but it is facing problems of deflation and recession. These problems are arising because, as we will see in the next section, the island is starting to hit the limitations of using a gold-backed currency.

III. FIAT MONEY AND MONEY SUPPLY

THE EQUATION OF MONEY AND MONEY SUPPLY

MILTON ADDRESSES GEORGINA'S economic council. "Our economy needs more money. Our economy can't grow because there is simply not enough currency. Prices are dropping, and this deflation is incentivizing people to spend less. People postpone their purchases because they are hoping for more price drops."

"More money? You mean we need to be wealthier? Hah, well no one would argue with that."

"No. I mean we need more actual cash. Money helps facilitate trade, and we need more money to enable us to trade more."

"Back up," said Georgina. "Why does the economy need more money? We have a pretty stable supply of gold."

"The bank is giving fewer loans," Milton glances at Bob. "So it is creating less bank money. Therefore, overall, there is less money than before. If our economy is going to grow, we need more money in order to make more transactions. But instead, we actually have less money, which is preventing growth."

"Well, don't be so vague then, Milton. How much money do we need?"

"Remember that John measured GDP in two ways, which came to the same total. One way was to add up all the transactions. The other way was to follow the actual money and measure how money circulated."

"Yeah, that reminded me of a cart—measuring distance traveled by adding up the trips—which is like adding up all the transactions." Georgina waved her hand back and forth. "Or measuring the wheels' rotations—which resembles the circulation of money." She drew circles in the air with one finger.

"I guess so," Milton said. "And those two methods should be equal. That calculation is the key to why we need more money. In any given year, our total GDP is given by either one of the following", and Milton started writing on the chalkboard:

$$GDP =$$

$$Number\ of\ transactions \times average\ transaction\ price =$$

$$Quantity\ of\ money\ in\ existence \times$$
$$number\ of\ cycles\ (velocity)\ of\ money\ circulation$$

"Call it the 'equation of money'. It's pretty simple. Either you add up all the transactions, or you follow the money—the nuggets and notes and checking account bucks—as they circulate. Either way, you get the total value of all transactions."

"Now I'm a bit confused," said Georgina.

"Look, it's not complicated. All I'm saying is that each week people offer their labor and capital to businesses. In return, they receive wages and profits as income; and then they spend their income on goods and services. That's our economy. So if wages are paid weekly, the velocity of money is one cycle per week. That means we need enough physical money for one week's worth of GDP. In other words, we need enough physical cash to cover the cycle of payroll and shopping each week."

"OK…" Georgina frowns at the board.

"Now. We want the economy to grow. We want a greater number of transactions. We'd like to see more products and services produced and consumed. So we need money for more transactions. But instead, we actually have a reduction in bank money. Look at the equation again. If we want more transactions, we need a greater supply of money. Let me make the equation even simpler by considering the GDP not in a year but in one cycle of money, which we estimate is a week. In each single weekly cycle, we have:"

$$\textit{Quantity of money in existence} =$$

$$\textit{Number of transactions per weekly cycle} \times \textit{average transaction price}$$

"But if I've got this right, Milton, we could get more growth by increasing the velocity of money? Could we have the same number of bucks circulating twice, instead of once, per week—and support a bigger economy that way?"

"In theory perhaps, but that's really unlikely. The velocity of money, cycling once per week, is pretty much ingrained in our economy, given that we are used to being paid weekly. If we had monthly payroll, the cycle would be monthly. It's unlikely to change."

Georgina frowned at the board and pointed at the equation once more. "Look, I have another idea. What if we let the average price drop? If the average transaction price is lower, the number of transactions can increase, even with the same quantity of money. Let's say prices drop by 10 percent across the board—then the number of transactions can increase by about 10 percent, with exactly the same physical money supply. Right?"

"Well, yes, Georgina. That's deflation. And that's the very last thing we want. When people think prices are dropping, they postpone non-urgent spending. Why buy something today when you might be able to buy it more cheaply tomorrow? In fact, that's exactly what we're seeing in the market. Prices are dropping and people are postponing purchases. The purpose of this meeting is to fight deflation."

Milton stands up and addresses the room. "Ladies and gents, our course of action is abundantly clear. An increased money supply is the oxygen our economy needs to grow. We can't increase the velocity of our existing money, and we don't want prices to drop further. If we want to have growth in our economy's production and consumption, we require more money—more buck banknotes out there circulating, or more checking account balances."

THE EQUATION WE SAW is called the *equation of money*. This equation determines the quantity of money that an economy requires. It can also be stated simply, as "the quantity of money must equal the number of transactions during one money cycle, multiplied by the average price of a transaction".

Believe it or not, this *quantity theory of money* was first described by Nicolaus Copernicus in 1517. Yes, the same Copernicus who postulated that the Earth circles the sun also introduced the theory of the circulation of money, which remains a central tenet of modern macroeconomics.

This equation of money is at the heart of modern monetarism, promoted most famously by Milton Friedman; as you may have guessed, our character Milton is a tribute to him.

FIAT MONEY

"OK, MILTON. More money." Georgina sighs. "You want the government to hire a team to dredge the river and find more gold?"

He shakes his head. "You won't be able to rely on finding gold. You—"

"Ah, you're thinking more bank money? Shall we push our friend Bob here to lend more? Maybe reduce the banking reserve requirement to 5 percent so he can give more loans and create more checking account balances?"

Milton frowns. "That would be rather risky. The last thing we want is another run on the bank. No, you should simply print more bucks."

"Sure, but as you know, each buck is a receipt for gold in the Fisc. I need more gold in order to print more bucks. I think we're going round in circles…"

Milton nods. "You could perhaps use fractional reserves, like a bank."

"I can't do that. A run on the government is scarier than a run on the bank. I'm not going to take the risk of only partially backing the buck with gold."

"Then don't back the buck with gold."

"Pardon?"

"Do not back the buck with gold. Have zero gold reserves."

"What? Not back it at all?" Georgina raises her eyebrows. "What will the buck be worth, if it's not backed with gold?"

"It will be a currency by fiat, by declaration. It will just be money by virtue of being declared to be money. Your government will declare that the buck is no longer backed by gold but remains the currency for trade. The government itself will lead the way by continuing to accept bucks as payment for public services and tax. People will soon believe that the buck can be money without being backed by anything."

The council members look at each other. After a couple of hours of heated debate, Georgina receives the green light from her council. During the next market gathering, hiding her trepidation, and doing her best to appear confident, she announces: "Fellow islanders, my government wishes to announce that the buck is no longer backed by gold. This will give your government more flexibility to increase the money supply, to provide oxygen for our economy to grow. That's all for now, please continue with your business as usual."

"Erm, Charlie, will you still accept bucks for coconuts?" Brody waves a buck note.

"I don't know what to say. That's just a piece of paper now. What about you Brody? Will you be accepting bucks for apples?"

"Tell you what, I will if you will. Most people don't even have any gold anymore, so I don't have much choice. Anyway, if I can still spend bucks on coconuts and the like, then I'm happy to accept bucks for apples."

"OK, Brody, same here. If I can still use bucks to buy apples and stuff, they work for me. But I can't live on apples. Let me do one more check. Give me the buck but wait right here. I'm not giving you the coconuts yet."

"But—"

"Just for a minute."

Charlie marches over to Arthur. "Will you accept this buck for a fish?"

"Sure, why not?"

"Because— OK, never mind, that's great."

"So, do you want the fish?"

Charlie marches back to Brody, "OK, all good. Here's your coconut."

And so, one transaction at a time, people gain confidence that the social contract is intact, and bucks are still accepted as money. After a few nervous hours, bucks are circulating just as before; and after some weeks, people pretty much forget that the buck, and by extension Bob's checking account balances which are IOUs for bucks, are no longer backed by anything more than social convention.

FIAT CURRENCY WAS BORN half a century ago, on August 15, 1971, when President Nixon announced rather suddenly that the U.S. dollar would no longer be convertible to gold. Until then a dollar was exchangeable for 1/35 of a troy ounce (1.1 grams) of gold. At that time, other major currencies were pegged to the dollar under the Bretton Woods system. For example, the British pound was always worth $2.40 (or about 2.7 grams of gold). With the so-called Nixon Shock, the dollar was unpegged from gold, and other countries responded by unpegging their currency from the dollar.

Overnight, fiat currency was born. Since most Americans had used dollars all their lives, without ever cashing in dollars for gold, most people accepted this change without question. Shortly afterwards, as other currencies unpegged from the dollar, floating exchange rates became the norm, with the exchange rate between pairs of currencies determined by open market supply and demand for exchange.

ZERO MONEY: THE MEANING OF FIAT MONEY

LATE ONE EVENING Georgina and Fred get talking.

"I've got to say, Fred, this transition to fiat money has gone more smoothly than I expected. Many islanders have barely noticed that the buck used to be backed by gold and now it's not. Pretty cool. But personally, fiat money confuses me. What is it? Why do people accept it?"

"You know, Georgina, in retrospect, I'm not sure gold money was all that different from fiat money. I suppose gold has occasional use in jewelry, so you could claim it has some inherent value. But regardless, to a very large extent, gold itself was only valued as money by social convention, unrelated to any inherent value. People accepted gold for purchases because they knew others accepted gold for purchases. And even when bucks were backed by gold, they accepted bucks primarily because of the social convention that you can buy all kinds of things with bucks. The fact that bucks were backed by gold wasn't that important."

"Hmm. Well that just strengthens my question about money then." Georgina takes a wad of 100 bucks in banknotes from her pocket and fans them between her fingers. "I know these are useful for shopping. But what is this fiat money, really?"

Fred stares at the banknotes. "You can trade those to buy all kinds of junk, right?"

"Right," she nods.

"OK. So, those are credit notes. The bucks are tokens proving that the people of the island owe you 100 units of stuff. Or you can use those same bucks to pay a salary, so you are owed 100 units of labor."

"That's absurd," she said. "Why should anyone owe me anything?"

"You can take those bucks to the market and come back with products, or you can receive services?"

"Sure."

"So, Georgina, people owe you stuff."

"But… but everyone has some cash. We can't all be owed. If some people are owed, other people must owe."

"Aha." Fred sits silently for a few seconds, counting the notes in Georgina's hand. "Well, everyone who has cash is owed. That's what the cash means. And everyone owes others. Some people owe more, some are owed more. In your case, it's exactly balanced. You're at par. You are owed exactly what you owe. Zero."

"Zero? I have 100 bucks here. How can that be zero?" Georgina stares at her bucks.

"Yes, I reckon 100 bucks is zero. There are some 100,000 bucks of actual government-issued cash on the island, not including bank money and other IOUs. There are around 1,000 adult citizens, so on average, each adult has 100 bucks in cash. Right?"

"Sounds right, Fred."

"So 100 bucks is average. It is zero. If someone has no cash at all, they owe 100 bucks of stuff. Admittedly, it's totally unsecured, unlimited credit, and they can keep owing it forever if they wish. But in a sense, they do owe. Until one day they sell 100 units of stuff. Then they have less stuff, and they are back to having the average of 100 bucks. Or they might work 100 units of labor and earn their way back to par.

"Now you have 100 bucks, so you're even. With 100 bucks, you are neither in credit, nor debit."

Georgina frowns. "Nah. That's ridiculous. How can someone without any cash be in debt?"

"OK, Georgina, let's take this in step by step. Say there was just me all alone on the island. On my own. And I print 100 bucks of banknotes for myself. Would you say that money represented wealth?"

"Well, no, of course not. Without anyone to trade with, the 100 bucks is clearly just paper. Zero. I get that. But what if there is someone to trade with?"

"Right," Fred says. "Now imagine just you and me on the island, just the two of us. Initially we barter with each other. We swap stuff and sometimes we trade labor for stuff. But we don't always have a coincidence of wants. So we invent a points system: one day I give you something worth a couple of points, or perform a few points' worth of labor for you; another day you repay me with some other item worth the same number of points. But we find it difficult to keep track of who owes whom how many points. So one morning we introduce money. We print ourselves 100 bucks of money each. Each buck is a point."

"Hmm. OK, I see your point. The cash that has just this second been printed isn't new wealth. It's just tokens to keep track of who owes whom. So, if there are just the two of us, I suppose I'd agree that 100 bucks would be par."

"Right. With the two of us on the island, it's clear that our only wealth is our actual stuff. We each have 100 bucks that we just minted, but that's not wealth, 100 is zero. Now suppose you want to take a chair which is worth 50 points off me. Without money, you would take my chair and we would remember that you owe me some stuff. But that's hard to track. Once we introduce money, I can instead 'sell' you the chair for 50 bucks. Now I have 150 bucks and you are one chair wealthier than before, but you have just 50 in cash. So those cash balances are really just a convention to keep track of the fact that you owe me 50 points' worth of stuff. You would still owe me that much, even without money. But money provides tokens to help us keep track of the fact that you owe me 50 units of stuff."

"Well, I guess." Georgina scratches her head. "I can see that when taking the chair—sorry, *buying* the chair—I suddenly have more than my fair share of stuff and I give up some cash to track that. I guess I have less than 100 bucks to remind me that I have more than my fair share of stuff. And I guess you having more than the average of 100 bucks is a record that you are owed stuff. Without money, I would just owe you stuff. With money, I don't need a mental note that I owe you because we have money to track that. But how can you claim your debt?"

"I can't. In that respect, cash is an unusual debt—I can't force anyone to repay it. Cash is an entirely open-ended unsecured debt. You can stay in debt forever if you like and leave me stuck in credit. But on an island with 1,000 people, that objection is purely theoretical. So—back to our world. I have 200 bucks right here. That's 100 more than par. Sure, I can't force anyone to give me stuff for my extra 100 bucks. But if I mosey on down to the market, lots of merchants will be more than happy to take my surplus 100 bucks and give me some stuff to fill my deficit. So in the real economy I am in credit, and in practice I will have no problem claiming that credit and obtaining stuff or hiring someone to do some labor for me."

"Wait a second, what if someone was born, or arrives on the island? Are they in debt?"

"Yes. Well, in theory we should introduce a rule that we print a new 100 bucks for every arrival. That would actually be fair, since 100 is the zero. But if we don't have such a rule, then the new arrival will be in debit. On our theoretical island, with just the two of us, when a third person arrives the average cash balance suddenly becomes 66.6 instead of 100. We each have 100 and they have none, so that new person will have to do some 33.3 units of work for each of us, or sell each of us something, in order to get to par. So, yes, they arrive in debit, but it's a small amount."

"Hmm. OK Fred, so in real terms, our fiat money system allows people to go into a small deficit of stuff, no questions asked, while others who have more cash are theoretically owed stuff. Why do we even want to allow that?"

"Because it facilitates trade. The average weekly salary on the island is 100 bucks. Each Friday, salaries are paid, and most people are cash-rich and therefore in credit on that day. They are owed stuff. Business owners are cash-poor on a Friday after payroll, so they owe stuff. Then during the week, people buy stuff from businesses, and go back into debt, while the businesses receive the cash and are back in credit. So the purpose of cash isn't to facilitate long-term debt—it's just to allow the short-term debt needed for the payroll-to-shopping cycle, the exchange of labor for produced goods and services."

"Gotcha. So, a buck means I'm owed a unit of stuff."

"Right, and when a business has a buck, it means they are owed a unit of labor or capital. And the money goes back and forth, as labor is exchanged for goods and services. The key is simply to understand that the average cash balance is the real zero. In that sense, we actually have zero money on the island—the people with above-average cash exactly balance the people with below-average cash. And all this fiat money is just a fancy way of keeping track of people who are slightly in credit or slightly in debt, of stuff. And we must have just enough cash to allow the trade cycle of salaries and shopping."

"But, Fred, that's just government money. What about bank money—what about the checking account balances? Doesn't bank money represent real value?"

"Well, your cash only allows you to go into 100 bucks of debt. That small amount of debt is interest-free and unsecured, but it's a pretty small amount—you can't go below zero cash so you can never be more than 100 down. If you want more debt, then you take out a bank loan. You owe the bank, and you receive bob, or rather a checking account balance, to spend. At the bank you can obtain a much larger loan, say 1,000 bucks. But it will require interest payments and security. So government money allows every citizen a very small debt, totally free and open-ended, mainly for the purpose of the payroll cycle. Banks facilitate bigger debts, which are interest-bearing and secured, and those debts are also money, bank money. But the bank only creates new checking balances in exchange for debt to the bank, so again the total of the credit and debit is zero. There is no actual wealth in money. Both cash and bank money are ways of tracking people who owe stuff and people who are owed stuff."

IN THE UNITED STATES, there is currently about $1.5 trillion in actual dollar banknotes in circulation. A complication is that approximately 60 percent of U.S. cash has found its way outside the U.S.,[23] including the dollars used for everyday trade in countries that don't have stable currencies of their own. In theory, these dollars abroad are a debt for Americans—those people could come to the U.S. one day and spend all their dollars and take away stuff. But this seems unlikely, so we can focus on the banknotes circulating in the U.S. There are around two trillion dollars of issued dollar banknotes.[24] Approximately 40 percent of that money is used in the U.S., amounting to about $2,400 in dollar banknotes per U.S. citizen. Based on the argument in this chapter, we can therefore say that $2,400 in cash is par in the U.S. Having more cash than that means you are owed stuff; whereas any less than $2,400 in cash means you actually owe stuff. This means that $2,400 is the average, and therefore the real zero. But the good news is that, if you have less than $2,400, there is no interest payment due, and no time limit on that conceptual debt.

And then there is bank money. The U.S. currently has only about $1.7 trillion in M1 checking account balances which isn't backed by cash—bank money.[25] Again, this isn't net wealth. All the bank money is matched exactly by debt to the bank, giving a net value of zero. So the amount of M0 and M1 available for trade is trillions of dollars, but the actual wealth directly represented by the monetary system is arguably zero.

A central theme of this book is that money isn't the *real economy*. In the real economy, income is the consumption of goods and services, and wealth is ownership of real-world capital assets. Credit is also a form of wealth, but again it should be thought of as credit for future money; or, more fundamentally, as credit for future consumption of goods and services, or credit for future asset ownership. Credit is always balanced by someone else's debt, someone who will one day have to give up some real income or real assets.

In summary, the total real value of money is zero. The main purpose of cash is to keep track of the exchange of labor and capital for goods and services. A laborer can receive their salary in cash and they will therefore, temporarily, have more than the average cash balance. This means that, conceptually, they are owed stuff. Then, during the following week or month, they spend the cash and receive the goods and services they wish to receive, in exchange for their labor.

Meanwhile, bank money provides larger, longer-term debt to finance investment in capital assets, such as factories, homes, or cars.

BUT WHAT THOSE people who have "too much money"? Strictly speaking, they probably don't. When we say that Jeff Bezos is worth more than $100 billion, he obviously has a tiny proportion of that in actual money, cash or checking accounts. He may have no more than the average cash amount. The vast majority of his wealth is in Amazon shares. This means that, along with other shareholders, he owns the physical and intangible capital of the Amazon business and is entitled to a share of Amazon's future profits. The specific value of those shares is assessed, based on the price at which they change hands on the stock market, where shares are traded for money.

When we look at the overall financial position of the United States, we similarly see that all assets have a net value well in excess of $100 trillion, while actual money, as we saw, is just a few trillion dollars, and arguably does not in itself represent any wealth.

INFLATION

FREED OF THE gold standard, Georgina's government can now print money at will. Just imagine a politician with a money printing press.

Martha gets her pension increase. Paula lands a government contract to construct two more bridges. Somehow Georgina even finds money for a nice pay increase for the governor.

Martha is the last to get to market one Thursday. The stalls are mostly empty. Almost all the goods produced on the island that week have been sold. All the haircuts and massages have been booked. The island has more money than before, but the same quantity of goods or services are being produced. So, at the end of the market day, Martha has money left to spend and nothing to buy.

Charlie has just a couple of coconuts left. "That's a buck fifty, Auntie."

"Young man, it's two coconuts for a buck. Always has been."

"Sorry, Auntie Martha. It's a buck fifty, take it or leave it."

With more cash around, consumers can buy the island's entire production of goods and services for the week and be left with extra cash, and no goods or services to buy. Merchants pick up on this instinctively and raise their prices, and the cash-rich consumers don't object as much as they usually would.

It starts sporadically, but soon enough most merchants are raising prices quite regularly, and the market settles into a pattern of prices increasing a couple of percent each month, in line with the increasing money supply.

Milton demands an urgent meeting with Georgina.

"You were supposed to gradually increase the money supply, Georgina. Gradually! Just enough to let the economy grow naturally. A few percent a year at most. You're flooding the island with cash. Don't you remember the equation of money? If there is more money circulating, there will be more transactions, or... higher prices per transaction. Obviously, production on the island can't possibly grow that quickly. More cash is chasing the same goods and services, and pumping up their prices. And this inflation is reducing the value of everyone's cash."

"Still, Milton, GDP is growing, isn't it? There is more spending each market day. I was tasked to grow GDP."

"Growth? This is not real growth. It's just growth in the nominal buck value of the transactions. You only get credit for real growth when you get more production and more consumption of actual goods and services."

Georgina is up for reelection in ten months. Somehow she feels this would not be a great time to cut back on infrastructure projects. Or to cancel pay rises for her staff. She continues printing money. For the good of the island.

Soon inflation is plaguing businesses and consumers, and the political cost of inflation is catching up with the political benefit of generous government spending. Prices are changing at a rapid rate. The food stalls are writing out new menus twice a month. People hate the fact that the cash in their wallets is worth less with each week that passes. They rush to spend their salaries in the market on payday for fear that prices will increase the next day.

Milton continues to campaign against money printing. "It's a simple enough equation," he tells anyone who will listen. "If there's more money circulating each week, then either production increases or prices increase. Everyone's already producing as much as they can, so real production can only increase very gradually. Georgina's money printing is forcing nominal prices up, and forcing the value of our money down. With no benefit."

And then Milton starts an organized campaign. More and more market stalls have signs saying "Georgina, hand over the keys" with a small diagram of the mint, or money printing press.

FOLLOWING THE ABOLITION of the gold standard in 1971, many economies fell into the trap of printing money, and experienced significant inflation in the seventies and early eighties. You might call this the adolescent phase of fiat money. The U.S. saw inflation in the range of 3–

15 percent per annum.[26] Some countries had hyperinflation reaching hundreds of percent per year.

It is worth clarifying that, although we use the term *printing money* loosely for the creation of new government fiat money, most modern money is in fact electronic. Only a small percentage is physically minted, and this is a point we will return to.

Hyperinflation was not invented in the 1970s. There was hyperinflation in the Roman Empire's Crisis of the Third Century.[27] Another famous bout of hyperinflation was in the German Weimar Republic of the 1920s; in December 1923, the exchange rate was over four trillion marks to a single U.S. dollar.[28] More recently, Zimbabwe suffered 79.6 billion percent inflation in a single month[29] and Venezuela experienced over a million percent annual inflation in 2018.[30]

There have actually been many theories about inflation other than an excess of money supply. Keynesian Economics talks about three causes of inflation:

Demand-pull inflation is caused by increases in demand—i.e., a negative side-effect of growth—also known informally as an *overheated economy*.

Cost-push inflation is caused by a drop in supply—for example, a natural disaster reducing production and causing goods to be rarer and their prices to increase.

Built-in inflation can arguably develop over time. Once there is an expectation of inflation, businesses develop the habit of raising prices, and their workers demand salary raises to afford the higher prices. The result is a price/wage inflation spiral, which may become ingrained as a social norm.

Milton Friedman denied these theories and famously stated: "Inflation is always and everywhere a monetary phenomenon." Friedman and other *monetarists* presented significant evidence that inflation is caused primarily by an excess in the supply of money. The equation of money teaches us that too much money, assuming the velocity of money is stable, inevitably causes inflation. As implied in our story, price inflation will typically arrive with a time lag after the printing of excess money, a point which will be significant later.

Another way to think about all of this is that an abundance of money, just like an abundance of any good, makes money cheaper. Therefore, the monetary price of everything else becomes more expensive.

Today, there is a consensus that excess money supply is the key cause of inflation, and so our story focuses on monetary inflation. But there is no denying that there can be other, secondary, factors in inflation. For example, in the seventies, there was an oil crisis which caused a spike in oil prices, and this *cost-push* was probably a factor in the notorious inflation of that period.

THE INDEPENDENT CENTRAL BANK

FINALLY, GEORGINA AGREES to hand over the keys to the mint to an independent authority. Fred is hired as the central banker, tasked with controlling how much money the government prints.

"Listen Fred. You have one job," Milton says. "Keep prices stable. And you have one tool: manage the money supply. In other words, keep Georgina away from the mint. Print money, gradually, to allow economic growth. Never print money just because the government wants to go on a spending spree. Print just enough to allow real economic growth, without allowing prices to increase."

"Agreed. But I'm not sure absolute price stability is such a great idea," Fred says. "If I keep the average price completely stable, we're just a hair's breadth away from deflation. If there's any change, like an uptick in production, we'll have deflation."

"He's right," says Georgina. "Also, if we keep the average price stable, not all goods will be stable. We may have some goods or services getting more expensive, while others become cheaper. So at least some goods will still suffer from the deflation problem—people will postpone buying them."

"All right," says Milton. "Can we agree on 2 percent a year as an inflation target? That will keep us safe from deflation, while limiting price increases to a glacial rate."

And so the island's government now has an independent central bank, and the central banker, Fred, has responsibility for controlling the supply of money. He prints money and gives it to the government to spend, but not based on how much the government would like to spend, rather based purely on the goal of stabilizing prices, targeting a gentle 2 percent annual price inflation.

IN THE U.S., the Federal Reserve, which is the central bank, was founded in 1913, although the history of central banks can be traced back to the Swedish Riksbank and the Bank of England in the 1600s. The Bank of England evolved modern central banking functions in the 18th and 19th centuries.[31]

Following the inflation of the 1970s, the *Federal Reserve Reform Act of 1977* made *price stability* an explicit goal for the Federal Reserve. And other countries set similar goals for their central banks and reinforced the independence of the central banks from the government.

Recently the independence of central banks was back in the news, with President Trump publicly pressuring the Federal Reserve to print more money. The Federal Reserve is affectionately known as the *Fed*, and their economic data, published by the Federal Bank of St. Louis, is called FRED.[32]

There was some reexamination of monetarist theory after massive money printing during the financial crisis of 2007–2008, and the Covid-19 crisis of 2020, failed to trigger inflation. We will return to this at the end of the book.

Explicit targets for inflation were adopted by New Zealand, Canada, the U.K. and the E.U. in the nineties. It was only in 2012 that the U.S. Federal Reserve joined other countries and adopted an explicit inflation target of 2 percent per annum, as in our story.

INTEREST RATES AS A MONETARY POLICY TARGET

A COUPLE OF years later there are three banks on the island, Bob's Bank, Barbara's Bank, and Bill's Bank. The banks all practice fractional reserve banking, and so they all create bank money for the island. The banks also start lending each other money on a daily basis—any bank which is not managing to lend out its available funds to clients, may lend funds to another bank instead.

The interest rate for loans between banks, on a yearly basis, is around 3 percent. The banks are trusted to return their loans, so this interbank interest rate pretty much represents the pure cost of borrowing money, with almost zero credit risk. Businesses and homeowners, on the other hand, are now paying around 5 percent, to cover the extra credit risk they pose, as well as the bank's profit.

Fred has laid out his monetary policy. He knows there are around 200,000 bucks of government cash in circulation. That's the base money supply, which he calls M0. Fred polls the three banks and learns that a total of some 50,000 bucks of physical cash are in the vaults of the three banks. The other 150,000 must be circulating between people's wallets. Bob, Barbara, and Bill inform Fred that they have a total of 250,000 bucks in all the checking accounts held by the three banks. Fred notes with satisfaction that the 250,000 bucks in checking accounts is backed by 50,000 in cash reserves, which is 20 percent. This is well above the 10 percent minimum reserve.

Fred introduces the term M1 money supply for the 200,000 in government cash, plus 200,000 unbacked bank money. The M1 supply of 400,000 bucks is the total money available for commerce.

Fred convenes the economic council to discuss how he should grow the money supply responsibly.

"Don't get clever," says Milton. "The population is growing at 1 percent each year. The economy can perhaps get 2 percent more productive each year, due to accumulating capital and new technology. So we should aim for 3 percent real growth of the economy. Therefore, I recommend we increase the money supply at a steady rate of 5 percent per year. We can allow 3 percent to enable the real growth, and an extra 2 percent to allow for our target of 2 percent price inflation."

"You realize I can only grow M0," says Fred. "I can't actually control the total M1 money supply."

"I wouldn't worry too much," says Barbara. "As more cash becomes available, some of it will find its way to the banks, and we will use those reserves to create more loans and more bank money. If you increase M0 by 5 percent a year, it's a decent bet that bank money and the total M1 money supply will increase by 5 percent too."

"OK." Fred points at the rudimentary printing equipment in the next room. "I will print new money at a steady rate of about 10,000 bucks per year and give the new cash to the government to spend."

For a few months, things are stable. The economy is growing gently. Prices are creeping up at a barely perceptible rate. Everyone is content with the new central bank.

Spring arrives. Suddenly, most farmers need money to buy seeds and hire temporary laborers to sow their fields. The economy goes into overdrive as farm hands work overtime. Farmers line up outside Bob's Bank to take out loans. Bob is not one to miss a business opportunity. Seeing the strong demand for borrowing bank money, he starts to increase his interest rates—5 percent becomes 6 percent, then 7 percent and then 8 percent.

Now other people can't afford loans for their businesses. People can barely afford to buy homes, and those with mortgages are suddenly hit with a painful increase in interest payments. In the meantime, Barbara's Bank has fewer farmer customers, but she can now lend money to Bob at 6 percent, for him to loan out at 8 percent, so she also benefits from the increase in interest rates.

Summer follows spring and interest rates ease back to 5 percent. And then, in the fall, farmers need loans to finance the harvest, and interest rates are on the rise again.

This time political pressure mounts, and Georgina summons Fred.

"Fred. What's this with 8 percent interest rate? People can't afford loans for their businesses. They can't afford mortgages for their homes. Some might lose their homes. Can't you bring interest rates down?"

He thinks for a moment. "I probably can. Money is like anything—if I print more money, it will become more plentiful and therefore cheaper."

Georgina pauses. "Simple as that? More money will give us lower interest rates?"

"It should. Think of it another way. Cash is effectively an open unsecured loan. So more cash slightly reduces the demand for bank loans, because the farmers can make more purchases from cash in hand."

"Well, OK, that's great. Fire up the printing press."

"No, I won't. Georgina, you gave me one job: keep prices stable. One job. And you gave me one instrument—the keys to the money mint. I'm trying to keep inflation at a gentle 2 per cent per year. I can only do that by being very restrained with the printing of money. Come on now, you know that."

"But then every spring and fall we're going to have a shortage of money and prohibitive interest rates? People will take mortgages in the summer, only to find interest rates getting hiked up in the fall. Fred, there must be a better way."

"Georgina, I'm not going to randomly print money and risk inflation. That would be neglecting my primary job."

Georgina paces for a minute. "OK, Fred, let me get this straight. If you print money, interest rates go down. If there is less money around, interest rates go up?"

"Yes."

"OK. Well, right now you are using the printing press to grow the money supply at a constant rate. But that doesn't make any provision for seasonal needs. Perhaps you should be using the money mint to stabilize interest rates instead. That way, when there is a seasonal need for more loans and more money, you can print extra money and keep interest rates stable."

"Hmmm," Fred pauses. "That might not be such a crazy idea. Instead of managing the quantity of money, I should manage the price of money?"

"Exactly. Manage the interest rates."

"But then how will I do my job of keeping prices stable, with gentle inflation?"

"Well, I guess you should still make sure our money supply grows at around 5 percent per year on average. But as the seasons change, adjust the money supply to smooth out the interest rates."

He frowns. "That would make my job much more complex. Printing money at a stable rate is simple. But interest rates are set by the banks to match supply of savings with demand for loans. I can influence that, but I don't control it directly."

"Guess what, Fred. No one ever said it would be easy."

And so later that week, after consultation with the government's economic council, Fred adopts a new policy. Rather than directly managing the quantity of money, he manages the cost of money: in other words, the interest rates, which represent the cost of borrowing money. This leaves some flexibility for the quantity of money to adjust seasonally.

"OK, now we will have stable interest rates. How do we choose an interest rate target?" Georgina asks the council.

IN THE NEXT CHAPTER, we'll see exactly how the money supply is used to manage interest rates.

Milton Friedman, the father of modern monetarism, urged the Federal Reserve to adopt the simplest possible monetary policy—printing cash at a fixed steady rate—just like Fred in our story. Friedman, a strong libertarian, preferred this strategy in order to minimize government involvement in the economy, by giving the Fed no discretion regarding how much money to create.

However, such a simple policy has obvious disadvantages. Firstly, as we saw, there are seasonal fluctuations in the demand for money. And an inflexible money supply will lead to seasonal fluctuations in interest rates, as occurred in the U.S. before the Fed started its operations in 1914.[33]

An even more serious issue can occur in the long term, as changes in economic growth rates and demographic growth rates require changes in the rate of expansion of the money supply.

In practice, therefore, central banks have always pursued a more complex strategy. The actual strategy has varied. There have been times where central banks set targets for the M1 money supply. The Fed pursued such a policy briefly from 1979 to 1982. But the consensus policy of central banks for many years now has been to set *nominal interest rate* targets from time to time, and to manage the money supply based on the current interest rate target. We see this in the headlines periodically, with the Fed, the European Central Bank, and other central banks announcing that their target interest rates are going up or down a percentage point.

Note that *nominal* in economics always means measured in terms of money, while *real* always means measured in terms of stuff.

We will now see how interest rate targets are achieved.

IMPLEMENTING INTEREST RATE TARGETS

THE NEXT DAY, Fred makes an announcement. "The island's central bank is going to aim to maintain the interbank interest rate at the current rate of 3 percent. We will adjust the money supply to keep this rate stable. The central bank may revise this interest rate target from time to time, based on the money requirements of the island."

The three bankers all demand an urgent meeting with Fred and Georgina. "You don't have that power," Barbara says to Fred. "We will negotiate interest rates between us, thank you very much. We banks can best judge our book of borrowers and lenders, and then decide at what rate we wish to borrow from or lend to other banks." Bob and Bill nod their agreement.

"Don't worry, banker friends," says Fred. "I won't force you to do anything."

After they leave, a rather confused Georgina asks Fred. "Does that mean mortgages will now cost 3 percent?"

"Not quite—3 percent is the target rate for loans between banks. That's the closest thing there is to a risk-free loan. But if banks borrow at 3 percent, they will then lend to businesses and homeowners for no more than around 5 percent. In other words, 3 percent will be the pure cost of borrowing money; but loans to consumers and businesses will always have some extra cost to allow for risk and for bank profit.

"Also, remember that 3 percent is the nominal interest rate. If a bank lends 100 bucks, it receives back 103 bucks after a year—3 percent in nominal terms; that is, in pure monetary terms. But we're targeting 2 percent inflation so those 103 bucks will only be worth about 101 old bucks in terms of purchasing power. The real interest rate—the growth in the actual amount of stuff you can buy—is just 1 percent."

"Huh?"

"Georgina, just remember that the real interest rate is the nominal interest rate, minus inflation. When you save money, the nominal interest rate is how much your bucks grow per year. The real interest rate is how much the *purchasing power of your bucks* grows per year. Real interest rates therefore capture the real reward for delayed gratification, in terms of how much stuff you can buy later. Now Georgina, my job has just become way more complicated, I had better get back to work."

Fred checks on loans between banks. Spring is in the air, and the demand for loans is high. Bob's Bank is strong in the agricultural sector, and Bob now has many farmer customers requiring loans. Barbara's Bank is strong in other sectors and does not have that many loans out. Her excess cash reserves are not earning her any money. Fred finds Bob and Barbara in the market discussing a short-term 2,000 buck interbank loan from Barbara to Bob, at an interest rate of 3.5 percent per year.

"Don't pay her 3.5 percent, Bob. I will lend you the money at 3 percent!"

Barbara's jaw drops. "That's not fair, Fred! How can you lend for just 3 percent? Hah! You're going to just print the money, aren't you? How can I possibly compete with that?"

"Next time, if you want to compete, offer Bob the loan for 3 percent. That's our target interest rate for interbank loans and we're serious about it."

"I thought your job was printing money. Since when did you get into the lending business?"

"It just so happens that reducing interest rates and printing money is the same thing. I used to print money at a steady rate. Now I have a more sophisticated policy and I print money whenever I see interbank interest rates going above 3 percent."

"Bob, you're not going to accept this loan from the central bank, are you?"

"Well…"

Sure enough, Fred mints 2,000 bucks of new cash, and lends them to Bob's Bank at 3 percent. He is using newly printed currency to stop interest rates rising during the season in which demand for money peaks. Bob uses the

2,000 bucks in cash as reserves and creates loans of 10,000 checking account bucks—newly minted bank money—which he lends out to farmers. The amount of money on the island has increased. M0 cash has increased by 2,000 bucks and M1—cash plus bank money—has increased by 12,000 bucks. Fred has succeeded in capping interest rates at 3 percent by printing money, and the farmers get their seasonal loans without an interest rate hike.

A few weeks later, going into summer, the demand for loans is waning. Bill's Bank is talking about borrowing money from Barbara's Bank for just 2.5 percent.

Fred now has the opposite problem. Interest rates are below target. This time he approaches the lending bank.

"Barbara, why lend cash to Bill for 2.5 percent? I will pay you 3 percent!"

"Hey, how unfair, Fred," Bill says. "You don't need a loan. I bet you're just going to lock up the cash. And you can afford to pay 3 percent interest for a loan you don't need, because you can just print that money when it's time to repay. You realize this means you are forcing up the interest rates my bank charges customers?"

After a few such operations, there is more cash locked up by Fred and less cash to go around, and the banks are borrowing from each other at a stable 3 percent. Fred doesn't interfere on a continuous basis. Having corrected the amount of money in circulation downwards, interbank interest rates stabilize at 3 percent without Fred having to compete for bank loans each day. Fred remains ready to add or remove cash from circulation the next time interbank interest rates show signs of deviating from his 3 percent target.

AFTER A COUPLE of years of stabilizing, the interest rate by lending to, and borrowing from, banks, Fred starts to appreciate the limitations of this system. Sometimes the banks are simply not in the market for providing or receiving a loan, and he is stuck without any way to adjust the money supply. So Fred develops a second strategy for forcing money in and out of the economy to stabilize interest rates—he decides to allow any islander to lend money to the government at the prevailing interest rate. He issues them an IOU, which he calls a bond. Now, instead of loaning money to and from banks, the island's central bank can borrow money from the islanders as well. When there isn't enough money, and interest rates go above the target 3 percent, Fred sells government bonds in the market. These bonds say "The government owes you 100 bucks in one year" and he sells them for around 97 bucks each, implying a 3 percent interest rate.

In September, demand for cash is high again. Paula had invested in a government bond, but now she needs cash to hire seasonal labor to pick oranges. There is a new corner of the market dedicated to trading government bonds and Fred often hangs out there. Her bond has a payout of 100 bucks in one year. Since demand for cash is seasonally high, several people are trying to sell bonds in the market that day, and Arthur offers Bella just 96 bucks.

"Hold it, Paula," Fred says. "That bond originally paid 3 percent interest. But if you sell it at a discounted price of 96 bucks, Arthur will be effectively making 4 percent. At the bank we call that a 4 percent 'yield.' And it's against our policy. Our job is to make enough cash available so that interest rates stay at 3 percent. So I will bid 97 bucks for your bond to make sure that the yield stays at 3 percent."

"You, Fred?" Arthur shouts.

"Well, not me personally. The central bank of the island will pay Paula 97 bucks."

"The government is buying its own loans?"

"When they're too cheap, yes we are. Just hold that bond for me."

Fred prints 97 bucks' worth of shiny new buck bills and buys the bond at this higher price, bringing the yield back to 3 percent. Paula now has 97 bucks in newly minted money which she can pay to laborers in her orchard, bringing more money into circulation.

Again, Fred is increasing the money supply to reduce interest rates to 3 percent, this time by buying back bonds for cash. Now that the bond debt is paid off, Fred simply stores it.

Come winter, cash needs are lower, and people want to buy government bonds as a safe way of saving. The price of bonds increases so that yields go down. Fred sees a bond trading for 98 bucks, representing an approximately 2 percent yield. "Hold on. I can offer you a similar bond for 97 bucks." After selling a bond from his vault, Fred locks up the 97 bucks, taking that cash out of circulation.

By buying and selling the government's own bonds on the open market, Fred is minting new money to lower interest rates, or he's taking cash out of circulation to increase interest rates. Either way, he's always keeping the interbank interest rates close to his target 3 percent, and there's no need for him to negotiate directly with the banks.

AS IN OUR STORY, the Fed, like other central banks, uses two main tools to move interbank interest rates towards their target rate. The first and most important is *open market operations*, buying and selling government bonds, and the second is setting the *discount rate* at which the Fed lends to banks, thereby competing with interbank loans. Both strategies involve printing money to reduce interest rates, and withdrawing cash from circulation to increase interest rates. Using these tools, the Fed is tweaking the base money supply on a daily basis. The Fed makes a public report on these open market operations.[34]

In theory, the Fed has other tools, like changing the 10 percent bank reserve requirement in order to influence how much money banks create. But in practice, this rate is rarely touched. It remained at 10 percent, with certain exemptions, from 1992 to 2020, when it was reduced to zero during the Covid-19 pandemic.

We see here again the concept that money represents zero wealth. Central banks regularly create or destroy money, but they don't directly create or destroy wealth. When the Fed prints cash, it swaps the cash for a bond or vice versa, replacing one form of debt with another. Similarly, if the Fed lends out newly minted cash directly to a bank, it is making a loan in exchange for the bank's indebtedness and commitment to repay the Fed.

SETTING INTEREST RATE TARGETS

FRED'S SHORT-TERM target is a stable 3 percent interest rate. But his long-term goal is price stability, with just 2 percent inflation. The short-term policy helps to smooth over seasonal fluctuations in the island's cash needs while keeping interest rates stable. But Fred is not yet entirely sure how we will decide on updates to the 3 percent interest rate target.

Fred pays a teenager to survey prices in the market. The prices cover a basket of the typical goods and services that an average family consumes in a week: five oranges, four fish, three cups full of berries, one haircut, and so on. Every month, the teenagers walks around the market and adds up the total price of this typical basket of goods and services.

At one of his regular council meetings, Fred has received a report that the price of the shopping basket has been increasing at a rate equivalent to 3 percent per year. This is 1 percent above his target annual inflation rate of 2 percent.

"Let's nip this in the bud," Fred says to the meeting. "It is my job to fight inflation. According to the equation of money, excess inflation indicates that there is too much money around. I suggest we reduce the money supply. Since we use interest rates as our barometer, let's increase our target for bank interest rates to 4 percent. That 1 percent increase will in turn lead us to sell bonds for cash, thus reducing the money supply, which will combat price inflation."

Milton is scratching his head. "You know Fred, that's not a real increase. That is just keeping the same interest rate."

"Pardon? Isn't 4 percent an increase from 3 percent, Milton?"

"Actually no. Not in real terms. Previously we had an interbank interest rate of 3 percent and inflation of 2 percent. After adjusting for inflation, the real value of loans between banks, in terms of purchasing power, was only increasing 1 percent per year."

"Yeah, OK. But we're targeting the nominal interest rate paid in money terms. Who cares about the real interest rate?"

"Only everyone! When people decide whether to spend all their income now, or to consume less now and delay gratification and save for a year, it's the real interest rate they have to consider. In other words, they have to think about how much more they will be able to buy in a year's time; that's the real compensation for delaying gratification."

"So?"

"Well, now inflation has gone up to 3 percent. If you increase the nominal interest rates to 4 percent, the real interest rate is four minus three. So the difference is still 1 percent, just as before. You haven't tightened up money in real terms, so it won't help to reduce inflation."

At the end of the meeting, Fred announces an increase in the target interest rate from 3 percent to 5 percent. Milton agrees that this will bring the real interest rate, 5 percent interest minus 3 percent inflation, up to 2 percent. It represents a real increase in the cost of borrowing which, the council considers, should help to combat excess inflation.

Fred immediately starts to implement the decision by removing cash from the economy. He competes to borrow cash from the banks, and sells treasury bonds for cash, reducing the value of the treasury bonds and increasing their yield. He keeps taking cash out of the economy until interest rates stabilize at 5 percent. With less cash going around, the slightly overheated economy stabilizes, and prices go back to a steady 2 percent growth rate.

The sudden 2 percent change in nominal interest rates is a jolt to the economy. People have to scrap their planned business projects and home purchases. So Fred and his council resolve to meet more often and make smaller adjustments in future, preferably no more than half a percent at a time.

The island now has a sophisticated monetary policy. Cash is being added or removed from the economy on a daily basis, in order to maintain stable interest rates in the short term; this allows money supply to be adjusted flexibly according to seasonal needs. And target interest rates are themselves being tweaked from time to time in an effort to keep prices stable, with the central bank raising interest rates when it sees signs of inflation, and reducing rates if there is a risk of deflation.

Fred hopes that this strategy will supply the island's economy with just enough money to allow steady economic growth, with only around 2 percent inflation, and with flexibility to allow seasonal changes in the money supply.

WHAT MILTON IS IN EFFECT arguing here is what became known as the *Taylor principle* from the 1990s. If inflation ticks up by 1 percent, central banks must respond by raising nominal interest rates by more than 1 percent, so that real interest rates will be increased.

This led to the *Taylor rule*, a proposed formula by which central banks can adjust nominal interest rates in response to indicators of inflation and growth; the formula ensures that nominal rates are moved by more than the desired change in inflation in order to shift the real interest rate.

For example, from 2003 to 2005, U.S. inflation rates were creeping above 2 percent and eventually above 3 percent.[35] And yet 3 percent is not a horrible inflation rate, and the official target of 2 percent inflation had not yet been adopted. But the Fed considered that inflation was too high, and trending up, and so responded aggressively, raising its target interbank rates by a quarter percent 17 times in succession. In this way, the Fed raised the rate all the way from 1 percent in 2004 to 5.25 percent in the summer of 2006.[36] As per the Taylor rule, the increase in the nominal inflation rate was greater than the excess inflation that it was combating.

The Taylor rule was an attempt to turn central banking into a science. However, central banks don't follow the Taylor rule strictly, as they like to have some human discretion when setting monetary policy. Setting interest rates therefore remains, in some sense, an art.

We have seen that the main goal of modern monetary policy is price stability, by ensuring there is enough money for commerce, but not much more. A secondary goal, which has been endlessly debated, is monetary policy as a tool for promoting growth. The consensus is that printing extra money can only have a short-term effect on growth; pretty soon, extra money just causes price inflation. This is sometimes expressed as: you can print money, but you can't force it to circulate. We will explore this argument again later when we discuss recessions, which economists regard as short-term phenomena.

Today, all central banks consider their main mission to be price stability—in other words, gentle steady inflation. And there seems to be a broad consensus around an inflation target of 2 percent. On the face of it, in order to achieve this goal, central banks simply need to grow the supply of money in line with the natural growth of the economy, plus an extra 2 percent.

If only it were that simple.

Monetary policy is complex for several reasons. Firstly, inflation does not respond immediately to changes in the money supply. So trying to control inflation is like playing a video game which responds with some lag to the joystick.

Secondly, the government only controls the amount of cash available (M0). The total amount of money, including bank money (M1), depends on how much banks are lending, which affects how much bank money is created. This can change fairly rapidly.

Finally, there are seasonal changes in the demand for money and occasional changes in the velocity of money. For example, some salaries are paid monthly, some weekly, and some employers are even experimenting with daily payments.[37]

Central banks seem to have reached a consensus that the best short-term barometer for the money supply is interest rates. On a daily basis, if interest rates tick upwards, central banks print a bit more money to bring them down. And if interest rates tick downwards, they remove a bit of cash from circulation to bring them back up.

And then every few weeks, central banks use a variety of imperfect indicators to assess the economy and adjust the interest rate target up or down accordingly. These key indicators include inflation, inflation expectations, employment, and growth.

As in our island story, central banks prefer to make gentle changes of a quarter percent or a half percent up or down. But the Fed can make more dramatic changes, like the drop from 1.5 percent to zero in two steps in March 2020 as the pandemic hit.[38]

We will come back to interest rates later and explore further the relationship between nominal and real interest rates.

FRACTIONAL RESERVE BANKING REVISITED

AS A QUICK aside before ending Section III, let's revisit the discussion about fractional reserve banking and bank money. As we saw earlier, in the chapter titled Fractional reserve banking and bank money, fractional reserve banking, together with the ability to spend bank money with checkbooks and the like, enables banks to create a large quantity of money and lend it out for interest.

Now we have also seen that in a modern economy with a fiat currency, the central bank itself can increase and reduce the supply of base money—cash—in a flexible way.

To my mind, this amplifies the question mark around fractional reserve banking. To the extent that banks can produce money for interest, and assuming the economy is not short of cash, the central bank will have to respond by removing base money from the system. Therefore, when banks use fractional reserve banking to create bank money, they are often replacing free money, cash, with expensive money, bank loans.

Let's think about this in terms of the real economy of stuff, rather than money. Simple bank loans based on long-term savings are clearly valuable to the real economy, matching the advance and delay of gratification. It gives some people the ability to postpone consumption and save for the future, while others are able to advance gratification and invest in building capital and pay for it later.

In a similar way, we can try to justify fractional reserve banking without bank money. The bank is aggregating casual delays of gratification, money sitting unspent in checking accounts, and matching them with advances of gratification, by providing bank loans. However, there are some question marks here. For example, if there is lots of money in checking accounts but it is moving from one person's checking account to another's, at least on a monthly cadence, then this money is actually in normal circulation and it's hard to find any societal benefit in allowing banks to lend it out. It might be preferable if banks could only lend out checking balances that have been static for more than 30 days, indicating that they do indeed represent a delay of gratification.

We will return to this point when we discuss recessions. In theory, when people decide to spend less and leave more money dormant in their checking accounts, fractional reserve banking, preferably without bank money, can help to get 90 percent of that money back into circulation. But is that what happens? Typically, no.

But my biggest reservation is about fractional reserve banking, combined with bank money, allowing banks to create money well beyond the amount sitting in checking accounts. We saw that with a 10 percent reserve requirement, banks can in theory loan out new bank money up to nine times the cash in checking accounts. These loans of bank money are not matched by any delay of gratification; it is just new money, and expensive money at that, which will compete with cash for buying the same amount of goods and services in the marketplace. The central bank will end up compensating for any such increase in bank money by removing cash from the economy. This is profitable for banks, but I have failed to find any evidence that it helps the real economy.

NOW THAT WE KNOW all about fiat money and how it allows central banks to create an elastic money supply, we can explore how the economy grows. In Section IV, we will find out about economic growth in the long term, over many years; and later, in Section V, we will look at the trickier, more controversial topic of shorter-term economic fluctuations.

IV. THE LONG-TERM ECONOMY AND GOVERNMENT

TAX AND FISCAL SPENDING

AS GOVERNOR, Georgina introduces a 20 percent tax on all salaries. Fred collects the money in the government vault, the Fisc, as he calls it. The government spends this tax money on building a bridge across the river, and, of course, paying Georgina and Fred's salaries.

These measures are reasonably popular, although one citizen, Milton, objects vociferously. "If people want a bridge, then a business can decide to build a bridge and make money by charging a toll. We don't need our government forcing us to pay for services we didn't choose. This is virtually slavery."

"Slavery?" Georgina rolls her eyes. "Do me a favor, Milton. It's not like you've been chained up and forced to work on the bridge."

"I beg your pardon, but in a way, yes, I have. I work five days a week. But you take away 20 percent of my salary and spend it on the bridge. That means one day a week my labor is financing work on a bridge that I didn't ask for, just as surely as if I was forced to slave on the bridge under threat of violent punishment. Indeed, if I refuse to pay taxes, which are equivalent to one day a week of forced labor on bridge construction, I will face the physical punishment of incarceration. How does that differ from a slave being physically punished for refusing to do his work?"

"With all due respect, that's a bit of a stretch," says Fred. "You are being asked—ok, yes, forced—to contribute some of the income from your labor for the good of society as a whole. That's not quite the same as being forced to work to enrich some so-called slave owner, is it?"

They never quite reach agreement, but construction continues. John notes that the government building a bridge is also part of the production on the island. In some ways it's like a business investing in capital, except that all islanders are forced to invest, and the bridge belongs to the public.

John updates his measurements of GDP to include government spending, in addition to consumer spending and business investment. So GDP now comprises consumption, investment, and government spending.

THE FIRST KNOWN SYSTEM of taxation was in Ancient Egypt around 3000–2800 BC in the First Dynasty of the Old Kingdom of Egypt.[39] Taxation, of course, remains a hot political topic. Libertarians, such as Milton Friedman, have a strong aversion to taxation and a strong preference for "small government," which leaves every possible function to the private sector.

While Friedman was no fan of taxation and a strong proponent of small government, the argument that tax is slavery was actually made more explicitly by Tolstoy and others.[40]

Big governments are in many ways a twentieth-century phenomenon. At the start of the twentieth century, most governments accounted for less than 10 percent of their country's GDP. Today government spending in developed economies ranges from around 25 percent in the U.S. to over 50 percent in Scandinavia. Not surprisingly, the biggest tickets in government spending are invariably education, healthcare, social security, and defense.

In this book, in order to keep diagrams of the economy concise, we include government services in the business box, by thinking of government services as public sector businesses.

REDISTRIBUTION OF INCOME AND WEALTH

A COUPLE OF MONTHS later, it's Martha's turn to lobby Georgina.

"Georgina, I'm barely surviving here. Other people have become wealthy. Yet we all pay the same 20 percent income tax. The government needs to help me."

"Well, it's a percentage. 20 percent means that rich people are paying many more bucks than you."

"Have a look for yourself. It's not working. I'm not suggesting we go back to sharing everything, but we can't have some people living in ostentatious wealth while others are on the verge of starvation."

Georgina convenes an economic council to discuss whether and how the government should redistribute income.

Bella, one of the wealthier islanders, is invited to represent businesses on the council. She herself knows people who are barely making ends meet. "I do agree that it might be fairer to have a system where not only the tax amount, but also the tax rate, progresses with more wealth. We can call it progressive taxation. A higher tax rate on the wealthy should finance social benefits for those who need them: poor people, the elderly, disabled and unemployed.

"In addition to progressive taxation on income, I don't think it's fair that some people are born with huge wealth and some with little or nothing. We need to redistribute wealth but that's difficult to do while people are alive. My solution would be an inheritance tax on the larger estates so that some of the wealth can be redistributed between families once per generation."

John adds an economic argument. "If there is too much income concentrated in too few hands, it may limit consumption and reduce economic growth. There are only so many goods and services that the wealthy will be inclined to consume, while everyone else may be stuck without disposable income. Move some bucks from a rich person to a poor person and there is an increased chance that those bucks will be spent in the market."

Fred talks about the risk of social unrest. "A big gap in wealth may ultimately prompt the poor to revolt, out of desperation and frustration. Let's consider long-term stability here."

And Arthur is concerned about happiness. "Huge gaps in income and wealth will obviously make the poor feel unhappy and may actually make the wealthy feel insecure too. If there is too much inequality the wealthy will always have some concern of theft or even of a social revolution. Less inequality should mean more happiness."

Milton stands up. "All your arguments are baloney. You can't just toss freedom to the wind. Everyone should be free to start a business and become wealthy. They should have the right to bequeath their wealth to their own children. The government has no ethical right to move money by force of law from one person to another. Charity should be voluntary. That is freedom."

He sits down. "Secondly, increasing taxes on the rich will reduce their incentive to build up successful businesses. It is precisely those businesses that increase the production of goods and services and create jobs. Any taxation on the income or wealth of the rich, even an inheritance tax, will dampen the incentive for entrepreneurs to invest in capital and create jobs. That won't only harm the poor—it will harm everyone."

"So," Georgina says, "you would not have us help the most disadvantaged in any way?"

"Look," Milton says, "I am in favor of supporting the poorest islanders. Not because of fairness and certainly not for any economic reason—it's actually bad for the economy. But purely out of compassion, I suggest a system whereby the government pays money to the poorest citizens with an income below 1,000 bucks per year. Call it a negative income tax for the poor."

In the next few hours, the council crafts a political compromise. The 20 percent tax is replaced with a progressive tax, which rises from zero percent on small incomes to 40 percent on higher incomes. They also agree to a 10 percent inheritance tax on estates of more than 100,000 bucks.

These taxes will finance a small social security stipend for any islanders who cannot support themselves, such as the elderly, disabled, and unemployed.

REDISTRIBUTION OF INCOME and wealth remains a hotly debated topic. As in our island story, the key arguments in favor of redistributing wealth are:

- Compassion for the needy

- Avoidance of social unrest

- Increasing happiness

- Economically, encouraging consumption by moving income to those who are likely to spend it.

Many of these are discussed in the somewhat controversial book The Spirit Level.[41] And the key arguments against wealth redistribution are:

- Protecting individual freedom

- Economically, taxing the wealthy reduces economic incentives to create successful businesses that produce goods and services and generate jobs.

In the real world, high taxation may simply drive wealthy people and businesses to emigrate to other countries; many countries currently compete to provide an attractive environment for the wealthy, and especially for entrepreneurs.

Thomas Rustici argued the "freedom case" against taxation particularly potently in an exercise for his economics students. [42] He asked them to compare a poor person mugging a rich person (under the threat of violence) to a poor person voting for a politician who will tax the rich person (under threat of the violence of forced incarceration) and redistribute the tax to the poor person as social security.

Of course, the equivalence, while intriguing, is far from perfect. A thief randomly mugging the most vulnerable wealthy person they can find, is not the same as society voting to tax all wealthy people.

Milton Friedman, and his wife Rose Friedman, wrote: "A society that puts equality—in the sense of equality of outcome—ahead of freedom will end up with neither equality nor freedom.... On the other hand, a society that puts freedom first, will, as a happy by-product, end up with both greater freedom and greater equality."

However, even Milton Friedman, who held some extreme libertarian views, did favor a negative income tax for the poorest citizens, out of compassion.

The Friedmans' theory, that economic freedom inevitably brings greater equality as a happy by-product, is dubious. In recent decades even though economic freedoms are expanding, inequality has grown in the U.S. and within most developed economies, especially in the years since Milton's death in 2006. Empirically, it's becoming increasingly hard to argue that a purely free and open capitalist market will naturally tend towards equality; and there are some good theoretical reasons to question this too. We will return to the issue of inequality in detail when we look at twenty-first century issues in Section VII.

Today, all modern economies have progressive taxation and social benefits, but the extent varies greatly. For example, Norway and Switzerland are as rich as the U.S. but have more social benefits and less inequality.[43] They also rank higher than the U.S. on happiness. In general, there does appear to be a correlation between inequality and unhappiness. However, the data is complex, with some outliers—like Costa Rica, which is very unequal and very happy.

Debates about the redistribution of wealth are always colored by people's personal circumstances. Not surprisingly, poorer people tend to be much keener on redistribution of wealth than wealthy people. To avoid this bias, it's helpful to consider John Rawls' *Veil of Ignorance* thought experiment:[44] imagine yourself as an unborn person, not knowing if you are going to be born to a rich or poor family, and whether you will be born with low or high intelligence, with athleticism and good looks, with robust health, or with physical disabilities, and not knowing whether you will have good or bad luck with your career.

In this situation, under a veil of ignorance, most people would probably favor of a policy of significant redistribution of income and wealth as a way of hedging their bets, in case they end up amongst the unlucky ones, with poorer life chances. They would almost certainly object to policies leading to a highly unequal society, since they would only have a small chance of ending up amongst the wealthiest. Then again, even behind the veil of ignorance, most of us would probably also wish for a society that provides decent incentives for success, entrepreneurship, and job creation, so the economy can flourish and people feel motivated.

Some degree of self-interest is inevitable in policy debates. But it would be far more productive if politicians and citizens could debate and negotiate the right compromise based on the theoretical objective perspective offered by the veil of ignorance, rather than basing their arguments primarily on individual personal circumstances.

Then again, some politicians are driven by ideologies of conservative libertarianism on the one hand or socialism on the other hand. However, it is amply clear that both ideologies in their purest form, where no wealth, or all wealth is redistributed, respectively, are untenable. Debate must focus on the complex issue of finding a pragmatic compromise which delivers the most benefit to the most people.

COMPONENTS OF THE ECONOMY

THE ISLAND'S ECONOMY is growing. Capital is accumulating: the islanders now have more ladders, nets, tools, houses, and buildings for workshops. This capital, in turn, increases productivity. From time to time, there is also a technological breakthrough, and people invent new methods of making production more efficient. Barbara's Bank makes a loan to a business which is constructing a watermill over the river. Overall, the same number of islanders are able to produce more goods and services using better tools, and better technology, together with continued specialization. As a result, the islanders are producing and consuming more stuff than before.

Fred keeps printing money at a gentle pace, to enable the gradual growth of the economy. He continuously adjusts the money supply to achieve his interest rate target, and periodically adjusts the interest rate target to achieve the inflation target.

One Monday, Charlie finds a dusty 10-buck bill on the floor of the market. This gives Charlie a little bit of extra credit—he is now owed some stuff. John spots Charlie picking up the note and follows him from his perch.

What will Charlie do with his windfall? He walks around the market and considers spending the money on goods—perhaps a toy for his daughter? He also considers a service, such as a haircut. John is ready to chalk up 10 bucks to the consumption part of the island's GDP.

But Charlie walks on past the toy stalls and the hairdresser and enters the business-to-business section of the market, where tools are sold. John reckons Charlie might use the money to buy some capital, such as a hammer for cracking coconuts. That would be a delay of gratification, an investment in the future, so John would chalk up the spend in the business investment component of GDP.

Then again, John thinks, Georgina may consider the cash find to be taxable income. She might take away part of the money and spend it on government programs, adding to the government spending component of GDP.

Any of these three would be direct contributions to GDP.

But then again, John muses, finding a 10-buck note doesn't change production on the island. It's just a tiny bit of money that was out of circulation and is now back in circulation. If Charlie buys a good or service or tool, then someone else doesn't get to buy that good or service or tool.

The find just transfers 10 units of income to Charlie, at the expense of everyone else. But it's just money; it's not a real addition to GDP.

Finally, Charlie walks over to Barbara's Bank to deposit his find.

John smiles to himself. Charlie is delaying gratification, but he is not making an investment himself. Instead, he is waiting in line to deposit the money as savings in the bank. Soon Barbara's Bank may match Charlie, who wants to delay gratification, with someone else who wants to advance gratification. That person wants to make a capital investment now, which they can't afford from their own pocket.

And so, John reflects, the island's economy consists of many thousands of such small personal choices each day. People barter their labor for money and then choose whether to spend the money on consumption, investment in their own business, or saving. If they choose to save, this may enable another business to invest now, while the saver can spend the money at a later date. And, whether people like it or not, some of their income is taxed and becomes government spending too.

John smiles to himself. Charlie's decision is benefiting the island's economy. Assuming the bank lends out his money wisely, it will be invested in producing capital, which is the surest way to increase the production capability of the island's economy.

LET'S TAKE A QUICK LOOK at the components of the economy in practice.

At the time of writing, the U.S. economy comprises 69 percent household consumption, 17 percent government spending, and about 16 percent business investment. Other developed economies have broadly similar ratios, although many European countries have bigger governments. In China, on the other hand, household consumption is just 39 percent, and government consumption 15 percent, while business investment is a whopping 43 percent.[45] So China is delaying gratification massively, and investing heavily in its businesses. Then again, the U.S. and the EU already have a lot more accumulated capital than China, which is playing catch-up.

We will see later that once international trade develops, there is one more element of GDP, namely net exports, although net exports are a rather small component amounting to just 2 percent of the economy in China and net imports are just 2 to 3 percent of the economy in the U.S.

How are the components determined? Clearly the size of government is determined by politicians, and in democracies this is influenced by electorates. Key factors in the size of government spending include the number of years of free education, the extent of free healthcare, size of military, and the relative generosity of social security and pensions.

But what determines the balance of consumption versus investment in an economy? Who decided that the U.S. should reinvest 16 percent of its production capability in producing capital, while China reinvests 43 percent?

Before wrapping up this section on the long-term growth of the economy, we will address this question, which brings us back to interest rates and a more in-depth examination of how they work.

SAVINGS/INVESTMENT AND REAL INTEREST RATES

BARBARA'S BANK HAS EXPANDED. She now employs two bank tellers, one dealing with deposits and savings, the other with loans.

Charlie is in the bank to deposit his 10-buck windfall. He is being offered a savings account paying 3 percent interest, which sounds reasonable to him.

"But 5 percent is a stretch," he hears Bella saying to the other teller who is offering her a business loan, not far from Charlie. "Sure, best case my business investment may pay off more than 5 percent. But there is risk too. It might not pay off at all."

"Don't think of it as 5 percent," Charlie hears the bank teller saying. "Remember, there's some inflation. Fred's target is 2 percent inflation. For every 100 bucks you borrow now, maybe you pay back 105 bucks in a year. But in real terms, that's about 103 bucks' worth, in today's bucks. In terms of purchasing power, what you repay us in a year is just 3 percent more, so 3 percent is your real interest rate."

"Wait a second," Charlie says to the teller serving him. "You kept very quiet about inflation when you offered me 3 percent interest on my savings. Are you telling me that my real interest rate is just 1 percent?"

"Hmm, I wish my colleague would keep her voice down. But, well, yes sir, it's true that if inflation stays on target at 2 percent, what you can actually buy with your savings in a year will be just 1 percent more than what you could buy today."

"Hah, well it's going to take more than 1 percent to persuade me to postpone my shopping. Goodbye."

"Sir, maybe we can stretch to 3.5 percent."

But Charlie is already on his way out of the door, thinking about what he can buy in the market right now.

Waiting behind Charlie in line is Arthur. Arthur has decided to save for a pension. He overhears Charlie's conversation and is disappointed to discover that his money will probably only grow about 1 percent a year in real terms. But his motivation to save is not primarily about the interest he will earn; rather, it's about ensuring his ability to sustain himself in his future retirement. He proceeds with his saving.

On the other side of the room, behind Bella, is Paula who wants to buy a bigger hut but only if the mortgage is affordable. Behind her is a corn farmer. Unfortunately, the corn crop has been poor this year, and he can only justify a loan to buy more sickles if the interest rates are not too high. Behind them is a line of people who want to ask about taking out loans. And each person has a different tolerance for interest rates, depending on how much their business investment is likely to pay off, or how much rent they will save by buying their own home.

Barbara watches both the lines from her little corner office. If she had the only bank in town, it would be her job to set the interest rate so as to balance the two lines, to match the supply and demand of loans. But matters are more complicated than that. Firstly, she can offer loans of bank money with only partial reserves, which are not matched by savings. And she can also lend to and borrow from other banks, so it's fine if she has more savers than borrowers, as long as another bank has more borrowers than savers.

John has followed Charlie to the bank. He surveys the scene too. Clearly, the banks are making loans more aggressively. They are granting more mortgages and bigger mortgages; and borrowers are using those loans to bid up the prices of houses.

John thinks again about how Charlie was at first inclined to save his money, but then switched to spending it. Every person in the bank that day was making decisions about whether to spend, save, or borrow. An economy based on thousands of personal choices has flexibility, John reflects, but also an inherent vulnerability. People's tastes are fickle. What if there is a sudden shift?

THIS CHAPTER CLOSES the section on the long-term economy.

We saw that the three components of an economy are consumption, investment, and government. Later we will add an adjustment for net exports. These are the goods an economy produces which are consumed abroad.

As usual, it is preferable to think about GDP primarily in terms of the *real economy*: the physical production of goods and services, of new capital tools, and of government services. Money is a secondary mechanism which is used to track trade in the real economy, and also as a yardstick to measure the real economy.

Of these three components of an economy, government spending is directly determined by government policy. But the balance between consumption and investment in the economy is more organic: it's a balance of willingness to save, versus the relative attractiveness of the available investment opportunities. This balance determines how much of the economy's production goes into goods and services for consumption today, versus resources invested in building capital tools for the future.

A key factor is the real interest rate, which effectively determines the price of time: the price paid for advancing gratification to an earlier time, and the reward for delaying gratification to a later time. The real interest rate should float, based on supply and demand, to ensure that savings equal investment; that is, delay of gratification equals advance of gratification. These should always be balanced so that the economy can reach its full production potential, thus ensuring full employment. Ideally, every person who is not employed providing goods and services for today, should be employed building capital for tomorrow.

How do real interest rates balance? The higher real interest rates are, the more people will be tempted to save, and the less people will be tempted to invest in business projects. When interest rates are high, a business project has to offer a really attractive *return on investment* to justify the interest payments on the loan that finances the project. Even if the business owners can afford to make the investment without a loan—for example, if a business has enough profits to start building a factory without drawing a loan—the investment still has to offer better returns than saving in the bank. Otherwise, the owners of the business will likely choose the simpler option of saving their money in the bank.

When real interest rates are lower, more business investments become attractive, but people are less tempted to save. Like every price, the price of time, the real interest rate, will find the market level that balances supply and demand for loans; that is, balancing the delay of gratification— saving—with the advance of gratification—investment.

How DOES THE PRICE of time evolve as societies get richer?

As people's income increases, they find it easier to save, and generally require less incentive to do so. In fact, some may want to save whether or not they have an immediate incentive—for example, saving for a pension. On the other hand, as societies get richer and accumulate a stock of capital, there tend to be diminishing returns available on new investments. The hundredth ladder will simply create less benefit than the first. Slam-dunk business investment opportunities are executed first, leaving business opportunities with lower risk-adjusted returns. As economies develop, we therefore expect real interest rates to drop, and the price of borrowing for investment drops.

What about the proportion of GDP which is investment versus consumption? This is less obvious. On the one hand, people will find it easier to save as they get richer; on the other hand, interest rates will drop, making saving less attractive. So will savings grow or diminish over time?

In practice, we see that wealthier countries usually save and invest less. The proportion of U.S. GDP dedicated to business investment is lower today than it was in 1950, and much lower than China's today. This is why as countries get richer, they generally experience slower economic growth, since investment in capital is the primary engine of growth.[46] For example, for decades now, China has been investing proportionally more than the established economies and has been growing consistently faster too.

BEFORE CONCLUDING THIS section of the book, let's clear up one major point of confusion. We have seen two types of interest rates, each with its own story. *Nominal interest rates*, the simple interest rate measured in terms of monetary balances, are controlled by the central bank, by adjusting the money supply. These nominal interest rates are what we see advertised every day by the banks and in the news.

Then again, *real interest rates* reflect the real price of time, which balances the delaying versus the advancing of gratification in society. Real interest rates are supposed to be based not on monetary policy, but on the real economy; that is, they balance the current appetite for saving with the available opportunities for borrowing to make business investments.

Is this a contradiction? Do central banks control interest rates? Or does supply and demand for delayed and advanced gratification determine interest rates? The answer is subtle and important—and not without controversy, because the short-term answer differs from the long-term answer.

The *Fisher equation* can be written in two directions. In one, the equation is a straightforward definition to derive the real interest rate from the nominal interest rate:

real interest rate = nominal interest rate - inflation

According to this simple equation, the central bank determines the nominal interest rate; and the real interest rate is derived from the nominal rate by subtracting the rate of inflation. This seems to imply that central banks control the real interest rate and determine the price of time. But that's misleading, as central banks cannot directly control inflation.

In this book, we are learning to think about the real economy first. So the Fisher equation should be rewritten as a prescription for central bank policy:

nominal interest rate = real interest rate + inflation

According to this approach, the real interest rate reflects the real price of time which balances modern society's propensity to save and invest versus spending now or even borrowing to spend ahead of time. And the central bank doesn't really have discretion in controlling interest rates; rather, it must set nominal interest rates so that they are equal to the prevailing real interest rates plus the inflation target. For example, if 3 percent is the real interest rate that balances people who want to delay, rather than advance, gratification, and if the central bank has a target of 2 percent inflation, then the central bank must set their nominal interest rate target to 5 percent and adjust the money supply accordingly.

In this view, it is the real interest rate, the market price of time, that controls the actions of the central bank, and not the other way around.

What if the central bank chooses a different nominal interest rate—not 5 percent? Inflation doesn't respond instantly, so the central bank may move the real interest rate in the short term. But soon enough, the real interest rate will return to its natural rate; and the misjudged nominal interest rate will translate into inflation which is too high or too low.

This *neutrality of money* principle is accepted by most economists. In the long term, the real interest rates will not be influenced much by the quantity of money, but rather will reflect the true market price for advancing gratification. In fact, neutrality of money does not merely refer to interest rates; it posits that in the long term the real economy is not influenced by the money supply.

For example, if there is too much money, then prices will eventually inflate to balance that out; and the real economy of physical jobs and goods and services will not be affected in the long term. If there is too little money, prices will eventually deflate, and the real economy will eventually get back to where it would have been.

That's the principle of neutrality of money: the real economy isn't affected much by the money supply in the long term. Double the quantity of money, and eventually prices and wages double, and any effect dissipates.

In conclusion, in the short term the central bank controls nominal interest rates, which determine real interest rates and the price of time. But in the long term, the situation and tastes of society determine the real interest rates, which then dictate the appropriate nominal interest rate the central bank must set.

ONE FINAL THOUGHT on interest rates. The problem is that real interest rates have traditionally been hard to assess. You can walk into any bank and see the nominal interest rate, but how do you measure the real interest rate? In the past you could only measure real interest rates in retrospect, by taking the nominal interest rates in the banks, and subtracting inflation, after measuring how much prices had increased in the shops.

To measure the real price of delaying gratification, you had to take the nominal interest rate and then guess what inflation would be in the future.

However, in recent decades governments have issued index-linked bonds. These are bonds that pay an interest rate, and also return the investment adjusted for inflation. In the U.S. they are known as *Treasury Inflation-Protected Securities (TIPS)* and there are equivalents in other countries. So now there are actively traded bonds which determine the real price of delaying gratification.

On any given day, the financial markets reflect exactly how much reward there is for delaying the purchase of a real basket of goods by 1, 5, 10, or 20 years. This means that the real price of time is no longer a mystery. It is traded in the financial markets.

Inflation-protected bonds, also known as *index-linked* bonds, give central banks a direct measure of real interest rates looking forward as well as in retrospect. These bonds give central banks a more direct way to set nominal interest rates in response to the observed real interest rates, and not the other way round.

We will return to TIPS at the end of the book when we discuss the quirks of the twenty-first century economy, and how TIPS yields, which represent the real price of time, are now—rather bizarrely—negative.

WE HAVE NOW SEEN how the economy grows in the long term, through the accumulation of capital. The real interest rate adjusts to help society find the right balance between consumption and investment. When everything works well, the economy remains at full production and more or less everyone is employed, either producing goods and services or producing capital tools.

But, unfortunately, things don't always work well, and that is the subject of the next section.

V. THE SHORT-TERM ECONOMY

ECONOMIC FLUCTUATIONS—RECESSION

CHARLIE RUNS INTO trouble and defaults on his mortgage payments. Barbara's Bank repossesses his home and dumps it on the market to recover their loan. A couple of other people default and lose their homes too, and the bank starts to find it harder to sell the properties. The banks quickly tighten up on new mortgage lending, making it harder for people to buy new homes. With fewer buyers, and with the bank dumping some properties, house prices start to drop, creating something of a panic which then causes home prices to drop more sharply.

While everyone feels instinctively that the island is once again in recession, John is the one who is objectively measuring the economy from the vantage point of the hill, and he confirms that GDP is down, and the island is producing less stuff than before.

As the recession takes root, families take precautions. Barbara is worried that her bank's losses may affect her personal income and she cancels an order for Paula's jewelry. Paula lays off Brody. Brody decides he had better cut his own hair instead of going to the salon. Bella is laid off from the salon.

For the first time in the island's history, there is significant unemployment. Within a couple of months, some 15 percent of the people are without jobs, creating great hardship for them and their families, and making everyone around them even more nervous. Almost all businesses are feeling the pinch because all the islanders, both unemployed and employed, reduce their spending.

John is observing all this with increasing frustration. Finally, one Tuesday morning he ventures down from his hill into the market. He perches himself on a rock. "Ahem. People, listen up. Yes, all of you. This recession is on you. You had better all start spending more. Just spend and consume, like you did last year. That's the solution. If you consume less, then businesses will produce less, and we'll have this awful unemployment."

Arthur pipes up. "Mind your own business, John. My job is hanging from a thread! Are you denying it's sensible for me to be thrifty and save some money just in case?"

"We're just looking out for our families," Paula says.

"Well, erm, yes." John waves his arms. "I suppose for each one of you, perhaps it makes sense to be cautious and cut back on spending. But do you see the paradox? All of you cutting back on consumption is exactly what's creating the recession! You think the recession is causing you to spend less, but actually your reduced spending is causing the recession. If you all start spending and consuming more again, the aggregate demand for goods and services will recover and people will get their jobs back."

Paula walks up to him. "So you expect us to spend recklessly just because you throw around fancy phrases like aggregate demand? I think I'll look out for my kids, John. No matter what you say, I am definitely going to spend less and save more."

John slinks back up his hill. What can he tell them? He can't really deny that for each family it makes sense to save if their jobs are at risk. But then, halfway up the hill, John changes his mind, does an about-turn, and heads right back to his makeshift pedestal.

"Listen up again, everyone. Don't you see, you cannot all save! Every saver needs a savee, if you will. You advance gratification and consume less, while someone else spends more. Later they repay you. Saving together with investment works, like two sides of a coin. But if everyone tries to save and consume less today, all on their own, then who is going to repay them in the future? If everyone saves, then no one is saving. No one! You are all just reducing your consumption now and no one will pay you back for it later."

"What are you talking about? I'm putting some cash aside. That's saving, isn't it?" Brody says.

"No, it is not. Forget money, Brody. Think about real stuff. If we all consume less, businesses will produce less. There will be fewer jobs and fewer goods and services now. Who will repay that later? No one."

"John, you're not making sense. If I save cash, who's going to stop me from buying extra stuff later?"

John exhales. "Think this through. We all consume less than we can afford right now and we put some money aside. Then, say in a year's time, we bring our saved money to market. But there are only so many goods and services to buy at that time. We can all pull out our extra saved cash, but we cannot buy more stuff because there are only so many goods and services to go around each month. Brody, if you save money in Bob's Bank and Bob lends the money to me, then today you consume less, and I spend more. In a year I pay you back and then you get to consume more, while I consume less. I swap my delayed gratification with your advanced gratification. But if we all save, then no one is saving."

Fred joins in. "He's right. We can't all pass consumption to our future selves. Saving is really lending and someone else has to borrow and later repay. If you really want to think about it in terms of money, I have long argued that the average cash balance is effectively zero. If everyone has more money, then no one has more money."

John and Fred's speeches have little effect, and many people go home from the market that evening with lighter shopping baskets.

Charlie finds another 10 bucks on the floor. This time he doesn't even think about spending it—he marches straight to Barbara's Bank and puts it on deposit. But Barbara is scared to provide more credit; so she doesn't use this cash to create any new loans and issues no new bank money.

THIS CHAPTER INTRODUCES the *paradox of thrift*. No one wants to be the one who is overspending in a recession. So consumers spend less, and businesses respond by producing less and investing less and downsizing, which only leads to a vicious downward spiral. At the same time, banks lend less and this adds to the gloom. People's natural response to a recession is exactly what makes the recession worse.

The paradox of thrift also exposes what one might call a *paradox of money*. Money makes it much easier to trade. But paradoxically, money also makes it easier to not trade. If Paula were bartering the oranges she grows, she would always receive other products and services in return immediately. But when she sells her oranges for money, it becomes easier for her to choose what to buy. Money also makes it easy to buy nothing— because money can easily be put aside for later. Paula just pockets some cash, or deposits it in her bank account, and walks around with un-pedicured feet.

Except that when everyone is saving, the saving is an illusion. If one person delays gratification and another advances gratification, that works. In fact it's highly valuable for the economy if the advanced gratification is invested in capital creation. But if practically everyone tries to delay gratification, they all just cancel gratification. They consume fewer goods and services than they could afford today, and there is no one to repay them with extra goods and services in the future.

The paradox of thrift was referenced back in 1714, in *The Fable of the Bees* by Bernard Mandeville:

"As this prudent economy, which some people call Saving, is in private families the most certain method to increase an estate, so some imagine that, whether a country be barren or fruitful, the same method if generally pursued will have the same effect upon a whole nation, and that, for example, the English might be much richer than they are, if they would be as frugal as some of their neighbors. This, I think, is an error."

John Adams may have been referring to this passage when he wrote: "What is prudence in the conduct of every private family can scarce be folly in that of a great Kingdom."

It was the British economist John Maynard Keynes who popularized the term *paradox of thrift* in the 1930s; and in our island story Keynes' ideas are roughly represented by John.

This is an example of the fallacy of composition—what is true for the parts may not be true for the whole. Consuming less may be prudent saving for one family; but if everyone tries to save, it reduces production and causes a recession.

An interesting analogy for the paradox of thrift is the *Prisoner's dilemma* in which each prisoner chooses what is good for himself, which results in the worst outcome for everyone.

CAUSES OF A RECESSION

GEORGINA CONVENES an emergency meeting of her economic council which now consists of John, Milton, Fred, Arthur, and the bankers Bob, Bill, and Barbara.

"I need answers. What triggered this recession?" she asks her advisors.

"I blame the credit crisis," John says. "During the good times, banks made loans liberally to businesses and homeowners. Then we started having defaults, and banks tightened up credit rather quickly. The sudden lack of loans made businesses invest less in capital, and people invested less in homes. This reduced aggregate demand, triggering the downward cycle."

"Sure, it's easy to blame us bankers," Bob says. "But maybe the central bank had a hand in this. The crisis is all about asset prices. In the good times, home prices kept increasing. You printed money, Fred, and reduced interest rates contributed to that. Eventually prices got so high that people panicked, and prices crashed."

"Why does it matter if house prices crashed, Bob?" says Georgina. "Even with the price of houses dropping, there's just as much actual stuff on the island as before. The homes are still there."

"True enough," replies Bob. "But the recession is about psychology. When house prices drop, people feel less wealthy, and so they spend less. Secondly, a drop in asset prices causes a credit reduction—when asset prices drop, my bank has less security for providing loans. That means there is less credit in the real economy."

"I have another theory," says Barbara. "You know we had a poor corn crop this year. Supply of corn was down, and corn prices were up. Corn is our staple food. The sudden hike in the price of corn left people with less money to spend on other stuff. This recession was triggered by a supply shock."

Georgina puts her head in her hands. "Each of you can explain how a recession starts but each of you has a different theory: a credit crisis, a bursting asset bubble, a supply shock. Which is it? We're just fumbling around in the dark."

"Don't worry too much, Georgina, I believe that a recession is not a natural situation in a free market," John says. "Almost everyone would like to be employed, producing stuff. And, on the other hand, our islanders have an unlimited appetite for consuming stuff. So in the long term, in an efficient open market, more or less everyone will be employed, the island will be producing stuff at the maximum possible rate, and people will be buying all that stuff. But right now, aggregate demand by consumers has got stuck below the potential output of our economy."

"I hope you're right," Georgina sighs. "But, whatever triggered this, what I really want to know is how we fix it. Council, I need you more than ever. How do we get people spending again and businesses producing again? I want solutions. Go!"

ECONOMISTS GENERALLY CONSIDER recessions to be short-term phenomena. In the long term, as John argued, a free market should enable close to full employment, with just a *natural rate of unemployment*, since there are always a few people who can't work, choose not to work, or are in transition between jobs. The free market should achieve this by setting prices and wage levels such that everyone who wants to work has a job. In this way, the economy is producing and consuming at maximum capacity, with everyone trading their labor for goods and services.

In the short term, however, the economy will, from time to time, get stuck in recession for a year or two, producing and consuming at less than its full potential, and therefore providing less than full employment. By modern convention, a *recession* refers to at least two consecutive calendar quarters of shrinking GDP.

Periods of economic growth punctuated by recessions used to be called *the business cycle* or *economic cycle* or *boom-and-bust cycle*. However, recessions have no cyclical regularity: the U.S. economy sometimes goes for a decade with no recession—for example, in the decades starting 1961, 1991 and 2010. Other times a recession comes shortly after another recession, as in 1974 and 1981.[47] Therefore *economic fluctuation* is a more accurate term, which has gradually been gaining acceptance.

While economic fluctuations are not regular, there may be a certain cyclical aspect to the growth of an economy. During periods of strong growth, there tends to be an exuberant buildup of asset prices and credit lines. Given human psychology, this may become what Alan Greenspan called *irrational exuberance*,[48] where people bid up the prices of an asset based on fear of missing out, known as FOMO. This creates a bubble in asset prices, such as property or shares, and a single piece of bad news can trigger the bursting of the bubble and a sudden fall in the prices of those assets.

Although in the real economy a bursting bubble doesn't destroy any stuff, it has a strong psychological effect—it also causes a real and sudden reduction in credit. Thus, the seeds of the bust are sown during the boom.

The *Great Recession* of 2007–2009,[49] for example, was triggered by the bursting of a U.S. house price bubble in 2005–2006, compounded by the unsustainable subprime mortgage credit practices which this burst exposed. The recession of 1973–1975 was largely blamed on a supply shock, with the oil crisis of 1973[50] causing oil prices to spike 400 percent. The recession of 2020 was unique, in that the Covid-19 pandemic suddenly shut down the production and consumption of several types of goods and services.

FISCAL STIMULUS

JOHN SPEAKS FIRST. "As I said, aggregate demand by consumers has gotten stuck below the potential output of our economy. And now, Georgina, your government must step in and spend more, and increase aggregate demand from the government's side. Increased government spending will compensate for decreased consumer spending."

"Hmm. Suppose I spend some government money. How much impact can that have?"

"More than you think. Whatever you spend gets multiplied. You pay 10,000 bucks to laborers to build a bridge. They spend much of that money on products and services in the market. Now the businesses have extra money; they buy some more capital tools or hire new staff. And so on and so forth—every buck you spend is likely to circulate and add several bucks of GDP to the economy!"

Georgina leans forward. "That sounds great. I love the idea of my government's spending being multiplied. But where do I get the money? Tax revenues are actually down since the recession set in. The Fisc is virtually empty."

"You can raise taxes."

"Hmm. But then I'm taking away money from citizens or businesses, some of which they might otherwise have spent. I'll be forcing them to spend less. Won't that further reduce aggregate demand, as you call it?"

"OK, I suggest you borrow it. Borrow money from all those citizens who are spending too little and saving too much. Then you spend it. Borrowing works well because people tend to lend you money that they were planning to save anyway. The government can borrow their money and spend it, and get that money circulating. Georgina, we elected you to govern, and now is the time we need you to step up to get the economy going again."

"That's all very well, John, but what this government borrows now, we have to pay back in a year or two. I hope to still be governor then. Aren't I just setting a trap for my future self?"

"No, because by then the economy will be growing. You can stabilize the economy in a recession by running a fiscal deficit—spending more than the tax revenues you collect. Then you can pay back the debt in the boom years, with a fiscal surplus."

And so Georgina instructs Fred to issue more government bonds, borrowing money from the citizens for periods of one to three years, in exchange for interest payments. Georgina's government spends the money on more public works.

Now Milton demands a meeting with Georgina. "What is this about increased government spending? Don't you know we're in a recession?"

"That's precisely the point, Milton. Our citizens aren't spending enough, so the government is picking up the slack and spending more. There's a multiplier—every buck your government spends gets re-spent again and again, ultimately creating a few bucks of GDP. So... you're welcome."

Milton pulls an incredulous face. "I didn't thank you. You think your spending is multiplied? That's just fabulous. And where are those bucks coming from? I assume tax. So you are taking those bucks away from the citizens by force of law. More slavery. What about the multiplier effect of tax?"

"I'm not following you, Milton. Why should tax have a multiplier?"

"Sure, it does. A negative multiplier. You force me to pay you a buck in tax. So I don't spend that buck on a coconut. And Charlie doesn't get a buck to spend on a haircut and—"

"Hmmm, I didn't think of that. But also, your assumption is wrong. Most of our spending is based on a fiscal deficit. We are actually spending more than we get in from taxes, and funding the deficit by borrowing from citizens. I reckon the money they lend the government is money they are probably not planning on spending anyway."

"And how exactly are you persuading our good citizens to lend their hard-earned bucks to the government?"

"I think you know. We issue them a bond, an IOU promising to return their money with interest. We're paying a nice interest rate to encourage people to buy government bonds."

"How much?"

"We started at 5 percent and now, in order to encourage more borrowing, we're paying 6 percent."

"So, Georgina, you're pushing up interest rates in the market to entice citizens to lend money to the government. That means it's now even harder and more expensive for businesses to get loans to create capital. Mortgages are even pricier. The government is crowding out private investment by raising interest rates. So, yes, Georgina, your spending has a positive multiplier, but your taxation and your borrowing both have a negative multiplier." Milton points a finger at her. "Don't meddle in the economy. Government spending just means that you are forcing our good citizens to spend on projects you choose; but they will repay you by spending even less elsewhere. You can't force your way out of this recession."

JOHN MAYNARD KEYNES, whom we met earlier, was the most influential economist of the first half of the twentieth century, best known for his magnum opus, *The General Theory of Employment, Interest, and Money*, published in 1936. Keynes visited the White House during the great depression in 1934 and urged President Roosevelt to increase deficit fiscal spending. Thus, Keynes was a proponent of the *New Deal*, in which Roosevelt greatly increased public spending in 1933–1936, building bridges, airports, dams, post offices, hospitals, and roads. Keynes recommended financing public works primarily through a fiscal deficit, or government borrowing, while Roosevelt chose to rely primarily on increased taxation.

Keynes was of the opinion that in a recession the economy can get into a rut of unemployment and may not fix itself. Right up to the 1970s, most economies adopted the Keynesian approach, that a fiscal stimulus was needed to end a recession.

As we have seen, in our story Milton loosely represents the views of Milton Friedman, American Nobel laureate and the most important economist of the second half of the twentieth century. Friedman was a prominent critic of Keynes, and a libertarian who favored minimal government intervention. He was an advisor to Republican President Ronald Reagan and Conservative British Prime Minister Margaret Thatcher in the 1980s, advising them against using fiscal policy to regulate their economies and opposing almost all forms of government economic intervention. For some decades, Keynes' idea of fighting a recession with fiscal stimulus was out of fashion.

However, in the years after the financial crisis of 2007–2008, there was rekindled interest in Keynesian economics, with many world leaders and economists supporting the idea of an economic stimulus funded by fiscal deficit. In October 2008, the UK chancellor referenced Keynes when announcing a fiscal stimulus package, followed by U.S. President Barack Obama in January 2009. These efforts were helped by interest rates which were around zero, and remained around zero as the government started borrowing. In this particular scenario, it's therefore hard to argue that government borrowing was *crowding out* private borrowing.

Governments again created massive fiscal stimuli, and deficits, during the Covid-19 pandemic of 2020. In the U.S. President Biden is continuing with a massive fiscal stimulus even as Covid-19 abates in 2021. We will discuss the opening two decades of the twenty-first century again later.

To this day, economists and politicians actively debate whether fiscal policy—particularly governments borrowing money to spend on stimulating the economy—is a useful tool for promoting short-term growth and combating recessions. They debate whether fiscal stimuli were, in fact, an important factor in ending the great depression in the 1930s or in ending the 2007–2008 great recession.

It is fascinating that such a fundamental question of macroeconomics remains undecided.

MONETARY STIMULUS

GEORGINA RECONVENES HER COUNCIL. "Milton has ruled out fiscal stimulus. What do we do now?"

Barbara clears her throat. "Your central banker is sitting right here. Fred should walk back to the mint and start printing money. Having more cash will help people feel wealthier and spend more. More cash will also increase available credit."

"Barbara, economic activity is down. Prices are easing downwards. Don't we need less cash when there are fewer transactions and lower prices? Won't more cash just create pointless price inflation?"

"Not necessarily," says Barbara. "Yes, economic activity is down. But there has been a big decrease in bank money, as my bank, and the other banks, tighten up credit. So I'm not sure we have too much money. Fred can print money and push interest rates down. It might cause a bit of inflation, but lower interest rates will discourage superfluous savings and encourage investment, while the extra cash will encourage spending."

Milton sighs loudly. "You still don't get it, do you? Perhaps injecting money into the economy will have a short-term positive effect. With more cash around, businesses might sense that they can sell their wares at a higher price and may be tempted to hire people and increase supply. But soon enough, everyone will expect prices to increase. As soon as the price increase is expected, the effect will dissipate. Then we just have price inflation without any benefit. What will you do then—print even more money and inflate prices still further? That's insane. Any positive effect from a boost in money supply will be very short-lived. So, once again, Georgina, let the economy fix itself."

BILL IN THIS CHAPTER of our story is actually a nod to William Phillips. In the 1960s, Phillips discovered the eponymous *Phillips curve*,[51] according to which there is always a tradeoff between inflation and unemployment. The thinking was that printing money increases inflation, but it can also trigger spending and reduce unemployment. For some years, this idea was highly influential, and people believed there was an inherent tradeoff between unemployment and inflation.

It was again Milton Friedman, and Edmund Phelps, who attacked this idea.[52] Printing money and increasing inflation, they argued, won't reduce unemployment if the inflation is expected. True, an unexpected increase in money supply may encourage spending and production, and reduce unemployment in the short term, as businesses are temporarily fooled into thinking they can sell their goods for an increased price. But this effect will only last until inflation expectations catch up.

In effect, they were arguing for the long-term *neutrality of money*. If you increase the money supply, eventually prices inflate. And from the perspective of the real economy, you are back to where you started—more money and higher prices but nothing real has changed.

Friedman was arguing on theoretical grounds, but over time the empirical evidence backed him up. There is no long-term tradeoff between unemployment and inflation. In the 1970s, the West suffered from *stagflation*—high inflation together with high unemployment. In the 1990s and 2000s, developed economies enjoyed low inflation together with low unemployment. Both these scenarios contradicted the premise of the Phillips curve.

There is now a consensus that the tradeoff between inflation and unemployment is a short-term phenomenon. Over the years, employment will return to its natural level of near full employment.

Nevertheless, many governments responded to the 2008 and 2020 crises by greatly increasing the money supply. Surprisingly, on these occasions the money printing did not result in inflation, a point we will return to later.

THIS IS AN OPPORTUNITY to revisit the workings of fractional reserve banking and bank money. In general, one hopes that fractional reserve banking will have a positive economic effect by taking demand deposits and lending them out, thereby getting the money back into circulation. But we have already seen a few objections to this thesis. Firstly, demand deposits are not necessarily out of circulation so long as banks provide checkbooks and debit cards, thus allowing checking balances to be spent. Lending out reserves therefore does not necessarily mean the banks are loaning out dormant money; rather, they may be doubling up on perfectly active money.

Worse, with a 10 percent reserve requirement, banks can in theory loan out not just 90 percent, but up to 900 percent of demand deposits. Clearly, banks are in fact creating brand new money which may either result in inflationary pressures or force the central bank to compensate by withdrawing cash from the economy. If this happens, the banks are effectively replacing free cash with expensive bank money. And all this comes with the risk of a credit crisis and occasional bank runs, which are inherent dangers of partial reserves.

But having studied economic fluctuations, we now see a final objection to bank money. Bank lending and bank money creation are pro-cyclical, which means that banks lend more during economic booms. Just as a recession hits, and there really is cash sitting unspent, banks will start worrying about credit and will tend to lend less and reduce bank money. Ironically, the more dormant money there is, the less the banks tend to get money back into circulation.

In terms of the real economy, when an economy is at full capacity, banks create new money by providing a bank loan, but there is no spare production to be purchased. There is more money competing to buy the same goods and services. Either this drives up prices, or it forces the central bank to compensate by destroying cash.

And then when a recession starts to bite, and there actually is under-consumption and spare production capacity, and unspent money, banks tighten up credit and reduce bank money. In practice then, giving banks the power to create money is likely to exacerbate, rather than moderate, economic fluctuations.

The practices of partial reserve banking and bank money are very embedded in the world economy and are probably not going to disappear any time soon. But that doesn't mean they are right. I personally struggle to see how this financial mechanism actually supports the real economy. I also wonder if the Sovereign Money Initiative to eliminate bank money, which was rejected by the population of Switzerland, actually had significant merit.[53]

ENDING A RECESSION WITH PRICE DROPS

GEORGINA IS TAPPING her foot, waiting for answers. "So what do we do? Why is the free market failing us? People want to work more, to produce more stuff. And people certainly want to consume more. How do we fix this?"

"I want to share an observation," says Arthur. "I'm friendly with Paula. I noticed she gave up her 5-buck pedicures. And you may know that Bella lost her job at the salon. Did you know that Paula then went to Bella and offered her 3 bucks for a pedicure? At first Bella turned her down flat. But a few days later she agreed."

"Totally fascinating, Arthur." Georgina raises her eyebrows. "Are you suggesting I should interrupt the economic council meeting and treat myself to a discounted pedicure?"

"Erm, that wasn't quite my point. Don't you see? Bella accepted a lower wage and started working again. And Paula was tempted by the lower price to start consuming again. Isn't that exactly what we want?"

Fred stands up. "Arthur may be onto something. If prices drop across the board, people will feel wealthier, and they will feel able to spend more. That way, they may get," Fred makes air quotes, "'tricked' into buying more stuff."

"But Fred, that would really just be a trick," Georgina said. "If all prices and all wages drop, then it's just a nominal change. Each buck of our fiat currency will be worth more, but everything real—all the stuff—will be just as before."

"Well," Fred says, "our problem is consumers' state of mind. A nominal change in prices, even if there is no real change in the economy, may help nudge our consumers back into consuming. If people feel wealthier, that might kick off the virtuous cycle of more demand, more production, more employment, which in turn gives people the confidence to demand even more. Likewise, the opportunity to hire people at lower wages may nudge businesses to hire some of the unemployed people."

"So the government should introduce a price cut?" says Georgina.

Milton jumps in. "No, no, no. Don't do anything! The last thing we need is the government intervening. The market will adjust itself over time. You just need to get out of its way. You made a law against cutting a laborer's pay—you should repeal it. We have to allow prices and wages to adjust downward as needed. It will take time, but the recession may also be a turning point for our economy. It will force businesses to become more efficient. The deeper the recession, the stronger the recovery that will follow."

"Hmm. Allowing wages to fall won't be popular."

Fred stands up slowly. "Right. And even if you remove those legal barriers to wage reduction, I'm not sure prices and wages will drop so fast. Wages are sticky. There are social norms against cutting wages. People have their pride. Anyway, the whole idea of a drop in the overall price level is dubious. Don't you remember that a big part of my job is to avoid deflation? When there is deflation, it's true that people may be tempted to buy at cheaper prices; but they may also be tempted to postpone their purchases for longer because they hope prices will continue dropping. So it could take a long time for prices to drop; and longer still to get rid of expectations that prices will drop further, so that people finally decide to buy the cheaper goods. I guess it will happen eventually."

IF PEOPLE WANT one thing from economists, it is policies for avoiding recessions, and for fixing recessions when they occur. Unfortunately, there is still very little consensus amongst economists on if and how recessions can be avoided or fixed.

As Georgina said, in a perfect market people want to work and produce stuff, and people also want to consume as much stuff as possible. So the free market should match up supply and demand nicely so that everyone is employed producing stuff, and everyone is consuming as much stuff as the economy can produce.

But the market is not perfect—at least not in the short term. And this is where the debate comes in: what causes the painful market imperfections known as recession and unemployment, and how do we fix them? Economists' opinions have evolved over the last century and our island story alludes to some of the major developments in economic thinking.

Keynes argued that the economy won't fix itself and advocated fiscal stimulus. Another British economist, Arthur Pigou, loosely represented by Arthur at this point in the story, proposed the *Pigou effect* in the 1940s, namely that an overall drop in price levels can help to restore full employment. We saw a small example of this in the story, with Paula restoring her previous level of consumption, but at a reduced price; while Bella restored her previous level of employment, at a reduced salary.

The Pigou effect suggests that the economy will get back to full employment simply by reducing the nominal prices and wages. If all prices fall, this represents no change to the real economy, it's just a deflation of the currency. But prices and wages don't all fall in unison; typically, the unemployed will be the first to accept a lower wage and this can help them get back to work.

The Pigou effect contradicts the neutrality of money—the idea that having more money with a higher price level, or less money with a lower price level, is equivalent for the real economy. But the neutrality of money principle only holds true in the long term. Recessions are a short-term phenomenon, with a significant psychological aspect. In the short term, price reduction may have a significant psychological effect, helping to nudge people out of a recession.

However, a major barrier to the Pigou effect working its magic is that many countries have legislation, trade union agreements or social norms, which prevent a reduction in wages. They may also have agreed minimum wages, which limit the scope of wage cuts. Such laws and agreements, however well intended, and however well they may work during a boom, can actually hamper the free market's ability to reduce prices and wages during a recession and may therefore delay a return to full employment.

The real-world evidence for the Pigou effect is mixed and so it remains controversial. As we have seen, lower prices can encourage spending, but this deflation can also discourage spending, as consumers come to expect further price reductions and so postpone their spending. There is empirical evidence that the deflation in Japan during the so-called *Lost Score* (twenty years of Japanese economic stagnation 1991–2010) did not in fact help to restore Japan to full employment. It seems that the Pigou effect would work best if prices and wages tick downwards but somehow on a one-time basis, without creating any expectation that they would fall further.

Despite all this uncertainty, most economists agree that in the long term, say over a year or two, a recession will fix itself, one way or another.

So should politicians fight a recession? No one is really sure. Faced with a recession, governments feel intense pressure to act, and they continue to experiment with both fiscal and monetary stimuli. But both techniques remain controversial.

In this section we have discussed *classical unemployment*, also known as *cyclical unemployment*, which appears during recessions; that is, during the bust part of the boom-and-bust business cycle, which is more accurately described as economic fluctuation.

It is worth noting that there is also a certain *natural unemployment rate*, meaning people who can't work or don't want to work. And, in addition, there is some *structural* or *frictional unemployment*, when an economy changes, especially due to new technology, or changing consumer tastes. In this case, people may have the wrong skills and may take time to retrain or find new jobs.

In the first five sections of this book, we have explored the behavior of a single economy. Now that we are experts on how a single economy functions, it is time to explore the workings of international trade, in Section VI.

VI. GLOBAL TRADE

FOREIGN TRADE—BARTER

SHE CASUALLY FLOATS UP to the beach at sunrise on a raft. "Hua," she says, pointing at herself. The island has its first visitor.

Arthur, an adept seaman, volunteers to ride back with Hua to her island. Within a few days, rafts are paddling back and forth between the two islands. The other island becomes known as Huaxia after the first visitor, while our islanders simply refer to themselves as "us," and so the foreign islanders start calling them Us.

Huaxia has a larger population—about 4,000 islanders, compared to 1,500 on Us. But it turns out that Huaxia kept the system of sharing all resources for much longer than Us did, which had reduced the growth of their economy. The visitors from Us find that Huaxia has accumulated less capital—fewer tools and machines—and is producing less stuff per person.

Recently though, Huaxia has begun to follow the same path that Us followed years earlier. It now has its own fiat currency, the yon, and its own central bank which sets its own target interest rate.

Charlie is amazed that he can trade a couple of coconuts for beautiful hand-knitted clothes which would cost five times more back home. "Don't they pay you for your labor?" he asks Hua, who perhaps fortunately doesn't speak Usian.

John ventures forth on a raft trip and starts observing the Huaxian market. He reflects that, as each Huaxian laborer is producing less stuff per hour of work, the value of an hour's labor is relatively lower there, and labor-intensive goods are relatively cheaper.

And so rafts start to shuttle back and forth as the islands barter with each other, each enjoying an increased variety of goods and services.

FOREIGN EXCHANGE AND TRADE

THE NEWLY DEVELOPING international trade is hampered by the constraints of barter. Charlie wants to buy another beautiful, knitted sweater from Hua, who is visiting the Us market with her wares. But now that the novelty has worn off, Hua doesn't really care for more coconuts.

"Take... these... bucks," Charlie says, fanning out some banknotes in his hand. "Use... at... any... stalls," he points at the stalls around him in the Usian market.

Hua hesitates, then nods and takes the bucks. But she doesn't want to buy stuff from Us; she wants to take the money back to her family. So she carries the bucks back to Huaxia on her raft and seeks out Yating who is starting a business importing corn from Us. She sells her bucks to Yating for 10 yon each.

Initially trade is not balanced. There is more stuff being imported from Huaxia to Us than stuff being exported from Us to Huaxia. Soon Yating has a line of Huaxian exporters outside her hut, offering to sell her bucks. A shrewd trader, Yating responds to the demand and offers first 9, then 8 yon per buck. And still there are lots of exporters of knitwear and toys offering to sell her their bucks.

Yating is delighted. With cheaper bucks, Usian imports become more affordable, and she starts selling imported corn for fewer yon per bucketful. Her business takes off.

In the meantime, Hua's export business is in trouble. She buys a Huaxian toy for 50 yon. At 5 bucks, it was easy to sell it to Usians. Now the value of the yon has increased and the toy is worth 7 bucks: that's a harder sell. Her business shrinks.

And so, as the yon appreciates and the buck depreciates, exports from Us to Huaxia increase, while Usian imports decrease. As long as there are more Huaxian importers than exporters, Yating and her fellow importers keep offering fewer and fewer yon per buck and their imports from the Us get cheaper in Huaxia and grow ever more popular.

Finally, at 5 yon to the buck, the trade evens out and is completely balanced. The same value of goods flows in both directions. And the number of bucks leaving Us on the Huaxian exporters' rafts now exactly equals the bucks returning to Us on Huaxian exporters' rafts.

The balanced trade enriches both islands. The Usians love the novel Huaxian clothes and toys, even though they're not as cheap as before. Meanwhile, the Huaxians develop a taste for Usian corn and coconuts, and sometimes purchase the more sophisticated Usian tools for their businesses.

AS IN OUR STORY, a floating exchange rate adjusts itself to balance out the flow of money. You may be wondering why international trade isn't balanced in today's world, if the flow of money balances itself? In the next chapter, we will discuss the fact that money can flow for purposes other than buying goods and services.

In general, both sides will benefit from international trade. Just as trading between people on the same island can benefit both sides, trade between people in different economies will tend to benefit both sides. Nobody is forcing people to trade, and if two individuals decide to make a swap, whether within a country or cross-border, it is because both of them see a benefit in doing so.

Earlier on, we saw the argument for specialization within an economy. For instance, it was more beneficial to the economy for Charlie to specialize in picking coconuts, where he had the greatest relative advantage, even though he may also have been better than Martha at growing mushrooms.

The same argument for specialization applies to trade between economies. Specifically, the benefit of trade stems from *comparative advantage*. In our story, Huaxia has a comparative advantage in producing hand-crafted goods, while Us has a comparative advantage in producing more advanced tools and in growing certain crops that fit their climate. By trading, both populations produce what they are best at making. This increases total world production, while trade ensures that both populations can access goods from both islands.

Theory tells us that even if Huaxia is less efficient than Us in every type of production, or vice versa, the two economies still both benefit from trade because of comparative advantage. Us will actually benefit from doing less of the things they are just a bit better at, and more of the things they are way better at.

Global trade has its share of detractors, and even attracts some violent protests, but economists agree, with good reason, that trade generally benefits both sides.

International trade also depends, of course, on transportation. When Chinese silk was first transported to Rome, the journey was so long and dangerous that the price of the silk reportedly increased one hundredfold along the way. But today, ocean transportation is so cheap and plentiful that sending goods by sea across the globe rarely adds more than a few percent to their price.

Over the centuries, elaborate systems of tariffs were created by countries to tax and discourage imports. In time, countries learned the benefits of international trade, and this culminated in the establishment of the World Trade Organization, WTO, in 1994. The WTO now has 164 member countries and provides a basic framework for more open trade virtually worldwide and for resolving trade disputes. There is also a web of bilateral and multilateral free trade agreements, including the EU single market, the North American Free Trade Agreement NAFTA, now replaced by USMCA, and the recent Asia-Pacific Regional Comprehensive Economic Partnership (RCEP).

So the long-term trend has been to reduce and eliminate tariffs and encourage global trade, with notable exceptions such as the Trump administration trade war and Brexit.

BALANCE OF PAYMENTS FINANCIAL ACCOUNT

THE HUAXIAN GOVERNMENT disapproves of the newly balanced trade. They liked having goods flowing from Huaxia to Us. It provided plenty of manufacturing jobs for their larger population. But now the yon has appreciated against the buck, and money and goods are flowing equally in both directions. Huaxian President Wang summons a meeting.

"At 5 yon to the dollar, our exports are not particularly competitive anymore." President Wang is standing, directing his remarks at Zhou, chairman of the Central Bank of Huaxia. "If we get the value of the yon up a bit, say at least 7 to the buck, the balance of trade should tilt back in our favor. How can we get the buck up to 7 yon?"

"You really want to devalue our own currency?" says Zhou, chairman of the Central Bank of Huaxia.

"I do."

"Well, I think you know how to devalue something," Zhou nods slightly.

"Sell it?"

"Right, Mr President. Simple supply and demand. Sell yon and buy bucks, and keep buying them until you drive the price up to 7 yon."

"And then we're done?"

"Done? Not at all. At 7 yon, we will probably have a trade surplus again. There will be a net flow of goods from Huaxia to Us. That's what you want, but then bucks will be flowing in from Us to Huaxia. If you don't want our yon to appreciate again, we will have to keep buying the surplus bucks. Every month."

"Do it."

"Your excellency, what shall we do with the bucks?"

"Store them."

Zhou hesitates. "Well, with respect and deference, accumulating bucks in cash in our vaults makes little sense. If we don't want to buy Usian goods with those bucks, we should purchase Usian financial instruments. Or capital assets. Probably the safest plan is to buy Usian treasury bonds. But we could also consider buying other assets such as businesses or land."

"Make it so."

"But why should we buy Usian bonds with the export bucks, rather than allowing our citizens to buy and enjoy imported goods today, in exchange for the goods they export?"

"Huaxia needs a trade surplus to keep our workshops busy."

And so Zhou, at the Central Bank of Huaxia, takes some of the tax yon, plus freshly printed yon each month, and uses them to buy bucks from Hua and other Huaxian exporters. First, he buys bucks for 5 yon. Then as he buys more the price starts increasing and so he pays 6 yon and eventually 7 yon. He is reducing the value of the yon by printing yon, and forcing its value down against the buck by selling yon and buying bucks.

Consequently, the price of a 50-yon toy decreases from 10 bucks to about 7 bucks. Huaxian toys once again seem cheap to Usian shoppers, while Usian goods become more expensive when sold for yon in Huaxian markets.

Trade skews again, with more goods flowing from Huaxia to Us. And the rafts floating back from Us to Huaxia are carrying less corn and more Usian government bonds.

By and large, Usians aren't complaining. They are enjoying buying lots more inexpensive stuff. And Fred has a new customer for any bonds he wants to issue. Of course, Us exporters are unhappy. And in the short term, there is a crisis for some of the Us workshops and laborers who can no longer compete with Huaxia. But, over time, most find new jobs opening restaurants and introducing an increasing array of luxury services. Us becomes richer as a result.

"What do we do about this trade imbalance, Fred?" Georgina says. "We're sending money to Huaxia every month."

"To be accurate Georgina, the payments are completely balanced."

"Look at our market, it's full of Huaxian products. Much more than the other way round."

"True, but we are sending them bonds. If you look just at goods and services, yes, we have a trade deficit because we import more than we export. But in the end every trade has two sides, so an equal number of payments go in both directions. If we import more goods than we export, then that will be balanced because we will be selling them more capital or financial assets like bonds." Fred pauses to make a sketch. "Take a look."

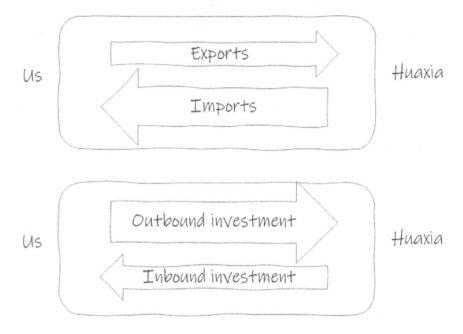

"Hmm. Why are they doing it, Fred?" said Georgina. "The Huaxians are sending us lots of cool clothes and toys today, and in return they receive bonds—pieces of paper with future debt. They are also depressing their own currency, which reduces what their citizens can afford abroad."

"Yup, they are delaying gratification on a national scale. Exporting more today, in return for debt which will allow them to buy more Usian goods at some unspecified time in the future. We get to enjoy more goods today but we're also accumulating some debt, which will eventually have to be paid off."

"But why, Fred? Why would the entire Huaxian people choose to delay gratification, years into the future?"

"Well Georgina, I don't believe the Huaxian people were consulted."

IN THE REAL WORLD, the U.S. has a consistent trade deficit with China. However, to put it in context, the net deficit amounts to about 1.5 percent of U.S. GDP so it is not a particularly significant part of the U.S. economy.

The effect of Chinese imports on the "decline" of U.S. manufacturing is often exaggerated—in fact, U.S. manufacturing output has not declined; it has continued to grow in recent decades. But even though manufacturing output has not declined, it is certainly true that the number of manufacturing jobs in Western economies has declined; the data suggests the decline has been primarily due to the fact that jobs have been replaced by technology, and only secondarily because of the trade deficit with China.[54] And the U.S. has maintained near full employment as more jobs have been created in other sectors. Nonetheless, such shifts do of course create considerable hardship for particular individuals and families, especially in regions which have traditionally been very dependent on manufacturing jobs. These regions may experience a slow and painful transition to creating employment in other industries.

As in our story, if the Chinese currency floated freely, it would appreciate and balance out trade. But China depresses its own currency by buying dollars. In the past, China purchased U.S. Treasury bonds. China holds over a trillion dollars' worth of U.S. Treasury bonds. And so, as in the story, China sends goods to the U.S., and part of the consideration they receive in exchange is debt that they can claim from the U.S. years in the future.

Recently, China has actually decreased its holding of U.S. Treasury bonds. Since 2013, it has instead used its dollars and euros to increase direct investment in foreign companies, with Chinese investors now owning such Western brands as The Waldorf Astoria, The Chicago Stock Exchange, GE Appliances, and Volvo.

Of course, China can't force the U.S. to lend it money or sell it companies. This strategy is only possible because the U.S. runs a large budget deficit and is constantly issuing Treasury bonds, while U.S. companies are always hungry for capital.

ECONOMISTS CALL THE FLOW of money between countries the *balance of payments*. And the balance of payments has two main components:

- *The Current account*—payments for imported/exported goods and services

- *The Capital account*—payments for investments (e.g., shares, bonds, real estate etc.; sometimes the Capital account is split into *Capital account* and *Financial account*).

We can add these names to Fred's diagram:

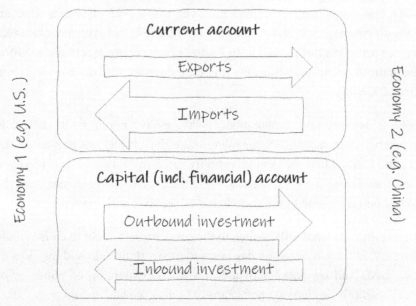

Balance of payments

The total *balance of payments* is always zero. For example, in U.S.–China trade, the U.S. has a *Current account deficit* (dollars flow out of the U.S.

because it imports more goods than it exports, shown as a thicker arrow); and this is balanced by a *Capital account surplus* (dollars flow back from China to the U.S. to buy U.S. Treasury bonds and companies, more than the other way round).

Similarly, the total balance of payments between any two economies is always zero. If a country is a net importer of goods and services, then it somehow has to pay for those imports. Either it is attracting foreign investment, which means it is exporting capital assets, or the country is borrowing money from abroad, or it is receiving foreign aid. Finally, in the short term, it might be spending and depleting reserves of foreign currency which it accumulated at an earlier time when it perhaps had a trade surplus.

As we saw, most economists agree that international trade, like any trade, is generally mutually beneficial. Over the last 50 years, international trade has rocketed from 12 percent of the global economy to 30 percent. Today, you can go to any downtown street in any developed economy and see goods that have been produced all over the world. There is also an international market in some services; for example, software development services are often outsourced to India and other countries, creating skilled jobs in those countries, while allowing their customers to develop software more efficiently.

There is an ongoing debate about whether having a trade deficit is necessarily detrimental. The growing trade deficit has not prevented the U.S. and Europe from achieving virtually full employment in recent years, other than during the great recession and the Covid-19 pandemic. And the West is better off due to the abundance of cheap Chinese goods.

The question is: what will happen to the growing U.S. debt to China in the future? Will the Chinese one day want to claim their debt and buy lots of U.S. goods and services? Will they use their ownership of bonds or of actual capital, including ports around the world, to gain political advantage? No one really knows. But today the $1.1 trillion[55] of U.S. debt owned by China, while huge, is still a small proportion of the U.S.'s overall debt of $27 trillion and a small proportion of the U.S.'s annual GDP of $19 trillion, so it's hard to see this as a massive threat.

Just as a matter of curiosity what would happen if China, or for that matter Japan or another country, did decide to dump their U.S. Treasury bonds fairly quickly. Firstly, with lots of bonds dumped on the market, the price of bonds would drop, meaning that the yield, or interest rate would actually go up. That would cause some loss to the Chinese government and would also drive up the cost of borrowing for the U.S. government. The Fed would respond by printing cash to buy back some of the bonds themselves and maintain their target interest rate.

Now China will have a lot of dollars. In theory, they could start buying American goods and services. This does not seem very practical. Chinese consumers are not suddenly going to buy another trillion dollars' worth of American goods. And even if they wanted to, the U.S. won't suddenly increase its production, so Chinese consumers would be competing with American consumers to buy the same goods and services, probably creating some inflation. So this does not seem like a particularly likely scenario. What is already happening, and may happen more, is that China sells bonds, or at least buys fewer bonds, and instead uses its dollars to buy American companies.

I do wonder what China's motivation is to artificially depress its currency in order to promote a trade surplus, that is a surplus in the export of goods, balanced by an "import" of ownership of American bonds and shares. I have not seen any convincing argument why China couldn't achieve full employment without running a trade surplus, as most developed—and many developing—countries do. And China would gain from investing more in capital creation within China, instead of buying up capital and debt abroad.

China clearly feels it gains some economic or geopolitical advantage by having a trade surplus, with a significant ownership of foreign assets. In the meantime, China's citizens are rather less wealthy than they could be, and many of China's trading partners are nervous about China's intentions.

IMPOSSIBLE TRINITY

OVER TIME, international trade becomes an important part of the economy for both Us and Huaxia. John adds exports to his calculation of GDP, as exports are part of what is produced on the island. He then subtracts imports as Usians spend money on imports, but these are not part of domestic production. John also notes that Usians are now net importers so overall this is a negative adjustment, as the island is consuming slightly more than it is producing.

Georgina makes her first state visit to Huaxia, accompanied by Fred, and holds an international trade summit with President Wang. They discuss how they can make trade smoother between their countries. After several hours of discussion, via interpreters, the two leaders agree on three goals that would help their economies to trade more smoothly:

1. A stable foreign exchange rate between the buck and yon
2. Free capital movement—citizens should be free to spend or invest their money in each other's countries
3. Independent monetary policy—each country will continue to set its own monetary policy, or interest rates, to manage its own price stability.

They shake hands and call in their central bankers to announce these three agreed policy goals. Zhou and Fred take a quick look at the goals and then look at each other with a slight smirk. "Will you tell them Zhou, or shall I?"

Zhou steps forward. "Esteemed leaders. These are noble goals. Unfortunately, these three goals are an impossible trinity—you cannot possibly have all three."

President Wang frowns. "We are leaders of two great islands. Agreeing on three common policy goals is a great diplomatic achievement and we certainly require all three."

"Let me explain, Your Excellency," says Zhou. "If we want to achieve our first goal of stabilizing exchange rates between the buck and yon, we have just two ways to do that. We can manage the flow of capital—like when Huaxia buys Us bonds but doesn't allow Usians to buy Huaxian bonds. By limiting our citizens' investment abroad, we can control how much money flows in the balance of payments capital account and use that to influence the exchange rates. But that means giving up on our second goal of free capital movement."

Zhou leans forward. "Or... we can allow capital to flow freely, as per your second goal, but then how will we stabilize the exchange rate? If both goods and capital are flowing freely, the exchange rate will fluctuate with supply and demand. The only remaining tool to stabilize exchange rates is to print money to intervene in the foreign exchange market, as I have been doing up to now, printing yon to buy bucks. But then I can't print money based on a domestic interest rate target so we would lose monetary policy independence."

"Finally," Fred continues, as soon as the interpreter has translated their conversation, "if we keep the second and third goals, we let capital flow freely, and we set interest rates based on our domestic targets of inflation and growth. In this case, we will have no control whatsoever over the exchange rates, which will fluctuate freely. Here let me sketch it:"

Free capital flow

Impossible
trinity of
int'l trade

Stable exchange rate   Monetary autonomy

"And so, my dear leaders," says Fred, "we have what we might call a trilemma. You must give up one of your three noble goals for the sake of trade between our nations."

WHEN IT COMES TO the *impossible trinity* of stable exchange rates, free capital movement, and independent monetary policy, different trading partners in the real world have made different choices about which of these three goals to give up.

Most of Europe has adopted the Euro so there is a fixed exchange rate between Eurozone countries. Europe also has free capital movement—citizens are free to travel with cash and to buy bonds, real estate, and companies in other European countries. Several countries, like Denmark, Bulgaria and Morocco, also peg their currency to the Euro, so they have made the same choice—stable exchange rates and free capital movement.

A steady exchange rate is stabilizing for trade, allowing importers and exporters to plan and budget. Free capital movement allows capital to go where it is most valuable. The downside of these two benefits is that countries in the Euro area cannot choose their own interest rate. For example, Latvia and Romania have higher inflation than Germany, but cannot fight this by increasing interest rates to reduce the money supply, since they use the same currency as Germany. Even Denmark has very little room to set interest rates for their Krone—they have to choose whatever interest rate supports their goal of a stable Krone–Euro exchange rate, which would typically be the same interest rate as in the Eurozone; Denmark is no longer free to set the interest rate that best suits their domestic goals, such as price stability.

The U.S., UK, Japan, and many other developed countries have their own currencies. These countries are free to set their own interest rates, and they allow for free movement of capital. But they cannot control exchange rates and their currencies float up and down, based on supply and demand for the currency, creating a rather unpredictable environment for importers and exporters, who account for some 30 percent of their economies.

Finally, China has chosen the third possible option of a mostly controlled exchange rate with the U.S. dollar and an independent interest rate. So China cannot allow the free movement of capital. China controls which investments Chinese citizens and businesses may make abroad, and how much foreign currency citizens may hold and spend. Overall, as we saw, China aims to make more investments than it receives, running a balance of payments capital account deficit, or an import of investments. This balances their current account surplus, or their surplus of exported goods over imports.

We can place these economies on Fred's triangle, showing which two policies each chooses, as shown on the next page.

Western democracies have limited their citizens' right to spend money abroad in the past, but this might not be politically acceptable nowadays. While China mostly gives up on the second goal of free capital movement, Western countries tend to give up on the first or third; either they don't enjoy stable exchange rates, or they sacrifice their independent monetary policy.

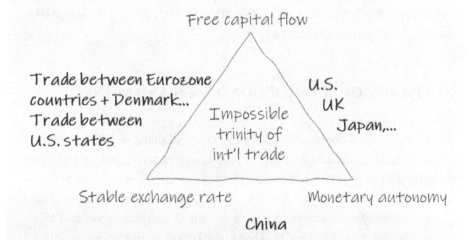

Of these two choices, the preferred choice is probably a matter of how much economies are inter-dependent. The economies of Europe have huge interdependence, and trade between them is a dominant part of their economies, so they prefer the common currency of the Euro, or stable exchange rates for currencies pegged to the Euro, at the cost of not having an independent monetary policy. Similarly, the 50 U.S. states share a currency, the dollar, and free movement of capital, but have no independent monetary policies. If prices in Alabama are inflating, and prices in Alaska are deflating, the Fed cannot help both.

On the other hand, the U.S. economy as a whole, while having significant imports and exports, is still more insular than an individual European economy. Americans therefore worry more about the freedom to manage their domestic price stability than about the need to facilitate smoother international trade. Since 1971, the U.S. as a whole has given up on the goal of stable exchange rates. Meanwhile, the individual states forgo an independent monetary policy.

AS WE REACH the end of Section VI, allow me to congratulate you—on knowing at least as much as I do about the basics of economics and money. In the final two sections, it's time to apply our skills to understanding current twenty-first century economic affairs First, let's briefly summarize the key concepts we have already met.

SUMMARY OF MACROECONOMICS AND MONEY

WHEN YOU THINK about it, the economy is not all that complicated. People organize themselves into *businesses*. The businesses hire people and equip themselves with *capital* tools, to produce *goods and services* and to invest in producing further capital. The goods and services produced are awarded to the *factors of production*: to people as *wages* for their *labor*, and to the owners of the capital as *profits*. That is the real economy in a nutshell!

Money should be seen as secondary to the real economy. Its primary role is to track the trade of goods and services, so that people have the flexibility to provide labor or capital to one business—and enjoy goods and services from other businesses.

Thus, units of money are tokens of entitlement, or credit. Specifically, instead of awarding goods and services directly to their employees and owners, businesses pay money as wages and as profits, and the laborers and capital owners then use that money to buy the goods and services they desire. In a society with money, people are still trading labor and use of capital for goods and services. But with money this trade is very flexible. People can earn their wages and profits in one business, and spend those wages and profits on goods and services from another business, without having to barter.

In a sense then, money is just a unit of debt—when salaries and profits are paid out, the businesses owe stuff, and the consumers are owed stuff. When the consumers go shopping, the money goes back to the businesses, showing that businesses are now owed labor.

A U.S. dollar bill says, "This note is legal tender for all debts, public and private" and "In God we trust." But it would be more accurate to write "This note may be exchanged by consumers for 1 unit of produced goods and services or exchanged by a business for 1 unit of labor and capital usage." and "In the social convention of fiat currency we trust."

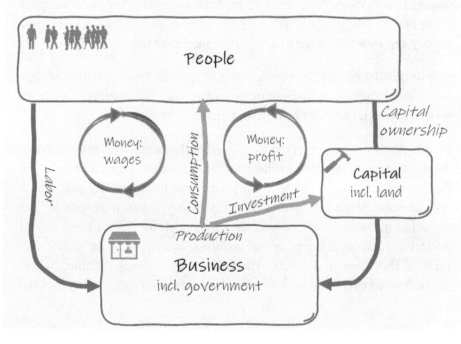

That was macroeconomics in a few paragraphs and then in a diagram.

If the economy is so simple, why all the fuss? Well, if everyone spent all their salary and profits each month, economics would indeed be pretty simple. In every payroll cycle, all the production would be exactly allocated to the laborers and capital owners, and money would cycle regularly from businesses to consumers and back to businesses. The economy would produce at maximum capacity, ensuring full employment.

The money supply would be also easy to calculate. We saw that *gross domestic product (GDP)* is simply the total amount of goods and services produced and consumed, including government spending, plus investment in new capital, plus net exports. The *equation of money* says that the supply of money should be equal to the GDP in the time period in which money cycles, e.g., there needs to be enough money for one cycle of salaries and shopping.

There are several complications though. First, there are seasonal variations in production—for example, farming, construction, and tourism all have different production outputs depending on the time of year. There are also changes in demography, technology, and consumer tastes. As capital accumulates, production grows. Clearly, even in this simple situation, the money supply would have to grow and adjust over time.

But by far the biggest economic complication is *credit*, or, put another way, *time shifting of consumption*. One way or another, much of macroeconomics ends up being about credit.

People don't want to consume exactly what they earn each month. Some want to consume more than they can afford today. Often they wish to finance the creation of capital for a business or home, a lofty goal which will increase future production of the economy. Even if people are not investing in creating new capital, they may wish to make a large capital purchase such as a home or secondhand equipment. The goods and services they earn in a month won't be enough to buy a home. In real terms, home buyers require a mechanism to under-consume for years and to pay for the home with lots of tokens. This will allow the seller, who gave up ownership of their home, to over-consume for years.

In the meantime, while some people are borrowing, others may wish to consume less than they can afford, either because they want to save for the future, or because they are attracted by generous interest payments.

With credit, suddenly the real economy is a lot more flexible, but also more complex. People are shifting their consumption forward and back in time. And yet, we want the economy to be constantly producing and consuming at around full capacity, so that more or less everyone is gainfully employed. This means that the advance and delay of gratification, which are constantly shifting, must be carefully balanced with each other.

Money is used not just to trade goods and services but also as tokens for tracking the real economy phenomenon of delayed and advanced gratification, which is credit. This is where banks come in. Simple bank loans are the easiest way of matching savers with borrowers. When the bank is able to match savers and borrowers accurately, it is a beautiful thing. A saver deposits cash in a savings account, instead of spending it, and promises not to withdraw it for some time. The bank lends it out to someone who then hires laborers to build a home or factory. The economy is still producing at full tilt, with full employment, but producing a little more capital for the borrower, while producing fewer goods and services for the saver's immediate consumption.

While the bank matches savers with borrowers, some jobs are shifted from producing goods and services for the saver, to producing capital for the borrower.

OF COURSE, it's not quite as simple as that—because banks cannot exactly match every long-term saver with a borrower for exactly the same term. And sometimes borrowers default.

But the main complication is that people often put aside money casually without committing to long-term savings. Some people are saving up for a few weeks for a medium-size purchase, but others are simply keeping their options open, or they are saving in case they lose their job. I call this the *paradox of money*, because money makes it easy to trade in a flexible way, but also makes it very easy not to trade, and casually delay consumption. This is the biggest threat to the economy. It is the easiest thing in the world to spend a bit less one month and leave a bit of cash in the wallet or checking account. But if a lot of people are putting aside a bit of cash in the same month, that has a bad effect on the real economy; not all the goods and services are being consumed and pretty soon you have downsizing and unemployment.

Viewed naively, fractional reserve banking appears to address this problem. Banks can take on demand deposits and lend out say 90 percent, so that even casual delays of gratification are aggregated and matched with loans which allow the advancement of gratification. However, due to the potent combination of fractional reserve banking and the ability of banks to create *bank money*, banks can actually loan out around 900 percent of checking accounts in bank money, when times are good. This means they are creating loans that may not be matched by savings. And it is hard to see how this extra bank money, which is expensive, is benefiting the real economy. Worse, at the first sign of economic trouble, banks worry about credit and the supply of bank money, denoted M1, may suddenly shrink.[56]

As far as I can tell, fractional reserve banking with bank money is therefore not a useful way to match the advancement and delay of gratification. And fractional reserve banking without bank money ought to work better.

Due to all of the above—not only economic growth and seasonal variations, but also cash coming in and out of circulation, and bank money being created and withdrawn—choosing the right supply of money is rather complicated. In fact, central banks no longer target a specific supply of money; instead, they set nominal interest rate targets and use these as a barometer indicating whether the economy needs more or less cash on any given day. Central banks, such as the Fed, control nominal interest rates by having a virtually infinite ability to print or withdraw cash from circulation, and buy and sell bonds on the open market, or lend to banks directly. So the Fed and other central banks set an interest rate target periodically—and usually independently of the government—and then adjust the money supply to achieve it.

BUT WHAT INTEREST RATE should a central bank aim for? This is a matter of ongoing debate, but I believe that monetary policy should always serve the real economy of goods and services. The real interest rate will balance the advance and delay of gratification. In other words, it will balance consumption now with investment in capital for the future. Real interest rates should find a level that ensures that the economy remains at full production and full employment. The people who delay gratification and consume less will be balanced by those who advance gratification and invest in capital.

Fundamentally the *central bank* should always set its *target nominal interest rate* to be the real interest rate, which balances the delay and advance of gratification in the real economy, plus the inflation target, which is typically 2 percent per year.

Inflation can only be measured accurately in retrospect but the market yield on inflation-protected government bonds is a very good barometer of inflation expectations. Nevertheless, central bank nominal interest rate policy remains hotly debated.

WE DISCUSSED SHORT-TERM economic fluctuations, and particularly the painful phenomenon of *recession*, a situation where the economy gets into a negative spiral of consuming less, producing less, and employing fewer people. This may be triggered by a collapse in asset prices, a credit crisis, or a supply shock. Or it may be triggered by an external force, such as a pandemic, that shuts down parts of the economy.

There is ongoing debate about whether governments can combat recessions using deficit fiscal spending or monetary stimulus—and many governments continue to experiment with both. Most economists agree that the economy will recover from a recession in the long term—perhaps with a nudge provided by a price drop—and reorganize itself with near maximum production and employment.

Finally, we looked at international trade, which, like all trade, is generally beneficial for both sides. There is an impossible trinity, though. Trading countries cannot enjoy stable exchange rates, free flow of capital, and independent monetary policy all at the same time. They have to sacrifice one of those aspects.

We saw that the *balance of payments* is always zero: if countries have a *trade deficit* in goods and services, which economists call the *current account*, they will have a surplus in the *capital account*. For example, Americans buy more Chinese goods and services; and China purchases more American bonds and companies.

Armed with all this background knowledge, we are now ready to jump to the present day and address some current economic dilemmas.

VII. MONEY TODAY: GOING OUT OF STYLE

TWO CENTURIES LATER...

CHARLIE V IS SITTING under a coconut tree, leaning back against the trunk. He looks up at the distant coconuts and recalls a family legend about an ancestor who used to climb the trees and pick coconuts all day, before collapsing of exhaustion in the evening.

Charlie V notices the first Spring blossoms appearing on bushes around him. He looks down at his jeans and frowns. They are ripped in all the wrong places. Anyone can tell they are left over from last Winter's season.

He pulls a smartphone out of the pocket of his jeans. Charlie frowns at the phone. He's had this phone for almost a year—there must be faster ones available now. He unfolds the phone. Touching the screen a few times, Charlie swipes through thousands of jeans and hundreds of smartphone models. He selects a pair of pants and a smartphone and taps to purchase them both for a few hundred bucks. He is offered credit to pay for his purchase over a year, with zero interest.

Young Charlie slides his phone back into his pocket, wondering if he made the right choice. He can't be sure; he couldn't possibly study all available options.

The new pants and phone will be delivered by a quadcopter drone within 60 minutes. He sighs and pulls his old phone out again and starts streaming media. He watches a clip about Arthur Jr. making plans to colonize Mars. Apparently, he's already launched a sports car into orbit around the sun.

He squints at the bright screen, trying to convince himself that he can see some fine pixilation. His new phone will have a way sharper screen.

IN TWO CENTURIES, the islanders have discovered coal and oil and invented the steam engine, the internal combustion engine, electricity, and the transistor. They drive around in electric vehicles on a network of roads. They have running water, an electricity grid, telephones, computers, and planes. Motorized cranes build skyscrapers.

Exponential economic growth has been working its magic.

Two centuries earlier, 50 percent of the islanders were farmers. Now only 3 percent make a living from farming. Using fertilizers, tractors, combine harvesters and genetically modified crops, these few islanders produce enough food to fill everyone's stomachs, fuel an obesity epidemic, export food to Huaxia, and still have food left over to put in the trash each day.

Semi-automated factories create millions of variations of garments, gadgets, and toys at an astounding rate. Now a mere 12 percent of the islanders are employed in manufacturing. Most of the goods produced in the semi-automated factories end up in landfill in a year or two.

With so few people needed in agriculture and manufacturing, the other 80 percent of the islanders work in services. People used to eat in restaurants once a year, then once a month, and now they expect to eat out twice a day. They have manicures and pedicures and massages. They drink lattes, slushy drinks, and pumpkin-vanilla fraps daily.

Every year the islanders invent yet more luxury services, and even more varieties of foods, fashions, and gadgets. And so almost everyone remains gainfully employed, producing services which, some would argue, are surplus to real requirements.

THIS CHAPTER REFLECTS the astounding transformation that has occurred in most of the world in the last 200 years. The story glances over the pragmatic problem that the archipelago's population is too small to support the complexities of the modern world economy.

Before the industrial revolution, economic growth was glacial. In the last 200 years, growth has been exponential, at a relatively rapid 1.5 percent per year, which compounds to 50 percent growth per 30-year generation. The key drivers of growth were the industrial revolution in the 1800s, mass production in the 1900s and information technology and world trade going into the 2000s.

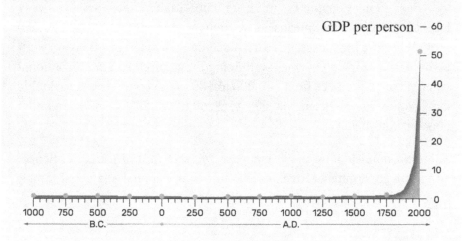

Long-term economic growth: GDP per person, thousands of today's dollars. By kind permission of the Bank of England.[57]

The employment proportions in the story reflect those in the U.S., which are similar to other developed countries. Around 3 percent of Americans are farmers, and they produce far more food than was produced back when 50 percent of the citizens were farmers. This productivity miracle is the result of capital accumulation, specialization, and technology.

Starting with the Luddites in the early 1800s, people have always worried that automation will create unemployment. But in fact, up to now, as productivity has grown, people have consumed more and more goods and invented new services. While in every generation many individuals suffered the hardship of losing their jobs from sectors that were being automated, most eventually found new jobs in growth sectors. Overall, society became wealthier through productivity, and succeeded in creating new job opportunities as fast as it replaced older jobs with machines.

The story hints at a modern concern: that above a certain level, increased wealth barely translates into increased happiness. In the U.S., one famous study claimed that any increase of income above $75,000 per year does not correlate with increased emotional well-being.[58] Another study claims that well-being continues to rise with higher incomes but only logarithmically. This means that, rather than every extra $10,000 providing extra happiness, it is each percentage increase that delivers well-being. For example, if average well-being is enhanced by a certain amount when income increases from $40,000 to $80,000, you then need to double the income again—from $80,000 to $160,000—to get another similar boost in well-being.[59]

Some economists now study happiness, aiming to turn it into a science; and some governments are experimenting with happiness targets for their countries.[60][61]

INEQUALITY OF INCOME

ANANYA AND ATKISH are roommates and seniors at a college in the island of Bharata. Atkish is studying computer science and Ananya is taking economics.

One evening Ananya says, "Hey Atkish, I'm sending you an invite to join Phasebook. A bunch of our friends are on already."

Atkish signs up and is rapidly absorbed by checking other people's statuses, tracking who is friends with whom, and perusing the content his friends have posted. As an engineer, he is also trying to analyze what technologies are used and estimate the size of Phasebook's database.

"Ananya, you're taking economics—what kind of a product is this?" he says eventually, "Why is it free?"

"Well, as one of my lecturers said, 'if you're not paying for the product, *you* are the product.' Those Phasebook guys over on the island of Us are selling you to their advertisers. More accurately, they are auctioning off the opportunity to influence you, Atkish, just a bit, to the highest commercial bidder."

"Hah. Well, who cares? It's free and it seems like a lot of fun."

The use of Phasebook spreads like wildfire across the archipelago.

Atkish graduates that summer and lands a software engineering job working for Phasebook. Phasebook is now competing with many other tech companies for the best engineering talent and paying top buck. Phasebook pays him the local equivalent of 50,000 bucks a year.

At the same time, there are too many economics graduates that year so Ananya doesn't find a job in her field and ends up taking a job as a cook in the Phasebook canteen, earning 10,000 a year. Over in Us, Phasebook is paying an average of 200,000 bucks a year to engineers and 50,000 bucks for less skilled jobs.

"They're paying you what?" Ananya says, raising an eyebrow as she spoons some curry onto Atkish's plate. There's no one behind him in the line so they chat for a while.

"Yeah, I feel kind of bad. I don't know how they can afford to pay me so much."

"Well, I admit I'm a bit jealous, but I do get how they can afford it," says Ananya. "Don't let this apron fool you, I'm still an aspiring economist. Look at their market opportunity. When you write software upstairs, they roll it out instantly across all the islands. We studied in class how products access global markets so quickly nowadays—in days, not years. So I guess they pay you good money to, well, transform curry into software, and then they have a well-oiled machine for turning software into user engagement. Then they sell that user engagement for money. Lots of it."

"Right," he lowers his voice. "But look at the inequality they are creating. Three months ago, we were roommates in college. Now I'm earning five times more than you just because my technical skills are in high demand."

"Yeah. Mind you, in a way they are reducing inequality too," Ananya replies.

"Reducing?"

"I guess they are increasing inequality here in Bharata. I mean, look at the two of us—"

"Right," he says, "but I bet they also have huge gaps between skilled and less skilled salaries in Us."

"No doubt they are also increasing inequality in Us," she nods. "But what about globally? In the past there was a massive gap between Bharatian and Usian salaries. But now you're in Bharata earning something close to an average salary in Us. Maybe you're not earning as much as an Usian engineer, but still, you, Atkish, are actually reducing the wage gap between the countries."

Atkish smiles and goes back to his food.

INEQUALITY IS RESEARCHED and discussed in great detail in a 2013 book by French economist Thomas Piketty which I have used as a major source for this and the next chapter.[62]

Inequality is of course nothing new. In fact, on the contrary, significant government intervention in the redistribution of wealth is relatively new. Until 1910, income taxes never exceeded single digit percentages, and governments barely acted to even out income inequalities. One can easily get a feeling for the prevailing inequality in the literature of the nineteenth century by contrasting, say, the landed gentry portrayed by Jane Austen, with the working-class and destitute characters in the novels of Charles Dickens.

Outside of perfect communism, some inequality of income is, of course, inevitable. Some people have highly desirable skills: they may be brilliant engineers, stunning models, inspiring orators, expert doctors, or talented sportsmen. Others are just very fortunate with the place and circumstances of their birth, or they get the right lucky breaks. The world's richest country in GDP per citizen is Qatar. But it is not due to any merit on the part of modern-day Qatari citizens that vast deposits of ancient plants decayed into fossil fuels deep below their shores, many millions of years ago.

And yet, as we saw, in the 1980s Milton Friedman wrote "a society that puts freedom first, will, as a happy by-product, end up with both greater freedom and greater equality." I wonder if he would still claim that today. Inequality of income within developed economies has widened in recent decades, most starkly in the English-speaking developed countries, as well as in China which has been developing rapidly and unevenly.

There are multiple ways of quantifying inequality of income. We can measure the percentage of income earned by the top 10 percent, or the top 1 percent. Or the *Gini coefficient* sums up all aspects of inequality on a scale, from perfect equality to perfect inequality. Since the *Occupy Wall Street* movement of 2011 used the slogan "We are the 99 percent," it has become fashionable to focus on the income share of the top 1 percent as a measure of inequality. Below are graphs of how that measure has developed in a number of wealthy countries in the past century,

This has been described as U-shape in the Anglo-Saxon economies, versus L-shape in other wealthy nations. However, even within the so-called L-shapes, one may discern increasing inequality since 1990, especially in France, and even an uptick in inequality in the relatively egalitarian Scandinavian countries.

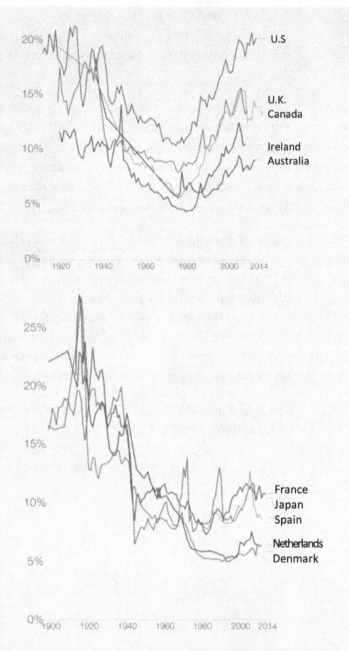

Share of total income going to the top 1 percent since 1900 (before tax)[63]

The U.S. and UK, in particular, have flip-flopped on their attitude to inequality in a way that must give high earners whiplash. The twentieth century started with close to zero income tax in all these countries. This had changed by the Second World War. From 1944 to 1963, the U.S. had a top rate of federal income tax above 90 percent and then at 70 percent till 1981. The top rate then dropped suddenly to 50 percent and later to 40 percent. The UK outdid everyone else with a top tax rate of 98 percent in the 1940s and again in the 1970s, later dropping to less than half of that at 45 percent. Both Anglo-Saxon economies were effectively capping salaries around the middle of the last century, and indeed this significantly reduced income inequality as seen in the first chart. But since the 1980s, both the U.S. and UK have gone in the opposite direction and adopted relatively low top tax rates, resulting in high income inequality.

As top tax rates came down, it started to become socially acceptable, especially in the English-speaking countries, for supermanagers, famous actors, supermodels, and outstanding sportspeople to earn multi-million-dollar salaries, while average actors and models and sportspeople struggled to make a living. This is sometimes called *hyper-meritocracy*. However, the emphasis on merit arguably belies the fact that success owes much to luck, starting with luck of the gene pool, luck of the country and location of birth, luck of family circumstances, and luck of happenstance during an individual's life and career.

Inequality has ticked up in recent decades, albeit more moderately, in most other large wealthy economies, that is in Japan, and continental Europe, even though their tax policy has remained more stable. For example, France and Germany always had top tax rates in the 50–70 percent range, never going as high as 90 percent or as low as 40 percent. Yet they, too, have experienced some rise in inequality since 1990. Economists tend to blame technology and globalization for this trend toward increasing inequality. Global markets allow managers and actors and models and sportspeople to rapidly build a brand and shine on a worldwide stage, increasing their financial value, creating global winner-takes-all opportunities.[64]

Many find the increasing inequality worrying because it doesn't feel equitable, because it reduces happiness, or because it may lead to social unrest, as indicated by the Occupy Wall Street movement. We will see later that inequality may also be to blame for some severe economic challenges.

HOWEVER, THERE IS a silver lining to this cloud. While income inequality within many individual countries has increased, global inequality of income has actually decreased in recent decades, with income in the world as a whole actually becoming more equal. This is primarily because many of the billion citizens of China (dark red in the graph below), and to a lesser extent India, have emerged from poverty to form a global middle class.

In 1800, the entire world was poor. Between 1800-1975 the world split into economically developed and undeveloped countries as evidenced by the two peaks in the 1975 chart, and this split continued into the 1980s.

By 2015, the gap was plastered over.[65] World income has increased overall and there is a massive new global middle class, primarily in Asia. So, income is becoming more unequal within many key countries, but more equal globally. This won't help domestic tensions, but it does paint a more optimistic picture for humanity.

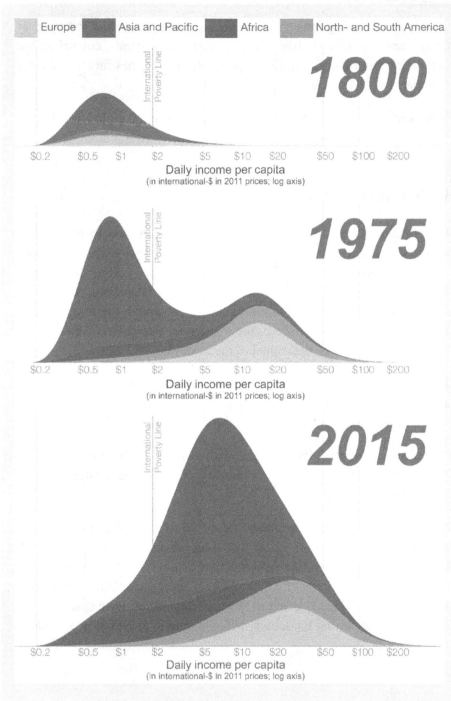

Distribution of income by region. OurWolrdInData.org[66]

This is an intriguing fallacy of composition: inequality has increased in China and America if they are considered as separate countries; but inequality has reduced in China and America if they are considered together.

However, while global income has become more equal, global distribution of wealth has continued to become more unequal...

INEQUALITY OF WEALTH

PHASEBOOK CONTINUES to grow rapidly. It sells access to its users to advertisers, and its revenues grow every month, as more users spend more time on the service, and therefore more advertisers are willing to pay more for the attention of those users. Like any business, Phasebook pays out its revenues to its workers and to the owners of its capital; the founder Zack is the main owner, but he shares the ownership with some investors who helped Zack to finance the capital of the business.

Barbara V, the banker, pays a visit to Zack. "Your company is red hot, Zack. It's growing fast and expected to grow for years to come. My bank would like to float your company on the stock market."

"Why would I do that, Barb? I like owning and controlling the company. All profits are distributed to me and a few other smaller owners. What's the advantage of floating?"

"Zack, when my bank arranges an initial public offering for your Phasebook company, there will be two huge advantages for you. The first is that your ownership of the capital of the business will be divided up into a million shares each one of which can be bought and sold on the island's stock exchange. There is going to be huge demand for those shares, based on the expectation that Phasebook will continue to grow fast and produce future profits."

"So?"

"So you can sell some of your shares today at a nice premium. The actual profits you receive today are small, but the value of each share, based on the expectation of future profits, is large. Yes, you will give up a proportion of your ownership and future profits, but you will have much more money today. You can buy yourself a second home or a yacht. And you will have complete flexibility on how much ownership to keep or sell on any given day."

"Hmm. And?"

"And, once your shares are traded publicly you will also find it easier to raise new capital for Phasebook. Say Phasebook has a million shares; you will be able to issue and sell say another 100,000 new shares, and Phasebook can use the money for new capital investments. At that point there will be more shares so each share will be a thinner slice of the pie, but the pie will be bigger. You can use the money to invest in capital, like building a factory."

"We're a social network."

"Well, right. You can use the money to acquire the capital of a messaging platform or a virtual reality company. Whatever you like. Our stock market creates a very flexible environment, allowing investment to flow to wherever capital creation has the biggest benefit for the economy."

Sure enough, Phasebook announces an initial public offering, or IPO. Up to now, Phasebook has been owned privately by Zack and a few investors who have financed the company's capital creation. Now the ownership of Phasebook is subdivided into a million shares, and members of the public are invited to buy and sell some of the shares to each other on the Usian stock market. Each share simply represents one-millionth of the overall ownership of Phasebook's capital.

As Barbara suggested, Phasebook issues some new shares to raise money for future capital investments, and Zack sells a proportion of his shares to the public. The IPO is a big success. Phasebook now has many new owners as well as new investors who have put money into the company to finance future capital investments.

Overnight, Zack's shares are worth billions. Zack and his original investors still own a large proportion of the company, but the rest of the ownership is now split between thousands of shareholders, with some shares changing hands every second, and the price fluctuating second by second—based on supply and demand for the shares.

Atkish and Ananya are having drinks after work to toast their employer's IPO. "Still think Phasebook is reducing inequality, Ananya?" Atkish smiles.

"Well, I heard Zack only takes a nominal salary of 1 buck per year. So, you can't blame him personally for increasing income inequality. In fact, I may have more income than him. But wealth inequality—well, that's a whole different matter."

"Yeah. Ananya, you studied economics. How can this IPO create such vast wealth overnight?"

She thinks for a moment. "Well, the real wealth in the world didn't change. There is still the same amount of actual stuff as yesterday. Phasebook has various capital assets. There is an expectation we will use this capital to generate rapidly growing profits for many years to come. We had all of that yesterday too. But today shares in Phasebook can be bought and sold on the stock market. So it's much easier to value that capital in terms of bucks. There is no new physical wealth, but certain capital assets that existed yesterday are a lot easier to value today; and a lot easier for their owners to sell if they wish to."

"And that newly liquid wealth isn't distributed very evenly, huh?"

"Well, no. By the way, we both work for Phasebook, but Phasebook actually has very few employees relative to its profits. We learned in class that the factors of production are labor and capital. But here at Phasebook, you could say our profits are associated less with labor and much more with our capital."

"But what capital? Our laptops? Our desks and chairs? We don't have any big factories or expensive machinery."

"Our capital isn't as tangible as that. Our main capital is our data, our software, and the goodwill of our users. As a user you may enjoy our free service, which is great, but consider that your data, your loyalty to the platform, well, your addiction to the platform, those are the capital assets of Phasebook. And let's face it, that intangible capital is a much bigger factor in Phasebook's growth and success than our labor as employees."

AS THE YEARS PASS, there are more IPOs, and the issue of wealth inequality becomes more political. Eventually Bharata decides to start moderating wealth inequality directly. The island introduces an estate tax of 20 percent on inheritances over the equivalent of a million bucks, and 35 percent on inheritances over a billion bucks. They also introduce a wealth tax of 1 percent per year on islanders owning assets above ten million bucks. The measures are controversial but generally fairly popular as a reasonable way to moderate wealth inequality.

However, some wealthy Bharatans start to emigrate to other islands. Several other islands are more than happy to have Bharatans move there, bringing their wealth with them. Some even create special tax haven status for wealthy immigrants.

The Bharatan government is furious and begrudgingly cancels their wealth tax in order to stem the emigration of wealth. They demand an international conference on coordination of tax policy, to avoid islands competing as tax havens.

THIS CHAPTER IS MAINLY about inequality of wealth, but we have taken the opportunity to review basic concepts such as an *initial public offering (IPO)*. This is the process of a company listing its shares for the public to trade on a stock market, while also raising new money for the company by issuing new shares. These are actually two separate processes that often occur together: raising capital by issuing brand-new shares; and listing shares so that the public can trade the shares with each other on a stock market.

Stock market listings have become one of the most dramatic mechanisms for creating wealth and increasing wealth inequality. We will discuss share valuations in a little more detail later.

Piketty points out that wealth is even more unequal than income, pretty much always and everywhere. At the time of writing, two Americans, Elon Musk and Jeff Bezos, have about $400 billion in wealth. In contrast, the bottom 32 percent of Americans have a net worth of zero, and the bottom 39 percent, about 127 million Americans, have less net wealth than those two men.[67] In fact these two men have about the same wealth as all of Peru, or Hungary, and more than most countries in the world.[68] To give credit where it's due, Bill Gates who for a long time was the wealthiest person in the world set an example by pledging to donate 95 percent of his wealth to charity, and Warren Buffett 99 percent, while Elon Musk and several other billionaires have pledged to donate at least half of their wealth.[69]

Inequality of wealth is certainly not new. We've all read novels or seen movies contrasting the aristocracy and commoners in centuries past. A new aspect, which is perhaps welcome, is that with modern technology and access to global markets, tech entrepreneurs can create vast fortunes in a decade or two, and their fortunes sometimes dwarf some of the largest inherited estates.

Inequality of wealth is also discussed in great detail in Piketty's book.[70] He claims that inequality of wealth will inherently tend to increase constantly, because the annual return on capital is generally greater than the rate of growth of the economy (which he writes as $r > g$). Therefore, people relying on savings from their income will never accumulate wealth at the rate of someone who already has an invested fortune.

Piketty argues that there was one exceptional period when wealth inequality was compressed—during the First and Second World Wars. But generally wealth tends to become more and more unequal, with some families amassing ever greater fortunes, while the bottom 50 percent have close to zero net worth, not even owning their homes.

The increase in wealth inequality becomes more pronounced when the economy is growing more slowly, as it has in recent decades—because of slower demographic growth, and because productivity growth has slowed. In the meantime, while income stagnates, wealth continues to provide a healthy return and fortunes continue to grow. Piketty further argues that the richest people can afford the best investment managers who will help their fortunes to grow even faster, thus increasing the disparity further.

AN INTERESTING INDICATION that something fundamental has changed with respect to inequality in recent decades is the breakdown of *Bowley's law*. Recall that the income in an economy is split between the factors of production—that is, it is paid to laborers as wages and to capital owners as profits. English economist Arthur Bowley observed empirically that the ratio of income awarded to labor versus capital owners is stable at around two-thirds and one- third. This seemed so stable that he proposed his eponymous law, also known as the *law of the constant wage share*.[71] This empirical law, however, has broken down in recent decades. The *wage share* in the U.S. is now just 59 percent.[72] So of all the production of the economy, more is awarded to the capital owners than before and proportionately less to laborers. In more and more cases, as in our island story, the capital owners possess data and a loyal user base, rather than factories and tools. This unprecedented increase in the share of income going to capital owners will of course further widen the wealth gap.

When looking at inequality of wealth, there is also no silver lining. Both nationally, in almost every country, and globally, the trend has been towards greater inequality of wealth.

Demographics plays a role here. European aristocrats used to avoid their family inheritance being divided by following the practice of male-line primogeniture, whereby all the wealth went to the first-born son. This practice was largely abandoned in the last century and, since then, sharing inheritance between multiple children has helped to dilute fortunes once per generation. However, birth rates in all developed countries have fallen, and many wealthy families may now have just one child, or at most two, thus keeping the wealth fairly concentrated across generations.

One of the most popular policies for moderating the inequality of wealth is an estate tax or inheritance tax. This ensures that, once in a generation, some of the wealth is redistributed. Several prominent American billionaires have appealed to Congress to retain and potentially increase the U.S. Estate Tax which today only applies to the top 2 percent.[73] Warren Buffett was particularly eloquent on the subject, arguing that repealing the Estate Tax was like "choosing the 2020 Olympic team by picking the eldest sons of the gold-medal winners in the 2000 Olympics... Removing the tax would lead to the creation of an aristocracy of wealth instead of a meritocracy." The OECD recently recommended more inheritance tax.[74]

A more dramatic proposal, by Piketty, is a global progressive tax on wealth levied each year—in other words, in addition to taxing income, the state would tax away a small proportion of wealth annually. Spain already levies an ongoing tax on wealth in most regions, and France has a tax on some forms of wealth. However, wealth taxes are not that easy to implement. Assessing wealth is complex, and people have difficulty paying a wealth tax if none of their wealth is liquid. Further, to be truly effective, such a tax would require international cooperation; otherwise, competition between countries would cause wealth taxes to trend to zero. Indeed, most countries have no wealth tax, and some countries have no estate tax.

The issue of tax havens is not limited to Caribbean island nations. The UK taxes inheritance of its citizens, but unashamedly appeals as a tax haven to foreign billionaires who enjoy a *non-domicile* exemption on inheritance taxes for non-UK assets when moving to reside in the UK. It is easy to see how this is beneficial to the UK, attracting wealthy oligarchs to London, even though not everyone appreciates the resulting hike of London property prices. But if all countries start competing as tax havens for the wealthy, there will soon be no moderation of wealth inequality at all.

As this book was going to press, the G7 wealthy countries were agreeing for the first time to work towards a global uniform minimum corporation tax of 15%.[75] This international consensus could be the first step towards an era in which tax policy is at least somewhat coordinated between countries, halting the race towards zero tax as countries compete to attract companies and wealthy individuals. This could eventually help the world to moderate inequality.

Therefore, moderating wealth inequality within a country is difficult, requiring controversial taxes, and risking the flight of capital to tax havens. Redistribution of wealth between countries is even harder. The most direct mechanism is foreign aid. Unfortunately, foreign aid is currently too small to make a huge difference. The most generous countries, Luxembourg, Norway, and Sweden, donate about 1 percent of GDP.[76] The world's wealthiest country, the U.S., contributes a paltry 0.25 percent of GDP, or less than 1 percent of the Federal budget, in foreign aid. A lot of this goes to political allies, such as Israel, and to subsidize the purchase of American arms.

For now, the best hope for global redistribution of wealth is private philanthropy, following the example set by the *Bill & Melinda Gates Foundation*, their recent divorce notwithstanding, whose website proudly announces: "All lives have equal value: We are impatient optimists working to reduce inequality."[77] A broader inspiring movement which is gaining momentum is *effective altruism*,[78] which rejects the notion that charity begins at home, and encourages donors to donate wherever in the world their dollar does the most good, based on evidence. Several organizations help donors to follow these principles.[79]

While consistent tax on wealth is the surest way to systematically address wealth inequality within countries, and significant foreign aid would be the surest way to level the playing field between countries, both these policies remain either absent or meagre. Meanwhile, mega-philanthropy, especially philanthropy following the rational principles of effective altruism, is making an increasing contribution to addressing extreme inequality of wealth.

DECLINING REAL INTEREST RATES

SEVERAL YEARS AND SALARY raises later, Atkish is a senior software architect. He finds that he is no longer spending all his income so he starts saving each month. Atkish is not saving for a specific purpose. He already owns a great house, and he has a generous pension plan at work. He is just saving because he feels no need to spend more.

Around the same time, Ananya finally quits Phasebook to utilize her economics skills and become an entrepreneur. She takes out a bank loan to set up her own restaurant business. With the loan, she rents premises and hires contractors to renovate the building and to design a menu. She acquires ovens, fridges, freezers, and other capital equipment for her business.

Finally, everything is ready, and Ananya invites some friends for a rehearsal dinner.

"Do you know that you financed this place, Atkish?" says Ananya over dinner.

"Come again?"

"Well, not literally you, but people like you. You earn so much that you're not spending all your income anymore, so you're saving, delaying your gratification. But someone like me can't possibly afford to buy this setup out of pocket." She waves at the elegant decor. "These last few weeks, I've been spending way more than my income investing in this place. So I've taken a loan. If you are delaying gratification by saving, then I am advancing gratification. Sometime in the future, I'll have to repay the loan with interest, and then I will also have to spend less than my income, to make up for the fact that I'm overspending now. The banks are simply matching people like you with people like me."

"Well, you're welcome," he says.

"No, you're welcome. It's only thanks to people like me, making investments and paying for business loans, that the bank is able to reward you for saving."

"Yeah, well, I bet your loan was pretty cheap, because the interest the bank is paying me is barely more than what I lose due to inflation."

AT AROUND THE same time, Charlie V is buying a house. He's been saving up for 10 years. His savings have been earning him just 2 percent per year nominal interest. Charlie V notes with frustration that, after inflation, his savings are worth no more year after year; the interest rate merely compensates for 2 percent inflation. The purchasing power of his savings is not growing, other than the extra he puts in. Charlie V reflects nostalgically on stories of his grandfather Charlie III who used to earn 3 percent interest, and who told how his own grandfather, Charlie-the-coconut-picker, would earn some 5 percent interest on his savings.

As soon as Charlie V has saved enough to put down a 25 percent deposit on the house of his dreams, he goes ahead and purchases it. With his savings not gaining any value, he doesn't wait another day. To finance the other 75 percent, Charlie V draws a mortgage, advancing gratification, which he will repay over the next 30 years. The bank has to make a profit and so it charges Charlie 3 percent for the mortgage, but Charlie notes that, after inflation, that's a real interest rate of about 1 percent. Charlie V, now a homeowner, has suddenly flipped from saver to borrower. He is now delighted that interest rates are at historic lows, and that his debt to the bank barely grows over time in real terms.

"If interest rates had been higher," Charlie V muses to the mortgage bank clerk, "I might have saved up for another five or ten years. But with no returns on delaying gratification, and a very low cost for advancing gratification, I might as well own my home sooner rather than later."

IT TURNS OUT that in the real world, real interest rates have been declining for a long time. In January 2020, Paul Schmelzing of the Bank of England published a remarkable study[80] with a tour de force of long-term trends in real interest rates. If you've been paying attention, you may have noticed that real interest rates in Europe have been dropping by an average of about 2 percent per century, at least since 1311. The data is on the next page.

The data is complex and there may be many factors contributing to the decline—for example, reduced credit risks due to more sophisticated banking. But the most likely primary reason for real interest rates dropping, as Schmelzing also mentions, is that over time capital accumulates and the economy's production increases. This will push interest rates down from both sides. Savers become wealthier and find it easier to save money, without requiring exorbitant interest rates as an incentive, so the supply of savings increases.

At the same time, the demand for expensive loans will decrease. Once all the business ventures that offer a 10 percent return on investment have been financed and realized, there will be no more borrowers at 10 percent and the demand for loans might max out at 9 percent. In order to match supply and demand, the banks will drop their interest rates as more capital accumulates.

We saw hints of this on the island—as the island got richer, it became easier for islanders to save. And the business opportunities became less lucrative—the hundredth ladder didn't boost production as much as the first.

Looking at the chart once more, we notice that, while the data is messy, there is an average trend line very roughly aiming towards real interest rates crossing zero around the 2010s. And here we are.

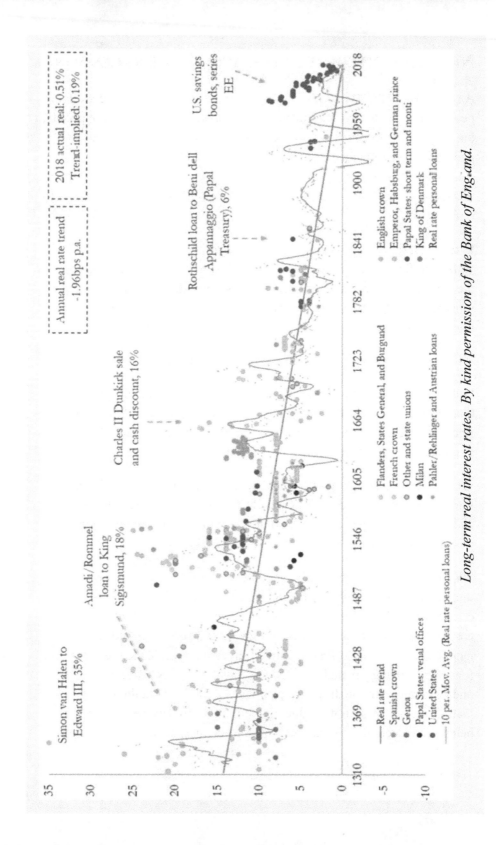

Long-term real interest rates. By kind permission of the Bank of England.

NEGATIVE INTEREST RATES, AFFLUENCE RECESSION

A DECADE LATER, Barbara's Bank is facing a challenge. There are more people lining up to save than to borrow. Well, not necessarily more people, but in total the people in the savers' line have more money to save than the people in the other line wish to borrow. The bank manager, Barbara V, is concerned. The bank will lose money if she pays even a paltry interest rate to savers, while much of that money is not being loaned out for interest to borrowers.

In the meantime, there is growing unemployment on the island. Barbara V walks the floor of the bank and chats with some of the people waiting in the long line of savers. Some are laborers who need to save up for their retirement. But some are people who simply have way more income than they can spend and want to put the excess in a savings account.

Barbara V schedules a meeting with Fred V, head of the central bank.

"Interest rates are too high," she says. "The bank is facing more saving than borrowing. I can't afford to pay the savers 2 percent interest if I can't find borrowers to pay me 3 or 4 percent. We need to lower interest rates by at least a percentage point or two to balance the market."

Fred V puts his shoes up on his mahogany desk. "I don't know, Barbara. Interbank rates are 2 percent. Consider our target of 2 percent inflation, and real interest rates are zero. As it is, savings gain no real value from year to year. How can we lower interest rates?"

"Well, Fred, maybe you don't care that the bank can't find borrowers for the savings, and us bankers are losing money. But think about the consequences for the economy. We have people saving, which means they are not spending all their income on goods and services. And if we don't lend that money out to finance capital investment projects, then there are fewer jobs being created by business investment. No wonder we have unemployment. If you drop interest rates, we can lend out the savings. And then the jobs lost by not producing the goods and services which are not being consumed, can be balanced by jobs created by investment projects building factories and homes. I know you care about getting the island back to full employment."

"But just think about it, Barbara. If we drop nominal interest rates further, then the real interest rate is negative. That means people's savings are losing value each year, after inflation."

"Tough luck for them, Fred. That's the market rate. Perhaps negative real interest rates will finally encourage people to save a bit less and consume a bit more. That will definitely create jobs."

"That's all very well, but will your bank really make loans at interest rates that are around zero or even negative in real terms? That means businesses will actually be paid to borrow money. Some companies may take loans to build factories even if they expect to lose a bit of money in the process. What is the point of that? Society will be paying businesses to make investments, whether they are profitable or not."

"I don't know, Fred, but it sure beats having unemployment."

And so nominal interest rates are reduced to 1 percent. And for the first time in the history of the island, the real interest rate, after adjusting for inflation, is well below zero, around minus 1 percent.

Sure enough, the line of savers gets a bit shorter—and the amount of money in that line reduces— as some people decide they might as well spend and consume more, rather than losing the value of their money by saving in the bank. And some business investment projects which have been on hold, because they were barely profitable, get the green light. The line of savers keeps getting shorter, and the line of borrowers keeps growing longer, until they balance. The new business investment projects employ people to build factories and infrastructure, and unemployment starts to go down.

REAL INTEREST RATES slid into negative territory in the 2010s. In reality, they did so without pausing to have the explicit conversation Fred and Barbara had. This chapter explores briefly what would happen if real interest rates were artificially kept above zero. This question will become important in our later analysis. The result could be a rather persistent period of unemployment.

I call this kind of hypothetical unemployment an *affluence recession* because, on the one hand, it is the result of wealthier people not wanting to spend their income. And on the other hand, it reflects a society where all the clearly worthwhile capital investments have already been made, and there is little demand for loans unless the real interest rate is negative.

How do we even gauge real interest rates? We have seen that there is a market in government bonds which represent real loans, in that they repay the loan adjusted for inflation. The amount repaid can purchase the same quantity of real stuff in the shops as the loaned amount.

Throughout most of the 2010s, U.S. government five-year treasury inflation-protected bonds (TIPS) mostly paid negative real yields.[81] Recall that the *yield* is the effective interest rate, based on how much the bond costs in the market relative to the amount it will repay. These bonds are actually trading for more, not less, than the amount to be repaid. So people have been investing in government bonds despite knowing that the money they receive back will be worth less than what they invested, in terms of purchasing power.

And it's not only government bonds—even some corporate bonds are in negative territory. In 2019, Toyota was able to borrow money at 0.0000000091 percent interest.[82] That's less than 1 yen interest per billion yen loaned, which—after adjusting for inflation—represents a negative real interest rate. Germany's industrial conglomerate, Siemens, borrowed for a nominal rate of -0.3 percent,[83] which net of inflation, is even more negative. In the U.S. in 2020, the parent company of Google borrowed money for a record low 0.45 percent nominal interest,[84] also representing a negative real interest rate after inflation.

You might think that negative real interest rates could only apply to governments and the most solid blue-chip companies. Perhaps you assume that, once banks add their profits and cover their credit risk, consumers would never see negative real interest rates—let alone negative nominal interest rates. But that perfectly reasonable assumption has been shattered. Denmark has seen negative nominal consumer mortgage rates.[85] Yes, people get an actual discount if they are willing to pay for their home over ten years instead of now. In Germany too, consumers can sometimes draw loans with negative nominal interest rates[86] and even lower real interest. This means they pay back fewer euros than they borrowed, and each of those returned euros also has diminished purchasing power.

So the market price for delaying gratification is now truly negative, in real inflation-adjusted terms. For the first time in history, people are paying to delay gratification, and being paid to advance gratification. This is a strange reversal in the value of time. Later is worth more than now!

This is not natural human behavior. Kids famously find it difficult to swap one marshmallow now for two marshmallows in 15 minutes.[87] It seems ingrained in human psychology that we prefer sooner rather than later. And yet today's average adult is willing to swap a product or service now for less than one in thirty years' time.[88] In the UK it is particularly extreme—you have to give the UK government two figurative marshmallows now for the privilege of being repaid just one marshmallow mid-century![89]

WE MENTIONED THE LONG-TERM accumulation of capital and wealth as the key reason for the current super-low interest rates. We will discuss later how inequality accelerates this trend. For completeness, several other explanations have been suggested for the paltry interest rates which have been prevailing.[90] One which seems convincing to me is that a lot of modern businesses are based on software and data, rather than massive physical infrastructure, thus reducing the demand for business loans. Our story previously touched on the example of Facebook.

Tyler Cowen has argued in *The Great Stagnation*[91] that during the 1800s and early 1900s the industrialized nations developed massive infrastructure including industry, electricity grids, skyscrapers, railway networks, roads and cars, and aviation. However, since the 1950s, while computing and computer networks have accelerated forward, the physical world has actually not changed all that much.

This shift may indeed be a contributing to lower demand for capital and lower interest rates; but this doesn't alter the potentially damaging consequences we are exploring.

Another argument worth considering is that China is saving massively, as we saw, buying U.S. Treasury bonds and other assets, making more debt available and reducing interest rates. Finally, people are living longer and need to save for larger pensions.

Notwithstanding these other possible factors, surely the major force driving down real interest rates is the accumulation of capital. Wealthier people are more likely to save, while more developed countries have fewer opportunities to make investments with very high returns. We will explore later on how inequality accelerates the downward trend of interest rates.

THIS BOOK IS ALL about understanding the real economy. Negative interest rates may sound like a technical monetary issue. But by thinking about what they mean to the real economy, we can appreciate just how bizarre negative real interest rates are, and how they are likely to be economically harmful.

An economy has a certain capacity to produce stuff. In a healthy economic situation, we would expect that plenty of people would be willing to consume all the stuff that can be produced. If people have no desire to consume all the stuff that can be produced, then we have entered some kind of utopia, or in some people's mind a dystopia, where the world is just too rich, and there will no longer be employment for everyone. We will return to this point when we discuss the future.

So what about real interest rates? In an ordinary economy situation, while people generally want to consume all the stuff that can be produced, some people may agree to postpone some of their consumption and save, in return for receiving interest. This will allow other people to pay interest and borrow. This way we still have full employment, but we have fewer people producing stuff for today. Instead, some are employed in realizing capital investments, building factories, homes, and developing new technologies, which will pay off tomorrow.

But what if real interest rates are zero? This means that people, on average, no longer require any incentive to save and delay consumption. Zero real interest rates mean that society has achieved such wealth that, on average, people don't really care if they consume more or not; many are happy to consume less stuff even with no reward for doing so. In the meantime, people can borrow for free, so society is willing to finance investments regardless of whether they are expected to be profitable.

In the puzzling situation of zero real interest rates, what would cause real interest rates to drop still lower into negative territory? In general, prices drop, of course, to balance supply and demand. Loans are no different. Real interest rates drop below zero, if at zero there would have been more savers than borrowers; that is, more people wishing to delay consumption—even with no reward whatsoever—than people willing to draw a free loan to invest in a business or bigger home.

Huh?

Once real interest rates are negative, we are in an even more bizarre situation. People are so keen *not* to consume that we have to penalize them for saving in order to perhaps persuade them to consume more today and not save. And on the other hand, we are *paying* people to take loans to build factories and homes, even if there is no expectation of a positive return on investment; or even knowing that the investment will make a slight loss.

Both sides of the coin reveal the problem of a society which has become too rich for its own good. Such a society is struggling to maintain full employment by incentivizing people to consume rather than save, and by "bribing" companies—such as Siemens—to borrow and invest, even in ventures that may be loss-making.

To be fair, one category of savers are pension funds, which by their nature must delay gratification. But pensions funds are also being redeemed, so the net increase in pension funds is not a huge part of the growth in savings.

On the other side of the bonds is Siemens, which may have already made all the investments that they expect to be profitable. And now they are building one more washing machine factory, or whatever, because investors are literally paying them to borrow money.

AS A QUICK ASIDE, a society with negative real interest rates actually reminds me of the fourth circle of hell in Dante's *Inferno*.[92] Here, guarded by Plutus, the mythological deity of wealth, two categories of sinners face eternal damnation and punishment. The first group are the misers who hoarded their possessions, and the second are the wasteful spenders who squandered their income. Both groups are punished by jousting, pushing heavy weights against each other for eternity. In some interpretations, the weights are bags of money.

Gustave Doré - Dante's Inferno - Plate 22
(Canto VI - Hoarders and Wasters)[93]

With a little poetic license, this macabre scene may remind us of a society with negative interest rates. It is in fact our society, where we have savers who are so thrifty as to postpone spending, even if they have to pay to do so; and we have borrowers who may be wasting resources on investments which are loss making, because they are paid to do so.

EVEN IF YOU LIVE in a wealthy country, you are probably wondering by now how it can possibly be the case that most people are so wealthy that they are willing to pay to *not* spend their income. In the U.S., the median income is $35,000 per year and this income is not difficult to spend. If anything, it may be hard to make ends meet with this salary. And so we now turn to investigating the connection between inequality and negative real interest rates.

THE INEQUALITY EFFECT

AFTER THE FOURTH international conference, the Bharatan government finally achieves an international treaty which partially harmonizes taxation across the archipelago. It is agreed that in every island the top 10 percent will pay at least 50 percent income tax, that fortunes above 10 million bucks will be taxed at a minimum of 1 percent per year, and that estates above 10 million bucks will be subject to at least 35 percent inheritance tax. Beyond this, each island is free to set its own taxation policy.

"Ananya, can you believe my income tax just jumped from 40 percent to 50 percent because of some international treaty," Atkish moans over drinks. "I guess you probably got a tax break funded by yours truly and my fellow members of the so-called top 10 percent."

"I did. Am I supposed to feel guilty?"

"Well—"

"Tell me something, Atkish. Will this tax hike change your lifestyle at all? Will you spend any less?"

"I will save less. I'll be buying fewer shares on the stock market."

"Oh, cry me a river. Really, Atkish, forget about your stock portfolio for a second. Forget about some vanity net worth number. Sometimes I think that, for people like you, having more money is like winning more points in a game. Right now, I'm talking about real goods and services that you physically enjoy, and which create real jobs. Will you change your actual consumption habits?"

"Hmm," Atkish takes another sip of his twenty-year-old single malt whiskey. "Probably not."

"Right. Well, I'm going to pay less tax now, and I can tell you that I will actually be spending more. Not on my savings account, but on real goods and services. I'm going to join a gym. I'm going to buy more takeout food. Real stuff that I physically enjoy, and which creates jobs for the service providers."

THIS SHORT CHAPTER describes a hypothetical coordination of tax policy which is arguably a prerequisite to addressing inequality effectively. This was written as a wishful hypothetical, but as the book was going to press, as referenced earlier, the G7 leaders were meeting in Cornwall, England, to start coordinating a minimum tax rate for the first time. So far, they have only discussed taxes on corporate profits, but it no longer seems impossible that one day governments will agree a minimum tax rate on personal income or inheritance.

Reading about negative real interest rates in the previous chapter, one can't help wondering how developed countries have possibly found themselves in a situation of negative real interest rates today. How can this have happened, given that even wealthy countries have millions of people living in relative poverty who would surely be delighted to consume more, and would likely appreciate a cheap loan to buy a home, or a car, or to start a small business?

Furthermore, there are 689 million people living in extreme poverty in developing countries, surviving on less than $1.90 per day.[94] The world is surely not yet too rich to consume all that it can produce, when hundreds of millions of people can barely afford food, a roof, or a $5 mosquito net to protect their kids from malaria. And the world still has urgent projects to undertake, like building renewable energy infrastructure, which should surely come before "subsidizing" business investments with no expected positive return.

This is where inequality comes in. Perhaps one day the world will be so wealthy that real interest rates will need to be negative. At that time, we may just give up on the goal of full employment and say that it only takes part of the population to produce every luxury that anyone could ever need, and the others should take it easy. But if such a day lies in our future, it is still in the distant future.

Rather, it seems to me that we have reached negative real interest rates many decades too early, due to inequality. It is surely not the case that a majority of people feel that they cannot spend their income, but it is apparently the case that *most of the income* is going to wealthy people who cannot spend their income. The result is that a lot of income is going to people who have no interest in spending it. This money is in fact searching for a home—so much so that it is now chasing loss-making government and corporate bonds.

It seems self-evident that if we moved more income to less wealthy people, they would be far more likely to spend it—to consume more and save less—and interest rates would ease back up into positive territory.

GIVEN THAT SOCIETY today finds itself in this surprising predicament, where most of the income is going to people who don't want to spend it, should we be grateful for negative interest rates saving us from the unemployment that would otherwise be inevitable?

My understanding is that negative real interest rates are a flimsy band aid. They are in fact an indirect form of *workfare*, whereby we pay to keep people employed doing work which may well offer no benefit to society. This does indeed prop up the employment figures, but I believe that negative real interest rates create a vicious circle which will tend to spiral downwards.

Why? Well, loans have to be repaid. If we pay Toyota to build a factory, even though the business case may be marginal to negative, then some people are employed for a while building that factory. But when construction finishes and the loan is repaid, they may be unemployed again. And now the world has even more cars, which are not wanted by the people who can afford them, making the problem worse than before. So now we need to pay Toyota, or another company, an even more negative real interest rate to build the next factory.

THE MOST SUSTAINABLE way to avoid negative real interest rates would be greater redistribution of income and wealth. In real terms, our economies can produce a certain amount of goods and services; if too much of that production is awarded to wealthy people who have already maxed out their consumption, then it won't get consumed, and we will have wastage and unemployment. Lending the excess income at ever lower interest rates, as society is currently doing, is not a sustainable solution—because loans have to be repaid. The data implies that we need to tackle the root cause—and moderating inequality will ensure that enough stuff gets to the people who actually want more stuff.

In the meantime, society is sustaining employment by punishing savers and subsidizing borrowers. Even if you think this bizarre situation is acceptable, we will now see that there is actually a limit to how low interest rates can go, after which this strategy will hit a brick wall.

THE REAL ZERO LOWER BOUND

Twenty-five years in the future

CHARLIE V, now in his fifties, has paid off his mortgage. He still earns more than he cares to spend, and wants to ramp up his savings towards retirement. Interest rates have been fluctuating across the years, but the long-term trend has continued downward.

He pays a visit to Bob's Bank. "I wish to open a savings account," he says.

"Welcome, sir. We would love to help you with that. I should warn you that the bank has many wealthy customers wishing to save money, even more than people who want to borrow money. Therefore, the interest rate we currently offer on savings accounts is -1.5 percent."

"Are you insane?" Charlie says. "I'm not going to pay you to save my money. And in addition to paying you 1.5 percent I might lose 1 or 2 percent to inflation every year!"

"I do understand your frustration, sir, but that is simply the prevailing market interest rate, which balances saving and borrowing." The clerk gestures at the line over at the loan desk. There is a sign on the wall offering business loans for -0.5 percent. But Charlie notices that the line for loans is no longer than the line for savings accounts; people are not exactly clamoring to borrow, even with a negative interest rate.

"Well, I am not going to pay for the privilege of delayed gratification."

"We'll be very sorry to lose your business, sir. The bank can put your savings to great use. I saw you glancing at the other side of the branch. We have many budding entrepreneurs wishing to borrow money to finance their businesses, and people wanting mortgages to buy homes."

"With a negative interest rate—I bet you do. Well, I'm so sorry to disappoint you and them. Perhaps I can simply accumulate my money in a checking account?"

"Certainly, sir, we have excellent checking accounts that pay a very competitive -2 percent interest."

Charlie storms out. He considers upping his lifestyle to spend all his income, but he already has everything he needs, and he really ought to save for retirement. So Charlie fires up his internet browser and orders a state-of-the-art safe and a security camera. He starts saving up cash at home in 100-buck notes. He reckons the security cost is at most 1 percent per year of his savings, which is better than the bank rate of -1.5 percent.

Meanwhile, Bob's Bank has to disappoint many aspiring entrepreneurs, some of whom now find themselves unemployed. For centuries, the island's banks were able to find the interest rate that balanced borrowers and lenders. But that rate has now trended down to the point where it is significantly negative, and many savers are choosing to accumulate cash, leaving businesses ventures unfinanced.

For the first time in its history, the island has unemployment, not because of a short-term recession, but because of a persistent inability to finance investment, caused by savers preferring to hoard their cash.

Over in the central bank, Fred V, unaware of Charlie's new safe, is addressing his team. "We keep printing money. It should be driving growth. Not only that, but we've printed so much money that it should be making prices go up and creating inflation. Where is the cash going?"

CAN INTEREST RATES, which are already hovering around zero in the real world, and below zero in some countries, continue their long-term trend downwards? As our story indicates, developed economies are now operating very close to the *zero lower bound (ZLB)* of nominal interest rates. The zero lower bound simply means that nominal interest rates can't go below zero because then people will prefer to store cash.

Mind you, ZLB is a slight misnomer: zero is not in fact an absolute lower bound. If nominal interest rates creep slightly below zero, people will still be willing to pay the bank to store their cash safely. Many banks in Germany do, at the time of writing, charge a slight negative interest rate on checking and savings accounts[95] and people are willing to pay for the safekeeping of their cash, just as people paid goldsmiths to store their gold in the 1600s. The central bank of Czechia has estimated that people will pay up to 1 percent to store their cash safely in a bank.[96] Banks not only provide physical security but in many countries bank deposits are backed by government guarantees such as the Federal Deposit Insurance Corporation.

Think how strange the current situation in Europe is—we even have negative interest rates on a checking account! This means that people in Europe are pushing to pay their bills as early as possible, while utilities may be encouraging them to pay later, to save on negative interest charges. Right now, such topsy turvy interest rates are needed to balance borrowers and lenders.

So the real lower bound on nominal interest rates is about -1 percent, rather than zero. But if it goes below that, banks will be unable to perform their most basic function of matching the advancement and delay of gratification, as people will switch to delaying gratification by storing cash. And as you might expect, as we brush up against the lower bound, some people are already starting to hoard cash. In the UK, £50 billion of banknotes are "missing."[97] Politicians blame the Bank of England for losing track of this cash, but the central bank counters that citizens are entitled to hoard cash at home without informing them.

ECONOMISTS USED TO WORRY that, once nominal interest rates reach the zero lower bound, central banks cannot lower them further, and are therefore unable to provide further monetary stimulus for the economy. This could create a *liquidity trap*.[98]

Milton Friedman famously countered this by saying that, even if interest rates are zero, the central bank can keep printing money. If necessary, they can drop *helicopter money*.[99] Sure enough in recent times, once central banks got interest rates to zero by printing cash and buying back short-term bonds, they sometimes kept printing money, buying other types of financial assets such as longer-term bonds and bundles of mortgages, a process known as *Quantitative easing (QE)*. Furthermore, during Covid-19 the U.S. and other countries mailed a check to every citizen, a process quite akin to Friedman's helicopter money idea.

AND SO CENTRAL BANKS aren't too concerned about having their style cramped by the zero lower bound on nominal interest rates. Zero interest rates don't prevent the Fed or other central banks from printing more money. But in this book we are committed to focusing on the real economy.

So what about real interest rates, the real cost of advancing and delaying gratification, measured in terms of goods and services, not money? I would suggest the term *real zero lower bound (RZLB)* for the lower bound on real interest rates. It's simple to calculate. You take the zero lower bound of nominal interest rates and subtract the inflation target, which is typically 2 percent.

The real zero lower bound (RZLB) is therefore about -2 to -3 percent, assuming ZLB is zero to -1 percent and inflation remains at around 1 to 2 percent. But if the market real interest rate that matches people's taste for advancing versus delaying gratification is less than -2 or -3 percent, we're in big trouble.

We saw earlier that if the real interest rate is prevented from reaching a level that balances borrowers and lenders, we could face unemployment—because people then save too much, rather than consuming, while businesses invest too little. As we saw in a previous chapter, this will lead to an *affluence recession*.

This is not a remote problem. At the time of writing, real interest rates are already well below -2 percent in the UK[100] and Japan[101] so they are right up against the real zero lower bound, with the EU, U.S., and others not far behind.

THERE ARE WAYS in which governments can stretch RZLB lower. One solution would be to legally limit the hoarding of cash by limiting the amount of cash that banks can dispense or criminalizing the possession of large amounts of cash. Another solution is to eliminate cash altogether. Many countries already limit cash payments.[102] Norway doesn't limit cash, but Norwegians only use cash for 4 percent of transactions. With cash hoarding outlawed, central banks could set nominal interest rates as negative as needed without facing any zero lower bound. In this scenario, people would have no alternative to keeping their money in checking accounts, even if interest rates were below -1 percent.

Alternatively, if inflation targets were increased to, say, 4 percent, nominal interest rates could stay around zero. Meanwhile, real interest rates could drop as low as -4 percent, thus helping to balance borrowers with savers. However, this may not be practical since, as our story hinted, and as we will see in greater detail in the next chapter, central banks are finding it hard to increase inflation even when they want to.

In any event, neither of the above solutions is very attractive. Banning cash or increasing inflation could allow real interest rates to keep dropping, and avoid them hitting a hard bottom, at which point interest rates can no longer drop to match savers with borrowers. But as we saw, negative real interest rates create a vicious circle, which is likely to spiral downwards. So central banks will then have to force people to keep their money in bank accounts with ever more erosive interest rates, which will not be popular; or they will have to keep making inflation higher, a policy which is also unlikely to attract a standing ovation.

It would seem far preferable to restore a "natural" environment where real interest rates are positive, reflecting normal human psychology.

To my mind, negative real interest rates are an alarm bell telling us that inequality has gone too far, both nationally and globally. This situation indicates that we must move some income and wealth from those people who are willing to *pay to not spend*, to those people who would be very happy to spend and consume more today.

PANDEMIC, MISSING INFLATION

BELLA V IS WALKING along the beach at sunset when she trips over a ball-like creature covered in a lattice of large, brown, overlapping scales. She recognizes this as a pangolin, a nocturnal scaly anteater, which spends its days sleeping, curled up in a defensive position. Free dinner, she thinks, as she puts the rolled-up animal under her arm and proceeds to build a small bonfire on the beach.

This will actually prove to be by far the most expensive meal in history, as unbeknown to Bella, the animal is harboring an invisible coronavirus. This virus can trick some of the cells in Bella's respiratory tract to abandon normal bodily functions, and focus instead on making millions of replicas of itself, which will then drift out on Bella's breath. Soon other islanders are infected and the disease spreads exponentially through the island. Each infected islander infects several others, each of whom in turn infects several more. Before long, the virus has spread to other islands.

Governments of individual islands rapidly introduce emergency social distancing. They also close down non-essential businesses, such as restaurants, theatres, and hair salons, while keeping open the supply chains for food, medicines, and other essentials.

Atkish works from his home office, while Ananya is forced to close her restaurant. Almost overnight, Ananya and many like her, forming significant proportions of the population on every island, are unemployed.

Fierce debates break out in the government on the island of Us.

Georgina V addresses her economic council. "The production of food and other essentials must continue as before, but other services are shut, and many citizens simply have no income. In normal circumstances we award the production of the island in exchange for labor and capital, but now we must ensure that all our citizens have food. I propose an emergency tax on those who still have jobs, in order to share the income with all those who—through no fault of their own—have suddenly lost their jobs."

Fred V stands up. "I oppose that. Our citizens hate new taxes."

"I don't know, Fred; this is an unusual situation. There are fewer services available to buy anyway. Those with a job should be cool with some of their income being transferred to sustain the unemployed, especially when they have limited options for spending that income in any case."

"Georgina, we're agreed on what will happen in the real economy. The people without jobs will receive some of the income so that they can survive this crisis. But citizens hate tax no matter what. You should borrow the money we need to sustain the unemployed, and to preserve some of our shuttered businesses, till after the pandemic. We will issue bonds and borrow from people who have jobs, and have spare income to buy bonds, and spend it on those who are on furlough. Same result with a less blunt tool."

"I disagree, Fred. It's not the same result. If it's debt, it implies that the people who receive aid now will have to pay it back in the future. Meanwhile, those who are lucky enough to have a job and less to spend their money on, will demand to be repaid with extra consumption in the future."

"But Georgina, it's public debt. We're not asking our unemployed people to borrow; the government is borrowing."

Bob joins the conversation. "Georgina is right. Public debt is still real debt. If the government borrows from the more fortunate citizens, the public at large is in fact borrowing from those citizens. And the people buying the bonds will call in their debt in future years. This means we are expecting our unemployed citizens to pay in the future for the assistance they get now. Also, borrowing on such a huge scale will increase interest rates, creating further hardship for businesses and mortgage holders."

"Well, don't worry about interest rates," Fred says. "We at the central bank will target zero interest rates. We will print money and buy up any bond which has a yield above zero, thus keeping nominal interest rates at zero."

"Hah," Bob says. "In that case, the borrowing is a complete fiction. One branch of the government will borrow with bonds; and another branch of the government will buy back most of those bonds in the market, in exchange for newly minted cash. So what we're really doing is printing money."

"Well, yes."

"I see, so that's a different story," Georgina says. "What I care about is that people impacted by the pandemic should receive sustenance as a grant, not as debt. If we're printing money for them, they won't be in debt; for me, that's an acceptable solution. But won't that cause inflation? More money chasing fewer goods and services?"

"It might. And if so, it will achieve the effect that you wanted another way. Salaries will be worth less, due to inflation, but still the income will be more evenly distributed. But we haven't seen high inflation in years. Maybe there won't be inflation. It's worth a try."

"And if we print money and there's no inflation, we have managed to create new income out of nothing?"

"People might feel like we have, but in reality, no we haven't," Fred says. "The average cash balance is the real zero. By printing more cash, we are reducing the real net worth of those people who hold more cash, but they probably won't notice. We are redistributing wealth in a much more subtle way than tax."

"OK, let's try it. I will announce a stimulus package."

"I'm not sure it's a stimulus. This is really money printing to redistribute income so the unemployed can survive the pandemic."

"Yeah, but maybe leave the optics of this to me, Fred."

And so the Usian government starts printing money and distributing it to the shuttered businesses and unemployed people as a stimulus, so that they can purchase a share of the food production and other essentials and survive the pandemic. They do it in two steps: the treasury issues more and more bonds to finance that spending; and the central bank prints money to buy back a proportion of those bonds, whenever they are trading at a yield above zero. The central bank resolves to keep printing money to keep nominal interest rates at zero at least until they witness a real inflation problem.

They keep doing this for months, but prices in the shops remain stable.

"It's working, Georgina," Fred says. "Yes, the economy has shrunk, but we have pretty much managed to keep our citizens' heads above water, and we've done it without direct taxation."

DURING THE PANDEMIC of 2020–2021, the U.S. government spent an additional $4.5 trillion on various Covid-19 "stimulus" packages or about $13,700 per citizen.[103] This included paycheck protection, direct payments to families, loans, grants, and government contracts. This spending was in addition to the fiscal deficit that was budgeted for fiscal year 2020 even before Covid hit, which itself further increased due to reduced tax revenue. Other countries pursued similar strategies, with some—like Germany and Japan—spending proportionately much more than the U.S. during 2020.[104]

What does this mean in real terms? The government was not spending most of this money on public works, building roads and dams. Rather, this was largely a redistribution of income from those lucky enough to have a job, to the businesses and individuals impacted by the worst pandemic in a century, allowing them to continue at least consuming essential goods and services.

There were no new taxes. So was all this spending a grant or a loan? Will all those people eventually pay back the aid they received during the pandemic by having to consume less than they can afford in the future? In theory, most of it was a loan; in practice, we will see. The U.S. government took on about $14,700 in extra debt per citizen in 2020 and then redeemed about $5,200 per citizen by printing cash.[105] This left each citizen with an increased debt of about $9,500 for the year, bringing the total U.S. public debt to a whopping $84,000 per citizen.[106] To put that in context, almost half of Americans have a share in the national debt, which is more than their net assets,[107] meaning in reality they have negative net assets.

So it's true that the well-off citizens and the foreigners buying U.S. bonds are owed a large amount, while every other American owes a considerable amount of money. However, the wild card is that real interest rates are negative. In this situation, the U.S. government is in no hurry to repay this massive debt on behalf of its citizens; and the real value of the debt actually edges down each year on its own. That is before the government's new borrowing of course. So it's not clear if citizens will repay their debt in practice.

Then again, this situation of borrowing more and more on behalf of the citizens is not necessarily safe and sustainable. There may be future periods when interest rates increase, and the massive national debt will become a real burden.

What about all the cash printing? The U.S. printed $5,200 in cash per citizen in 2020,[108] distributing some of it fairly indiscriminately to almost all citizens and spending some of it more selectively on supporting the unemployed and closed businesses. This cash was a grant, not a loan. There was a risk that this would simply cause inflation, devaluing everyone's cash, but this didn't happen for reasons we explore in the next two chapters. But as we saw earlier, the real zero of cash is the average balance, and the "par" cash holding went up by $5,200. So those who received more than $5,200 were actually getting a grant, at the expense of those who received less than $5,200; and the latter were effectively being taxed without even realizing it.

COVID-19 HAS BEEN a massive killer and disruptor. Yet it could have been a whole lot worse if it had "chosen" to hit the world earlier. Firstly, the world today has an improved arsenal of scientific products, such as PCR tests and mRNA vaccines, to fight back with. Secondly, much of the world has fairly recently rolled out fast internet and adopted cheap video conferencing tools, such as Zoom, allowing people to work remotely and maintain relationships online. At the same time, an unprecedented number of employees are knowledge workers,[109] who can work remotely when necessary.

And one more bit of good fortune, relevant to this book, is that Covid-19 hit while inflation was AWOL, allowing governments to sustain their people and their economies, and redistribute income, by printing cash, without the need for direct taxation.

The idea of taking advantage of low interest rates to increase government debt predated Covid-19 by a decade. It started as soon as interest rates hit zero in 2009:

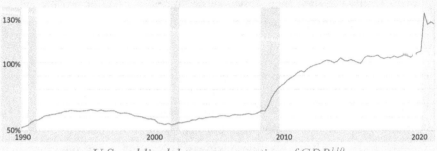

U.S. public debt as a proportion of GDP[110]

However, this situation—taking advantage of negative interest rates to build up excess debt and excess cash—comes with a long-term risk, and I would argue it should not be used once the pandemic emergency is over.

Clearly, the trillions of newly printed cash have created neither growth nor price inflation. So where is this money ending up and why?

STOCK MARKET INFLATION AND SINGULARITY

CHARLIE V IS LESS than delighted about saving for his pension by stashing cash at home in his makeshift vault. Every year his cash loses 1 or 2 percent of its value to inflation. Every year, as he saves more, the quantity of cash is greater, it requires more safe capacity, and the security risk is increasing. He purchases a second safe. He adopts a second dog. The dogs need a lot of dog food, not to mention expensive veterinary treatment.

Charlie is chatting about his predicament with Paula V, owner of the local supermarket, PMart.

"Charlie, why not invest right here in the supermarket? I'm approaching retirement, and ready to cash out part of my ownership."

"But you make a nice profit in this place, Paula? Why sell?"

"Yeah, not bad. Between you and me, we make a steady 100,000 bucks profit each year. Our prices grow with inflation, so our profit keeps up with inflation too. But by selling some of the ownership, I can sell off the future earnings today, and have more money to support me in a comfortable retirement. And that might suit you too because you are looking to save for the future."

"I'm listening. What do you propose?"

"We've split the ownership of the PMart company into 100,000 shares. We earn about 100,000 bucks profit per year, so that's 1 buck of profit per share. I reckon we have a stable business here, with a captive customer base in the neighborhood, and I think the business will be stable for the next 30 years. So you should pay around 30 bucks for each share, since each share will earn you a buck a year for at least 30 years. How many shares would you like to buy?"

"Wait a second Paula. Do you even distribute those profits to your shareholders?"

"You mean dividends? I don't think that should matter to you. Each share you own is one part in 100,000 of the business, and so each share earns a buck in profits. Whether we pay that profit out to you in cash, or we reinvest it in the capital of the business—in *your* business—say buying more freezers or renovating, it's still your earnings."

"I guess so. But honestly, I need to think about whether I believe your prediction that your business will be stable for 30 years. There could be market changes that cause PMart to decline..."

"And there could also be market changes that allow us to grow. Let's say, on average, we remain stable, with our physical sales about flat. And in money terms, our revenue and earnings do at least keep up with inflation."

"Let me sleep on it."

The next day Charlie pops back into Paula's office.

"OK, Paula. I've thought about it. And it seems reasonable to hope your business is stable for 30 years. But I'm still not paying 30 bucks per share."

"Why not?"

"Well, Paula, I'm not willing to pay 1 buck now in exchange for 1 buck in a year's time. I'll give you 0.95 bucks now for a buck in a year. Or two years? I'll knock another 5 percent off. Look, this is what I sketched, showing how much value I place today on each future buck. The longer it takes to earn each buck of projected earnings, the less I will pay for it today—each year the price is 5 percent less than the year before:"

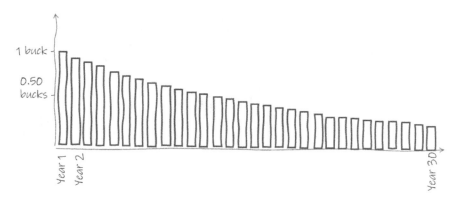

"I reckon it all adds up to about 20 bucks."

"Hmm. But you know, although we focused on 30 years, I actually hope and expect this business will last more than 30 years."

"Sure, but after all that discounting, any profits your shares generate more than 30 years in the future add very little to the value today."

Paula stares at the chart for a moment and then stands up. "Hold on a second, Charlie. Are you trying to trick me?"

"No, why?"

"Well, I guess my late grandma, Paula III, might have accepted your argument. In her day, you got a decent interest rate in the bank. There was a reward for delaying gratification and a cost for advancing gratification. No doubt she would have accepted 0.95 bucks today for selling a buck of profit in a year. But as you well know, today there is a premium for advancing gratification. Tell me the truth, Charlie. Isn't that why you're here in the first place? The bank pays you negative interest, and storing cash costs you money. If you want to use shares in my company to help you delay gratification toward your retirement, you have to pay me for the privilege. Here, give me that piece of paper." She sits and pulls out a pencil. "This is how I see the value today of future profits:"

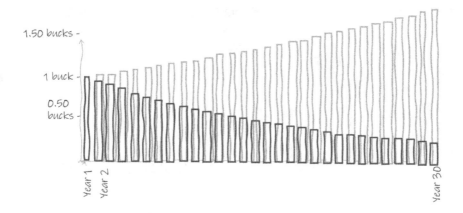

"So, now that I think about it, you shouldn't pay me 20 or even 30 bucks. The future earnings of 1 buck per share for 30 years are worth at least 40 bucks right there. Just add it up. And don't even get me started on profits beyond 30 years. those are actually the most relevant to today's value, since delayed gratification is at a premium!"

After some further debate, Charlie forks out 40,000 bucks from his cash stash and purchases 1,000 shares, or 1 percent of the PMart business, at 40 bucks per share. Charlie and Paula have agreed to value each share at 40 times more than the annual earnings per share.

WHILE MASSIVE MONEY printing in 2008–2020 failed to create inflation in the supermarket, it did create significant inflation in the stock market. We cannot discuss economics in the opening two decades of the twenty-first century without a glance at stock prices; that is, the value society currently places on business capital. Our island story gives us a framework for the discussion.

A *share* is of course a partial ownership of a business. A share in a business which is a going concern derives its value, not primarily from the company's capital assets today, but rather from the share's participation in the future profits of the company. Most investors, just as Paula V argued, will value a share based on expected earnings per share, regardless of whether the company plans to pay those earnings to shareholders as dividends or to reinvest earnings in the business.

As in our story, the value attached to a steady future cash flow depends on just one thing—how much value is attached to future income, relative to income today. This is called *net present value (NPV)*, and it is the value investors attach today to income in the future. So how much would you pay today to receive 1 dollar in a year's time, inflation adjusted? Historically, a typical real interest rate was, say, 5 percent, so people valued a dollar in a year at about $0.95 today as Charlie tried to argue. So if you get a dollar per year in perpetuity, each year discounted 5 percent more, what is the total value? There is a nice bit of math for adding up infinite sequences, and the upshot is that with the annual discount of 5 percent a year, that is a discount ratio of 0.05, the total value of adding up 1 dollar per future year forever is approximately[111] *1/0.05* or $20.

Stock market investors call this a *price earnings ratio (P/E ratio)* of 20. Indeed, historically, a typical way to value a share in a stable company was with a P/E ratio of about 20, that is 20 times the annual earnings per share. If the company had strong growth prospects on the one hand, or risk of decline on the other, the market value of the share is adjusted accordingly.

One more important note on historic valuations. It's obviously very hard to predict how a company will perform more than 30 years in the future. But when future income is discounted, the value of a share today is mostly based on the expected income in the coming 30 years, and any income more than 30 years in the future has a highly discounted value today and has little impact on today's share value.

But all that was true of the last century. We have already seen that today real interest rates are *negative* and have been for some years. At present, investors attach *more* value to the future than to the present. So today's investors look at the future earnings of a share in the local supermarket, as Paula argued, and each year of future income is worth 1 or 2 percent *more* than the year before. The exact rate of the premium attached to the future changes in the market, day by day and country by country.

As in our island story, when there is a premium for delaying gratification, 30 years of future earnings per share are not worth 20 times the earning, or even 30, but rather *more* than 30. Thus, the stock market valuations will be substantially higher when interest rates are so low. Indeed, at the time of writing, the Standard and Poor (S&P) 500 index of the largest 500 companies on U.S. stock exchanges is trading at a price reflecting an average price-to-earnings (P/E) ratio of 40, compared to an average of 15 in the last century.

So in the weird reality of negative real interest rates, it is rational for the price of stocks to double, relative to the underlying earnings. Buying such a share is a good way to delay gratification to the future, inflation protected, and people are willing to pay for that.

But there is a more serious issue here. We saw that, in a normal market, the value of a company's expected income more than 30 years in the future doesn't massively impact the value of the share today. But with negative real interest rates, the value of time is reversed, and the value of income in 30 years is actually at a premium today. Now we have a serious dilemma. What will happen to the company in 30 years? Will it close down, due to changes in the economy? Or will the company survive and perhaps grow for 40 or 50 years? If so, the company is worth way more than $40 today.

To take an extreme example, if you think a company will last forever, and that real interest rates will remain zero or negative, the company's value is infinite, as all future earnings are at a premium today. You see the problem. Nobody can really know if a company will last 30 years or 300 years.

From this perspective, negative interest rates create a mathematical *singularity*, which means that they create infinite values. When interest rates are negative, a future *annuity*—a regular future income—has an infinite value. We don't know if a company will last forever, so maybe its value isn't literally infinite; but there is really no upper bound for the rational valuation of a company when real interest rates are negative.

How can investors accurately update their expectations for stock market valuations, as real interest rates vary? I have proposed that we define PETRY$_{30}$ to be the P/E ratio which is implied by discounting the next 30 years' earnings, based on today's real interest rates.[112] Given the bizarrely low interest rates today, PETRY$_{30}$ indicates that 40 is a rational P/E ratio and stock markets are not necessarily overvalued, even though this is up from an average of P/E in the last century. And a P/E of 40 is rational, even assuming that we discard any income beyond 30 years.

THIS DOESN'T MEAN there isn't cause for concern. The problem with valuing stocks in an era of negative interest rates is that the value is highly sensitive to some very tenuous assumptions about a company's prospects decades into the future. As long as real interest rates are negative, the value of stocks will be very high and extremely volatile. This is another reason why, in my opinion, societies should attempt to get real interest rates back up into positive territory by addressing the underlying issue of inequality.

We saw earlier that super-low interest rates justify high stock prices. But in 2021, it's important to emphasize that, while negative interest rates do imply high unstable stock prices, not all share prices are high purely due to a rational evaluation of expected future earnings. Quite a few shares and other assets are currently experiencing pricing bubbles, driven by an abundance of money floating around, pure speculation, and *fear of missing out (FOMO)*. We will return to the subject of *asset bubbles* briefly in a later chapter about bitcoin.

MONEY: GOING OUT OF STYLE

IN THE GREAT RECESSION of 2009 and its aftermath, and again during the Covid-19 pandemic of 2020–2021, the Fed and other central banks minted money by the trillions. The textbook prediction is that extra money will chase up the price of goods and services. But, so far, this has not occurred.

Let's end this section by playing economic detectives using the concepts explored so far.

First, here is the amount of base money (M0 or MB) in circulation in the U.S. This includes physical cash and electronic cash balances which the banks hold with the Fed:

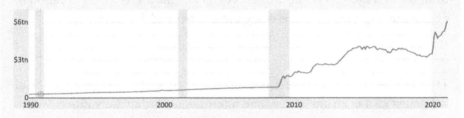

U.S. monetary base (MB). Shaded areas indicate recessions.[113]

In the 1990s and up to 2008, the money supply expanded slowly, as the textbooks recommend, allowing the economy to expand gradually, plus some gentle inflation.

Since 2009, things have been rather loopy. In 2009, in the wake of the credit crisis and the great recession that followed, base money doubled in just over a year. It then became quite volatile, with big increases in and around 2011 and 2013, although the economy was growing steadily in those years. In 2020 when Covid-19 hit, the best part of 2 trillion dollars was minted in half a year.

Ah, but we know that money isn't only created by the central bank. The commercial banks can provide loans, and as they only require partial reserves, they can create checking account balances which are perfectly good money too.

So we should look at the M1 money supply, which includes bank money. Here is the M1 money supply in the last 30 years:

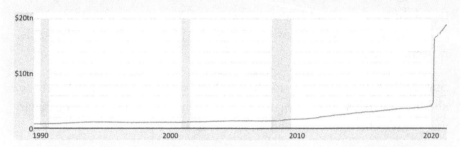

U.S. M1 money supply—cash plus bank money[114]

Well, prior to 2020, the M1 graph is certainly smoother than the M0 graph. To some extent, increases in base money were offsetting decreases in bank money. That solves one part of the mystery. The total money supply was not swinging wildly during the 2010s. Rather, the Fed was offsetting changes in bank money and the total money supply was growing fairly steadily. By the way, this underlines a point I made earlier that bank money creation may not be useful to the economy; we see here that the Fed is often working to counter bank money creation and destruction, in order to smooth out the growth of the M1 money supply.

But we are still left with two mysteries. M1 grew rapidly during the 2010s, more than doubling in a single decade. Secondly, in 2020 we see that M1 jumped up. And there was still no inflation.

Recall the equation of money:

*Number of transactions (per year) **X** average transaction price =*

*Quantity of money existing **X** # cycles (velocity) of money circulation*

If the quantity of money increases, there are only three other variables that can change to keep the equation balanced: more transactions—economic growth; higher transaction prices—inflation; or lower velocity of money. The U.S. economy was growing nicely in the 2010s, but nowhere near doubling. There was very little inflation. We are left with the only other possibility, a significant change in the velocity of money. This is contrary to all the textbooks, which say that the velocity of money tends to be stable, reflecting the payroll cycle.

Sure enough, the velocity of money declined throughout the 2010s decade, and then fell off a cliff during the Covid-19 pandemic. If there is one chart that justifies the title of this book, here it is:

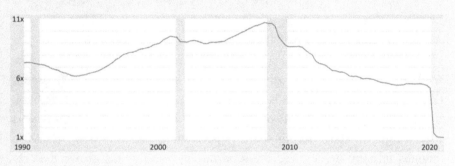

U.S. velocity of M1 money[115]

U.S. money started this century circulating around nine times a year; in other words, money was spent once every five or six weeks. In the 2010s, that dropped to a velocity of five or six times per year; and during the pandemic to less than four times a year. At the time of writing, an average a dollar is therefore spent less than once per three months.

We have now thrown a key tenet of Milton Friedman era economic textbooks out of the window. The velocity of money is not constant in any way. And printing money doesn't always cause inflation.

BUT WHY HAS THE velocity of money not been steady in recent years? Why is money going out of style and failing to circulate?

Analysts at the Fed have discussed causes such as technology, globalization, and aging populations.[116] Personally, I find these explanations unconvincing, as all these trends occurred in the 1990s too.

I would point instead to the increasing inequality and zero interest rates which we explored in the previous chapters. There is simply too much money in the hands of people who are so well off that they have zero propensity to spend extra cash. And with interest rates at zero, they have zero propensity to save or lend. So they hoard cash or they use the cash to buy and sell stocks.

It matters who gets the money that is printed. During Covid-19, the U.S. government mailed checks directly to most citizens, rather like helicopter money. But that is the exception. Most of the money the Fed prints is used to buy bonds. Bond investors and traders are typically not people who are saving up for their next supermarket visit. When they sell a bond to the Fed, they don't spend the extra cash on goods and services; they spend their cash on buying stocks.

So I would argue that inflation isn't missing. Rather, the Fed is driving inflation of stock market prices instead of inflation of the prices of goods and services.

Twenty years into the twenty-first century, we have something of a bifurcated economy. There is the economy in real goods and services. And then there is a growing economy trading financial assets. We can refer to the *real economy* and the *financial economy*. While the stock market, and the financial economy in general, is certainly not new, it *is* new that millions of consumers sit at home day-trading on Robinhood and other platforms. Stock market valuations are up, and trading volumes are also up.[117] As the Fed prints more and more cash, they are creating inflation in the financial economy so far, not in the real economy. The inflation in the financial economy includes high prices across the board and some pure asset bubbles like Game Stock.

FOR CENTURIES, the people who could afford to do so were teased for spending money as if it were going out of style; in the twenty-first century, money finally has gone out of style, in a manner of speaking. We now have a lot of money sitting in accounts, owned by people who have no interest in spending it.

As this penultimate section of the book comes to a close, here is a summary of the points I have made about the unprecedented economics of the twenty-first century so far:

Near zero nominal interest rates and negative real interest rates: These have become the norm for more than a decade now. In the long term, real interest rates are not controlled by the central bank; rather, negative real interest rates represent the average value society attaches to time, and they reveal something fundamental about the state of the real economy. Real interest rates have been trending downwards for centuries. Now they are mostly negative, and the value of time has been reversed, with delaying gratification coming at a premium.

Dante's fourth circle of hell: Negative real interest rates don't match natural human psychology. They indicate that a lot of income is being awarded to people who are hoarding it and are even willing to pay to save rather than spend. At the same time society is subsidizing loans, paying people to borrow, even for investments that may not be worthwhile.

The inequality effect: Inequality has become more pronounced in recent decades, with wealth inequality becoming extreme. This is probably a key factor in pushing real interest rates down into negative territory, long before society at large is saturated with wealth. Negative interest rates may be an alarm bell, warning us that inequality has gone too far and is having negative economic consequences, in addition to social consequences.

The negative interest rate spiral: Negative real interest rates are self-enforcing. Society provides subsidized loans for investments in business ventures that may not even be profitable. But loans have to be repaid, and then the problem becomes even more acute because there will be even more production of goods and services that don't get consumed.

Real zero lower bound (RZLB): Nominal interest rates cannot drop far below zero, because people have the option to store cash, unless holding cash is outlawed. Assuming inflation is limited to 2 percent, real interest rates cannot drop much below -2 or -3 percent. In several countries, real interest rates are pretty much at the RZLB lower bound already.

Affluence recession: If interest rates drop any further, people with excess income will simply hoard cash—indeed, some cash hoarding is happening already—and then there will be no way to provide loans for investment, resulting in a dangerous persistent recession.

The singularity of asset prices: Negative real interest rates mean that future income is worth more than present income; and the net present value (NPV) of a company's future earnings becomes infinite. This creates a mathematical singularity, where the value of a share in a company is unbounded and unstable, resulting in inflated and unstable stock markets.

Money going out of style: Recently, printing money has not led to either economic growth or inflation. This is likely again because too much money is going to people who have no propensity to spend more. In the short term, this gives governments a new tool to redistribute income by printing money, which was helpful in adjusting to Covid-19. In the long term, it has significant risks as there are trillions of dollars of money lying around that could come back into circulation and tens of trillions of public debt, which may one day incur punitive interest payments.

Economics, of course, remains a mighty force, but it is precariously close to the crisis which is threatened when interest rates hit the zero lower bound, and the market can no longer match savers with investors. We can hold this off by banning cash, but it would be more valuable to address the root cause of inequality.

While most of the newly minted money is not being spent on goods and services, it is fueling unstable stock markets with some assets experiencing a bubble. In the final section, we look at a few final topics related to current affairs, the first being the biggest and purest *asset bubble* of all.

VIII. FINAL THOUGHTS

CRYPTOCURRENCY

PHYSICAL CASH IS USED less and less on the island. Banks are now fully computerized. Most transactions involve credit cards, debit cards and electronic bank transfers. The banks keep computerized ledgers which track people's bank account balances. People trust the bank to keep track of how much money they "have"; that is, how much money the bank owes them. The banks in turn have smaller physical cash vaults than before; and instead they keep their reserves as electronic balances with the central bank. The central bank "prints" new money by buying bonds and paying for them in digital money.

While banknotes still exist, the buck is now mostly an electronic currency with balances managed by the central bank and commercial banks. With this, the anonymity of cash is gone. Almost every transaction between islanders, other than petty cash transactions, is recorded on a bank computer and available for government inspection. The Usian government quite likes this situation and is actively debating ways to further limit cash use. But some islanders resent the lack of financial privacy.

From time to time, various schemes are proposed for a cryptocurrency, where monetary transactions are recorded on a central ledger in an anonymous way. In such a system, only the payor and payee can decipher each transaction, while it is securely encrypted for everyone else. However, there is always a conceptual limitation that all participants have to trust a bank, or other central authority, to maintain the ledger. Thus, one scheme after the next is shot down because people cannot agree who will be trusted to manage the ledger of a cryptocurrency.

Then one day, out of the blue, an islander using the pseudonym Satashi publishes an anonymous paper describing a radical new fully decentralized cryptocurrency. According to Satashi's scheme, no central authority needs to keep the ledger at all. Instead, many people, called miners, will run computer systems that each keep a full copy of the ledger; and any islander who owns a computer can choose to become a miner and keep a ledger copy. The miners' computers will communicate with each other to achieve consensus on the ledger and root out any cheats who try to award themselves coins.

Satashi then publishes software for miners, and launches botcoin, the first cryptocurrency with no central ledger at all. This is all done in complete anonymity.

Many questions are asked of the brilliant anonymous inventor. To maintain anonymity, he, or she, communicates exclusively on the chat forums:

@Tomfool1234 Who says your botcoins are worth anything?

@Satashi Who says bucks are worth anything? It is a social convention. If people start to accept that botcoins have value, then soon enough they will have value as tokens that can be exchanged for goods, services, and labor.

@Tomfool1234 If there is no physical cash, how will we keep track of who has how many botcoins?

@Satashi There is a ledger - a record of transactions and balances. But instead of a bank or government keeping that ledger, many miners will keep copies which are synchronized with each other electronically, based on consensus. Once 51 percent of miners agree on the ledger, everyone else falls in line. If you have a computer, you can also become a miner @Tomfool1234.

@Tomfool1234 Hah! Well, what if someone manages to create so many mining rigs that they have more than 51 percent of all of them? Then they could just forge a ledger awarding themselves millions of botcoins and everyone else will accept it?!!

@Satashi Yes. But to avoid this, I have designed mining to be expensive. For each new block of transactions added to the ledger, the miner must invest a lot of computing power to solve an arbitrary hard mathematical riddle. I call it proof-of-work. This proof-of-work computation will make it prohibitively expensive to cheat.

@Hackr098 Expensive? I was thinking of being a miner. Why would I do that if mining is designed to consume expensive computing power?

@Satashi There is a reward. Every miner who publishes a proof-of-work showing that they have solved the next random problem, will receive some free botcoins. That's why I call them miners. Not only are the miners acting as the bookkeepers, by collective consensus, but they are also the ones "mining" new botcoins. In a sense, they are like gold miners who work hard and are rewarded with new gold coins.

@EnvironmentGal439875 So you are incentivizing miners to invest in heavy electricity-consuming computers and run them 24/7, solving arbitrary problems? To hell with the environment?

@ComputerScienceBloke3 Won't all this limit the rate of transactions? The world needs many thousands of commercial transactions per second. Can your software cope with the same volumes as credit cards?

@DescendantOfFred   What about the money supply? How will you make sure that the number of coins available matches the size of the economy?

@Satashi   I have adopted an idea originally advocated by Milton. The money supply will increase gradually. There will be no targeting of interest rates or inflation, just a steady increase in money supply for some years. Then eventually it will stop.

@DescendantOfFred   The money supply will eventually freeze? Do you realize that this will stunt economic growth?? The economy can't grow without more money, except by deflation, which also stunts growth.

@Anarchist!@#$ This is fantastic! Down with the government! Down with the banks! Bucks are another way the government spies on us and controls us. Botcoin will free us. There's no government like no government.

@PrivacyGuy8765   So the whole ledger will be public?

@Satashi   Yes the ledger is public but with no real names.   Everyone is only identified by a unique key. Every transaction is like #2349872134 sent 10 botcoins to #34871234234.

@PrivacyGuy8765   I like the use of random pseudonyms. But if someone did figure out my key, then every transaction of mine will be public thereafter?!   What about when I first use real bucks from my bank to buy botcoins? That might allow someone to identify the real me with my botcoin wallet? Once my key is revealed, this cryptocurrency is actually much less private than bucks, right?

@LawEnforcer3241234 Yes, but on the other hand if you do manage to keep your key secret, law enforcement has no way to investigate financial crime. I think it's too private.

@AbsentMinded999 What if I lose my digital wallet key? Then all my money is irretrievably lost? Lost not just to me but the money is effectively destroyed and removed from circulation forever?

The debate rages on. Despite a few efforts, the new botcoin crypto coin is not adopted for serious commerce in the archipelago. It is bought and sold by speculators and used by criminals to collect ransoms.

IN THE REAL WORLD, electronic money is already mainstream. Countries where the majority of payments are electronic include the U.S., China, UK, Scandinavian countries, and South Korea. A lot of continental Europe still prefers cash. Many countries actually limit the use of physical cash by outlawing large cash transactions, because they want more government oversight of payments. But electronic currency today relies on electronic ledgers kept by banks and central banks; that is not the same as *cryptocurrency*.

We have seen that modern fiat currency is issued by governments and commercial banks, but that currency derives its value from the entrenched social convention that it may be exchanged for goods and services, as well as for labor and use of capital. This raises the intriguing question of whether a currency could gain acceptance without any involvement by governments and banks.

It's perhaps unlikely that a non-government body would be able to manage the widespread distribution of physical banknotes and coins. But with a purely digital currency, a non-government currency might be feasible. However, there has always been the issue of whom, other than a government or bank, could be trusted by everyone to manage the electronic ledger tracking money balances. In particular, ones and zeros are easy to copy, so any digital currency would require a trusted ledger to solve the *double spending problem* and ensure that the money isn't duplicated and spent twice. A non-government currency would therefore require a conceptual breakthrough.

This conceptual breakthrough came with *Bitcoin*. The proposal for a cryptocurrency using a data architecture called *Blockchain*, was published on October 31, 2008, under the anonymous pseudonym Satoshi Nakamoto. Satoshi implemented the bitcoin network and executed the first transaction on January 3, 2009. Nakamoto disappeared in 2010 and has never cashed in his Bitcoins, which are now worth tens of billions. His, her, or their identity remains unknown.

Bitcoin received huge attention in 2016–2017 with its price growing twentyfold before crashing. Despite some publicized use of bitcoin to buy a pizza, its main use today is for speculation and crime. In October 2020, Bitcoin started another massive bubble, growing several percent most days for no reason other than the *greater fool theory*—the theory that I might be a fool to pay $50,000 for an amorphous bitcoin, but I'll be able to sell it at a premium to some greater fool.

The total value of bitcoins at the time of writing exceeds a trillion dollars, although some 20 percent of them are probably irrevocably lost due to misplaced digital keys. One man offered the city of Newport, Wales, the equivalent of $70 million to search a rubbish dump for a hard disk he threw out seven years ago containing bitcoins now worth $300m.[118]

Bitcoin and Blockchain are remarkable intellectual achievements, but bitcoin suffers from several serious design flaws hinted at in our story. The money supply of bitcoin does not respond to the economic situation, and in practice the value, or exchange rate, of bitcoin fluctuates wildly, making it unsuitable for real commerce.

Worse, the mining of new bitcoins will stop when they reach the limit of 21 million bitcoins in 2140. It is not clear why the bitcoin money supply was designed to eventually freeze, instead of continuing to grow a few percent each year, but in the very long term this seems like a fatal flaw.

Privacy is also a concern in both directions: when keys remain secret, law enforcement agencies cannot investigate financial crimes. Conversely, if keys are revealed, then there is no privacy at all, and people's financial transactions become public.

Furthermore, bitcoin miners working on solving completely arbitrary proof-of-work problems to facilitate speculators selling bitcoins to speculators, and ransomware, currently consume more electricity than most countries—more, for example, than Argentina or Netherlands. This makes bitcoin an environmental disaster.

Finally, bitcoin transactions, based on the blockchain architecture, are very cumbersome, as they require all the miners to communicate with each other and reach a consensus. In practice, only a few bitcoin transactions can be executed per second, whereas Visa processes many thousands of credit card transactions in the same amount of time. The bitcoin transactions are therefore also slow and expensive. Various schemes have been proposed, including one of my own,[119] to redesign blockchain so that it performs better, but right now bitcoin is several orders of magnitude too slow to be used as a serious currency.

Bitcoin inspired *Ethereum* and at least 6,000 other "altcoin" cryptocurrencies using similar Blockchain technology. For a short time, startup companies were raising money with *initial coin offerings (ICO)* where each startup created its own separate bitcoin-like cryptocurrency and issued coins to "investors" in exchange for cash. This bizarre practice has fortunately all but disappeared.

There is no underlying value to each bitcoin, and bitcoin long ago gave up any claim at being a serious currency for commerce. Bitcoin has arguably become the weirdest asset bubble since tulip mania in 1636.[120] At least back then, when you forked out a price equal to ten years' salary, you were the proud owner of a tulip bulb. And you weren't hurting the environment. Today when you spend tens of thousands of dollars on a bitcoin, you might as well pay someone to sell you the number 73, and to pollute the planet while they're at it.

In summary, bitcoin is a brilliant idea whose implementation suffers from fatal flaws, leaving it to function as a massive energy-wasting casino for speculators, while perpetrating an ongoing crime against the planet. But it is still possible that someone will adapt the idea of Blockchain one day to create a stable, energy-efficient cryptocurrency that can replace government currency.

BIASES

WE LEAVE THE ISLAND behind now, to discuss a few final topics which readers asked me to include, and to briefly discuss the future.

In recent decades, humanity has become a lot more self-aware when it comes to our own biases and tendency to behave irrationally. There is a whole discipline of *behavioral economics*, with experts studying the ways in which people make biased decisions. Pioneers of this work included Nobel laureate Daniel Kahneman with the late Amos Tversky.[121] However, most behavioral economics studies relate to *microeconomics*—that is, decisions made by individuals and institutions, and how their behavior may be irrational. I am more interested in macroeconomics—how the overall economy behaves—so I will leave the fascinating topic of behavioral economics to other authors.

However, some systematic biases do relate to broader economic issues. This chapter is a brief summary of a book about biases which directly affect macroeconomic policy. *The Myth of the Rational Voter*, by Bryan Caplan,[122] explores how voters tend to have biases which contradict rational economic thinking, and which push governments to adopt economically harmful policies. The book documents four biases: *anti-market bias, anti-foreign bias, make-work bias*, and *pessimistic bias*.

Caplan describes *anti-market bias* as a "tendency to underestimate the benefits of the market mechanism"—for example, an inherent distrust of large companies and resentment of their profits. Many people still haven't absorbed the central lesson of the foundational book of classical economics, *The Wealth of Nations* by Adam Smith. In this pioneering book, published in 1776, Smith explains that the "invisible hand" of the free market actually "pushes" selfish businessmen to serve the public good. As he so eloquently expressed it: "Every individual is continually exerting himself to find out the most advantageous employment for whatever capital he can command. It is his own advantage, indeed, and not that of the society, which he has in view. But the study of his own advantage naturally, or rather necessarily leads him to prefer that employment which is most advantageous to the society."

Caplan is reminding us of a basic lesson we learned when we saw Paula constructing a ladder, motivated by her desire for her own personal profit, but resulting in more abundant and cheaper oranges for everyone. Economists since Adam Smith have understood that the pursuit of profit drives entrepreneurs to make investments that best ensure economic growth, which ends up benefiting everyone.

It's not that I think free markets are perfect. There is often a need to regulate fair competition, break up monopolies, and moderate inequality. But I think it's useful to be reminded of what people often forget: fundamentally, free markets and the pursuit of profit are powerful forces for good, and as a rule we should not resent corporate profits.

The second bias is *anti-foreign bias*, particularly bias against foreign trade. While economic theory teaches us that trade between countries is, as a rule, beneficial for both sides, many people are only too happy to blame rising unemployment on foreigners "taking their jobs." Another variation of this is anti-immigration bias. Populist politicians find it easy to pander to this bias and get elected on the back of anti-foreign trade policies and anti-immigration policies that actually make little economic sense.

Economics teaches us that trade is inherently good. In general, whether we consider two people, or two nations, they trade because it benefits both of them; not because one is taking advantage of the other. Notably, the growing trade between the West and Asia in recent decades has helped to lift a billion people out of poverty in Asia and has also increased quality of life and economic wellbeing in the West, although it's true that certain people, industries, and regions went through painful transitions.

Interestingly, the concept of *comparative advantage* means that, even if one nation produces all goods more efficiently than the other, they both still benefit from trading with one another, as each specializes where they are *relatively* efficient. For example, if a nation produces cars a bit more efficiently, and computers a lot more efficiently than another country, that nation will actually benefit economically from *importing* more cars from the other country. This is because, even though the other country produces cars a little less efficiently, importing cars will free up more people to produce and export more computers, where they have a huge advantage.

There is arguably a long-term trend in the direction of free trade, with a growing number of free trade agreements and trade blocs around the world. And yet the world still has a messy web of tariffs and regulatory barriers to international trade. The Trump trade wars and Brexit were two recent high-profile examples of political movements which played on anti-foreign bias, even in countries which were historically pro-trade.

There are nationalistic and xenophobic undertones to many discussions about international trade. Americans are quick to get upset about a trade deficit with Asian countries, while never worrying about a trade deficit between Wyoming and Delaware and rarely worrying about the trade deficit with culturally similar Canada.

A common theme in these anti-market and anti-foreign biases is a misconception that economics is a zero-sum game. In fact, trades are most often win–win. Two sides engage in a trade because they both gain, not because one is taking advantage of the other. If a company is making a profit, it doesn't mean that its customers are losing out. If China is gaining from international trade, we cannot infer that the U.S. and Europe are losing from international trade.

Caplan calls the next bias: *make-work bias*. Back in the nineteenth century, Luddites were suspicious of technologies and efficiencies that they believed would cause people to lose their jobs. This is certainly understandable; however, it is short-term thinking. There is in fact a massive long-term benefit in replacing employees with machines because it frees up workers to be gainfully employed in other jobs where they contribute more to society by doing something which cannot be achieved by a machine.

Without a doubt, losing a job is a significant hardship, and making the transition to another job can take time and effort. Worse still, when a specific industry becomes automated or offshored, there may be pain for entire communities or even regions where the industry was centered. It may take a generation for the region to be revitalized by the growth of other sectors, as in the case of the *Rust Belt*[123] in the Northeastern and Midwestern United States.

But in the long term, the benefits of allowing layoffs are dramatic. The developed world went from having a majority of its population employed as farmers in the nineteenth century to about 1.5 percent today. If farms hadn't been allowed to automate jobs and lay off workers, we would all still be toiling in the fields today, and we wouldn't have any of the modern conveniences we now enjoy.

The same is true about the closing of unprofitable British coal mines under Margaret Thatcher, the automation of manufacturing in all countries, and countless other layoffs which freed workers up to contribute to booming healthcare, education, leisure, and travel sectors. Developed countries have so far maintained close to full employment over most of the last two centuries, even as they became more and more affluent, with people laid off from automated or declining sectors finding jobs in new growth sectors.

In the end, we are face with a dilemma: short-term hardship for some; versus a massive long-term benefit to society. Most developed economies resolve this dilemma rather sensibly by allowing layoffs and softening the pain with a social security net of unemployment benefits, and subsidies for disadvantaged regions. However, the bias persists; and some people feel understandable anguish about those losing their jobs, while losing sight of the huge benefits to society of allowing at-will employment and a flexible workforce.

Finally, Caplan talks about *pessimistic bias*, which he defines as a tendency to overestimate the severity of economic problems, and underestimate the recent past, present, and future performance of the economy. He has a point. Despite periodic recessions, inequality, and other blights, in the last two centuries, most people, in almost every generation, in almost all developed countries, have been significantly better off, and have lived longer and healthier lives, than their parents. Although there has recently been a sad dip in life expectancy due to drug overdose and suicide,[124] the long-term trend has been very positive. Yet the public is rarely satisfied with the performance of the economy.

ONE FINAL TYPE of bias, not from Caplan's book, but very relevant to this book is the *money illusion*[125] or *price illusion*. In this book we have tried to be careful to distinguish between nominal and real values. For example, we talked a lot earlier about nominal interest rates versus real interest rates. But people often mistake the face value of money for its real value over time.

For example, experiments have shown that people generally perceive a 2 percent cut in salary as unfair, but they see a 2 percent salary raise, even in a country with 4 percent inflation, as fair. And this holds true even though both scenarios equate to a 2 percent cut in real income.[126]

In times of high inflation, people are more aware of this distinction. In a country with 10 percent inflation, everyone is conscious of inflation and people realize that a nominal interest rate of 10 percent translates to a real interest rate of zero. But in the low inflation conditions that many countries have been enjoying, inflation is quickly forgotten, creating a money illusion that $100 now, and $100 in a couple of years, are equivalent.

Similarly, people forget that an interest rate just above zero represents a negative real interest rate. This may be partly why negative real interest rates have not received sufficient attention, particularly in countries like the U.S. where nominal interest rates have remained at or above zero.

BLACK-TO-GREEN: CARBON AND RAINFORESTS

I CANNOT WRAP UP a book about economics without touching on the precarious state of the precious planet we all call home. You could fill a library with books and articles on the subject, some of them excellent, so I will dedicate just one short chapter to how economics can be aligned with sustainability.

The remarkable economic growth of the past two centuries since the industrial revolution has not been merely the result of human ingenuity. Certainly, science and technology, entrepreneurship, the accumulation of capital, advancement of productivity, and hard work, have all played a role. But we humans must share credit for the industrial revolution and the economic miracle that followed with ancient phytoplankton, tiny, intricate, drifting aquatic plants. Zooplankton and ancient terrestrial plants played a role too.

Types of Phytoplankton, whose fossilized remains are a major constituent of fuels[127]

In fact, we owe a double debt to phytoplankton and other micro-organisms. Over eons, trillions of phytoplankton of various types spent their short lives absorbing the sunlight that streamed into the oceans, photosynthesizing atmospheric carbon dioxide into oxygen and carbohydrates. Over hundreds of millions of years, generations of these water plants transformed the Earth's atmosphere into the oxygen-rich air which is conducive to the evolution of animal life, including humans.

After providing this crucial service—altering the atmosphere to make it hospitable for future animal life—phytoplankton, and other ancient forms of flora, died and sank. Over the eons, mixed with mud and subjected to underground heat and pressure, they gradually fossilized into coal, crude oil, and natural gas.

In the last two centuries, these fossil fuels have been mined, drilled and fracked at a tremendous rate. The phytoplankton have performed a second crucial service to humanity, long after their death, powering our factories and vehicles and electricity-generating power stations. Their remains have been a key factor in powering two centuries of spectacular economic growth.

Unfortunately, by using fossil fuels as an energy source, we are undoing the crucial labor that the phytoplankton carried out in their lifetime. Every year, CO_2 that was gently sucked out of the air, over perhaps a million years, is spewed back into the atmosphere as we burn fossil fuels as energy sources in vehicles and power stations. Since the 1970s it has become increasingly clear that rapid emission of CO_2 is materially altering the Earth's atmosphere, creating a greenhouse effect, and leading to climate change. As we all know, climate change is now threatening natural ecosystems, and agriculture, and bringing with it the threat of extreme weather events such as storms and wildfires.

Bizarrely, some politicians still deny the reality of anthropogenic climate change. Others, driven by indiscriminate libertarian instincts, most notably in the U.S., argue that governments should not intervene. But most economists, however libertarian, would agree that, while it is generally beneficial to give businesses broad freedom to operate, that freedom should not include an inherent right to pollute the atmosphere free of charge.

Economics can absolutely help to solve the environmental crisis. In fact, only economics has the power to drive the massive changes required to solve the climate crisis. Today, emitting carbon dioxide is often free, and so long as it is, people will continue to burn fossil fuels and damage the planet. In pure economic terms, it makes perfect sense to burn carbon-based fuels, so long as there is no economic value attached to the atmosphere. In human terms, it makes no sense whatsoever.

But economics is a mighty force, which can be trained in the right direction. The Kyoto Protocol came into effect in 2005, capping emission of greenhouse gases in many industrialized countries, with the notable exception of the U.S. This agreement introduced a cap-and-trade scheme where a limited quota of emissions is allowed, and countries and companies can trade the emission licenses. It achieved moderate success in reducing emissions in signatory countries.

It is now broadly agreed[128] that a simpler and more effective approach is a carbon tax, which ensures that there is a cost associated with exhuming massive quantities of ancient carbon and, after combustion, spewing CO_2 back into the atmosphere. Several countries already have some form of tax on carbon in general, or at least on specific fuels.[129] Unfortunately, the world's largest polluter, the United States, has been subsidizing rather than taxing fossil fuels. At the time of writing, the Biden administration has started to address this.

If the countries of the world were to impose a high enough carbon tax, governments and entrepreneurs would be fully incentivized to switch their businesses to renewable energies and their innovation efforts to sustainability. Although renewable energies are ideal, there are also increasing voices pointing out that, even with all its challenges, the most accessible zero-carbon energy source is nuclear energy, leveraging safe new reactor designs. Regardless of the specific solution, it just takes a suitable tax structure, which truly reflects the toll extracted by carbon emissions, to ensure that the same free-market forces that drove the world to burn fossil fuels, drive the world to substitute other energy sources.

Today the situation is the opposite. The International Monetary Fund estimated that in 2017 the world subsidized fossil fuels, to the tune of $5.2 trillion, equal to roughly 6.5 percent of global GDP.[130] The world spends more money *encouraging* carbon emissions than it spends on education.[131] Here, subsidies include direct subsidies, as well as the indirect subsidy of allowing the petroleum industry and its customers to create economically harmful air pollution free of charge.

A positive case study may be found in Sweden, which levies the world's highest carbon tax at €112.08 ($132.17) per ton of carbon emissions, and has successfully reduced emissions, without any apparent economic harm,[132] proving that the strategy works. Mind you, even if all countries followed Sweden, the total tax raised from all global emissions would still be slightly less than the $5.2 trillion paid out in subsidies.[133] Clearly, the world must urgently tax carbon emissions and remove both direct subsidies and the right to pollute without paying for the consequences.

RAINFOREST IS ANOTHER precious resource which is being destroyed because the world has not attached a monetary value to it. Here, again, it turns out that an artificial negative value is often attached to rainforests. Between 2009 and 2012, for example, Brazil and Indonesia paid over $40 billion in subsidies to industries such as palm oil and soy, which drive rainforest destruction, with only $346 million dedicated to conservation.[134,135] If the rainforests ever stood a chance on their own, subsidies for their destruction are bound to seal their fate.

So we find ourselves in a bizarre situation whereby our governments and business leaders talk about sustainability, but actually *subsidize* deforestation and carbon emissions. However, if society put a suitable positive monetary value on rainforests, the economic incentive to chop them down would quickly turn into an incentive for preservation and reforestation. There should be a substantial international subsidy payable to countries who preserve or restore their natural habitats, or an agreed tax on destroying them. We all breathe the air emitted by rainforests, and we all treasure their biodiversity, so we should all be happily paying a suitable "rent" to Brazil, Peru, Columbia, Indonesia and other tropical countries, to preserve their rainforests. It wouldn't take that much.

Money may not grow on trees, but the trees of the rainforest will only grow with the right monetary incentives. To live, they need the monetary subsidies to be working for them, not against them.

WE PREVIOUSLY DISCUSSED inequality of income and of wealth. The world also has dramatic carbon inequality. According to the UN, "emissions of the richest 1 percent of the global population account for more than twice the combined emissions of the poorest 50 per cent. This elite will need to reduce their footprint by a factor of 30 to stay in line with the Paris Agreement targets"[136] of keeping long-term average temperature increases to well below 2°C (3.6°F).

The top 10 percent are already big emitters, running large cars, keeping big homes, and frequenting international flights. But the elites, the wealthiest 1 per cent, often with their private jets and yachts, take a massively disproportionate toll on the planet.

SAVING THE PLANET requires international cooperation. The Paris Agreement is a start, with its setting of international targets. But it is very light on specific commitments. If the world could agree on a uniform minimum tax on carbon emissions, while removing subsidies, and if the world would use even part of that tax to pay a uniform "rent" for preservation of rainforests and other wild habitats, then economic incentives would be realigned with real long-term human interests. The world's business community would do the rest of the work to find sustainable sources of non-carbon energy and alternatives to palm oil and timber from deforestation. Ideally, carbon tax money left over from a carbon tax could be dedicated to other global goals, such as moderating overpopulation.

I call this proposal *black-to-green*. The world can tax carbon emissions from black fossil fuels and use at least part of the money to subsidize the preservation and restoration of green rainforests and other natural environments. This double-sided measure, on its own, could enable us to start curing the biggest threats to our planet.

ECONOMICS IN THE FUTURE

THE DISCIPLINE CALLED "economics" has expanded in scope in recent decades. Professors of economics now study topics such as decision theory, education, family, law, politics, religion, terrorism, and war. Nobel prizes in economics are sometimes awarded to brilliant behavioral economists such as Daniel Kahneman and social scientists who have written nothing about money or the economy. In this book, however, we have focused on economics in the more traditional sense—and particularly on macroeconomic concepts of how an economy works and grows and the role of money.

Macroeconomics, I would argue, is in a bit of a crisis after the first two decades of the twenty-first century. The first half of the twentieth century was dominated by Keynesian ideas, most famously the prescription that governments should combat recessions with a fiscal stimulus—for example, borrowing money and spending on public works.

The closing decades of the twentieth century were dominated by Milton Friedman's libertarian ideas, shunning government interventions. When fiat currency emerged in the 1970s and inflation reared its head, Milton was a key advocate for stabilizing prices by applying a disciplined control of the money supply.

But these ideas have faced new challenges in the first two decades of the twenty-first century. Firstly, free markets are not bringing greater equality, as Friedman promised. While economic freedom has been increasing, income equality has been decreasing within most countries. Wealth equality has also been decreasing dramatically, both within developed countries and globally.

Friedman's pure libertarian view, that companies should be motivated solely by profit, is also a matter of ongoing debate, as more companies are being pressured to accept some degree of social and environmental responsibility.

Most dramatically, Milton's famous edict that "Inflation is always and everywhere a monetary phenomenon" is being challenged. The implied converse—that loose monetary policy will lead to inflation—is no longer true. In the years 2009 and again in 2020 and several times in between, central banks kept printing money, buying back short-term government bonds, until nominal interest rates hit zero or below. Then they kept printing more money, buying long-term bonds and mortgages and such assets under the banner of *quantitative easing (QE)*. Instead of inflation, we witnessed a reduction in the velocity of money. In other words, most of the newly printed money simply didn't circulate; and it certainly wasn't spent on goods and services. If the money did anything, it inflated the value of stocks and other financial assets.

In other news, the Keynesian idea of fiscal stimulus, so hated by Milton, is back with a vengeance this century, as governments adopt massive deficit spending once again, especially during the great recession of 2008–2009 and during the Covid-19 pandemic. Zero or negative interest rates are giving governments of developed countries unprecedented leeway to borrow. The U.S. government debt has increased from around 30 percent of GDP in the 1970s to 130 percent of GDP going into 2021.[137]

Strange as it sounds, the behavior of the economy has fundamentally changed, and central banks really seem to have no idea how money supply relates to inflation in today's economy. The *Taylor rule*, which used to model this, is out of the window. The Fed employs teams of PhDs to analyze the problem, and yet their policy is pretty much "Hey, we haven't seen inflation for a good while, so let's keep printing money, at least until inflation finally reaches our 2 percent target."[138] And, so far, every time they print money, the velocity of money drops, instead of prices rising. The money they print is not chasing up the price of goods. In fact, it's mostly not circulating at all, or it's being used for the day trading of shares.

This ability to print money without inflation has been a huge gift to a world combatting Covid-19, but it means that the economic theory textbooks have been thrown out of the window and new ideas are needed. There is *Modern Monetary Theory (MMT)*[139] which builds a theory around the de facto policy of unlimited printing of money to ensure employment, provided inflation does not result. This does not seem like a very solid strategy. Without a workable model, we don't know if the money will suddenly create inflation in the future, or if it will fuel asset bubbles that may be quite destabilizing.

Therefore, an updated economic theory is called for to model the era of negative real interest rates. However, I believe that any model of the economy with negative real interest rates will suffer from singularities and be unstable. I have shared my own intuition that money is going out of style because of inequality, with too much money in the hands of people who have no propensity to spend, as evidenced by negative real interest rates. While we could do with a new monetary theory for the era of negative real interest rates, it would be preferable to formulate new policies to reverse the trend of recent decades, moderating inequality, increasing interest rates, and bringing money back into style.

THE FUTURE WILL bring new challenges.

For two centuries, since the Luddites, job creation has kept up with job destruction. As agriculture and manufacturing became more and more automated, those manual jobs were lost, but rich societies compensated very effectively by consuming more and more goods and services, such as gourmet food, electronic gadgets, and fast fashion. They also invented new services, like takeaway food and pedicures, and more obscure services, such as, apparently, goat yoga, snake massages, fire facials, and sake and beer baths.

However, our remarkable ability to invent and enjoy new luxuries, and generate new types of jobs, may have its limits. Artificial intelligence (AI), after stagnating in the 1980s and early 1990s, has been making spectacular progress in the last couple of decades. AI outperforms humans at more and more tasks which we previously considered quintessentially human:

recognizing faces and voices, composing music, playing Jeopardy and chess and Go, translating texts, and diagnostically analyzing some types of medical images.

All this is happening in a very short time frame. It is not clear if society can continue to invent new goods and services which will create new jobs fast enough to employ all the drivers, passport control officers, bookkeepers, proofreaders, translators, and doctors who will be replaced by machines in coming years.

I personally love technological progress, and I do not wish to sound like a latter-day Luddite, but I think this time round the risk is real. It is perfectly true that historically 50 percent of jobs could successfully be switched from farming to other new types of jobs. But that took a century, or around four generations. But now 47 percent of American jobs are at high risk of automation within the next 15 years or so, and there is a similar situation in other countries.[140] Even if society can replace all the jobs that are automated with new high-touch services, there must be a limit to how fast we can shift employment as technological progress, particularly AI, keeps accelerating.

Of course, it may not matter all that much if AIs displace all our jobs, if shortly after that the AIs take control of the world and kill us all. This scenario, previously the stuff of science fiction, is actually not that far-fetched. However this book is focused on economics, and there are an increasing number of excellent books on the subject of existential risk from AI.[141,142]

If the creation of new goods and services eventually fails to keep up with automation, as seems likely, we will have to adjust to a world with partial employment. There will be plenty of highly automated production to sustain everyone, but we will have to share that production in a different way. Generous unemployment benefits are one obvious idea. But another idea which is gaining support is a *universal basic income (UBI)* to replace unemployment benefits. This scheme proposes that every citizen is given a basic income regardless of means. The idea of a *negative income tax* has a similar effect.

Some find UBI tasteless because even the top 10 percent would receive a basic income they certainly don't require. The counterargument is that unemployment benefits, a guaranteed minimum income, or any other means-tested benefits all reduce the incentive to work. A flat UBI ensures that people survive if they don't work, but always have an incentive to gain more by working. UBI is also much simpler to administer than a means-tested benefit, and of course 90 percent of a UBI doesn't go to the top 10 percent.

The idea of UBI was actually put to a referendum in Switzerland, although it was rejected.[143] In a way, UBI was piloted in a small way during the Covid-19 pandemic, with the U.S. and several other countries distributing flat cash grants to every citizen. At the time of writing in 2021, Wales is planning a UBI pilot.

Economists may be able to work out how a society can sustain itself in a future era when resources are plentiful, but employment is not, UBI being one available scheme. For many people, though, work provides a sense of worth and purpose so defining the future of humanity requires more than just economics.

IX. CONCLUSION

FREE MARKET ECONOMICS has totally, and positively, transformed the human condition in most of the world, especially in the two centuries since the industrial revolution. The basic mechanisms of the real economy are not all that complex; it is all about organizing labor and capital to produce goods and services and providing credit to allow investment in creating more capital. The accumulation of capital, together with improved production technologies, ensures that the world becomes exponentially richer. So far, automation and efficiencies have not caused long-term unemployment. Instead, as production becomes more efficient, we consume more and more goods and services.

That is the real economy. Money plays a critical secondary role in the economy, enabling flexible trade and sophisticated credit. The purest form of money is fiat money, which is not tied to any underlying commodity. Fiat money celebrates its fiftieth birthday in August 2021.

And yet, as it turns 50, fiat money is facing a deep midlife crisis. Money is just not as attractive as it used to be when it was younger. Trillions of dollars and euros and pounds and yen are sitting around in wallets and checking accounts, feeling unappreciated. Gone are the days when all money circulated vibrantly, from businesses to their employees and owners, and right back to the businesses, reliably every month. Many people will now pay a negative real interest rate to delay gratification, rather than spend more money and consume more today.

At the age of 50, fiat money is, if you will, reaching menopause. Gone are the reliable monthly cycles. Instead, the cycle of money has become erratic, just a few times a year.

For a number of reasons, the world needs international cooperation as never before. We must align the mighty power of economics with the need to sustain our planet, by coordinating a global black-to-green policy: a global minimum tax on combusting fossil fuels, combined with a subsidy for protecting rainforests and other natural environments.

And we need to moderate inequality of wealth and income. For this, we need basic international coordluation of tax policy, to avoid nations racing each other to the goals of zero inheritance and wealth tax, with ever bigger fortunes escaping to tax havens. Negative real interest rates are the alarm bell warning us that inequality has gone too far; we can still get back to the more natural situation of positive real interest rates, where the present is at a premium to the future, by applying a coordinated approach to addressing inequality and getting money into the hands of those who wish to spend it.

The G7 meeting of June 2021 may offer some hope that the world's largest democracies are finally tackling some of these issues together. But in the meantime, the world keeps printing money at an alarming rate, which may yet have unwelcome consequences such as the return of hyperinflation, and/or further asset price bubbles. One thing is for certain, the vast majority of money in existence today, is not being used for its intended purpose of paying wages and purchasing goods and services.

Money has been going out of style; it is time for the world to join forces in designing its comeback.

AFTERWORD

CHARLIE V FINDS a memory chip on the market floor rather close to where, unbeknown to him, his ancestor had found a 10-buck bill. Charlie V pops the chip into his phone and discovers that the memory chip contains a digital wallet with 100 bucks in cryptocurrency, which has about the same purchasing power as his great-great-grandfather's tenner.

Charlie looks around the market and considers spending the money on goods and services, but he already has everything he wants, and then some.

He thinks about saving it in the bank. Charlie has friends who are unemployed and would love a small business loan to become productive again. If he saves the money in the bank, he muses, the bank might lend the money to finance the capital for one of his friend's projects. Charlie would delay gratification, while someone else advances gratification, creating jobs and increasing the capital on the island, which would pay off with future growth.

But interest rates are negative, making a bank account very unattractive. Storing cash earns zero interest but is now illegal. But the government can't track this cryptocurrency, so he could store it and earn a market-beating zero percent interest rate. But, then again, he would probably never spend it.

Charlie considers donating the money. But would the donation be real? Actual production isn't going to increase suddenly because he donates. If he gives the money to someone to spend on goods, there will inevitably be fewer goods available for someone else. He will just be increasing the money in circulation, and shifting consumption from one person to another, without any increase in the real economy of goods and services.

So Charlie V throws the device in the recycling bin. Money has gone out of style, but at least the physical materials can go back into circulation.

Author's note: IF YOU ENJOYED *Money, Going Out of Style*, please consider leaving a review <u>on Amazon.com</u> and check out my other book, *Fizz, Nothing is as it Seems*, also available on <u>Amazon</u>.

ENDNOTES

[1] Wikipedia, *Reliability of Wikipedia*.
https://en.wikipedia.org/wiki/Reliability_of_Wikipedia retrieved May 2021.

[2] See for example the chart in
https://en.wikipedia.org/wiki/Economic_history_of_the_United_Kingdom – the UK has
some of the best available historical data on growth.

[3] *When Boris Yeltsin went grocery shopping in Clear Lake*, Houston Chronicle, Sep. 13,
2017 https://www.chron.com/neighborhood/bayarea/news/article/When-Boris-Yeltsin-
went-grocery-shopping-in-Clear-5759129.php

[4] David Ricardo. 1817. *On the Principles of Political Economy and Taxation*. Also see
Wikipedia, *Comparative advantage*.
https://en.wikipedia.org/wiki/Comparative_advantage

[5] David Graeber, 2011. Debt: The First 5000 Years.

[6] This is the total non-financial assets owned by non-financial corporate businesses as of
2014. Wikipedia. *Financial position of the United States: Estimated financial position,
Q1 2014*
https://en.wikipedia.org/wiki/Financial_position_of_the_United_States#Estimated_financ
ial_position,_Q1_2014 retrieved December 2020.

[7] OECD Data. "Self-employment rate." https://data.oecd.org/emp/self-employment-
rate.htm retrieved January 2021. However there seems to be different definitions of self-
employment floating around as this articles talks about 30%, possibly in part due to
Covid-19: Elaine Pofeldt. May 2020. "Survey: Nearly 30% Of Americans Are Self-
Employed." *Forbes*. https://www.forbes.com/sites/elainepofeldt/2020/05/30/survey-
nearly-30-of-americans-are-self-employed/?sh=448748572d21

[8] Wikipedia. *Wage Share*. https://en.wikipedia.org/wiki/Wage_share retrieved November
2020.

[9] Wikipedia. *Bowley's law*. https://en.wikipedia.org/wiki/Bowley percent27s_law
retrieved November 2020.

[10] Leonard E. Read. December 1958. "I, Pencil." *The Freeman*.
https://mises.org/library/i-pencil retrieved December 2020.

[11] Mark Catanzaro. April 2020. "A Snapshot of Record-High U.S. Household Debt." *St.
Louis Fed*. https://www.stlouisfed.org/open-vault/2020/april/snapshot-record-high-
household-debt retrieved December 2020.

[12] Wikipedia. *Shell Money*. https://en.wikipedia.org/wiki/Shell_money retrieved
November 2020.

[13] Wikipedia. *Goldsmiths of London.*
https://en.wikipedia.org/wiki/History_of_banking#Goldsmiths_of_London retrieved November 2020.

[14] Jesus Huerta de Soto. *Money, Bank Credit, and Economic Cycles.* Translated by Melinda A Stroup.

Ludwig von Mises Institute, pp. 73-74,
https://cdn.mises.org/Money_Bank_Credit_and_Economic_Cycles_De%20Soto.pdf

[15] Wikipedia. *Fractional-reserve banking.* https://en.wikipedia.org/wiki/Fractional-reserve_banking retrieved October 2020.

[16] Joshua N. Feinman. Federal Reserve Bulletin. June 1993. *Reserve Requirements: History, Current Practice, and Potential Reform.*

[17] Wikipedia. *Reserve Requirement.*
https://en.wikipedia.org/wiki/Reserve_requirement#Required_reserves retrieved November 2020.

[18] https://monneta.org/en/momo-modernising-money-association-switzerland/ retrieved November 2020.

[19] Wikipedia. *2018 Swiss sovereign-money initiative.*
https://en.wikipedia.org/wiki/2018_Swiss_sovereign-money_initiative retrieved November 2020.

[20] For convenience, Nocheck Bank might have a separate cash account, with full reserves, which allows checks. The important point is that the accounts with fractional reserves don't allow checks.

[21] William L. Silber. July 2009. "Why Did FDR's Bank Holiday Succeed?" *Federal Reserve Bank of New York: Economic Policy Review* 15:1.
https://www.newyorkfed.org/research/epr/09v15n1/0907silb.html retrieved December 2020. JEL classification: E42, N22, E58.

[22] Leland Crabbe. June 1989. "The International Gold Standard and U.S. Monetary Policy from World War I to the New Deal." *Federal Reserve Bulletin.*
https://fraser.stlouisfed.org/files/docs/meltzer/craint89.pdf retrieved January 2021.

[23] Ruth Judson. April 2017. "The Death of Cash? Not So Fast: Demand for U.S. Currency at Home and Abroad, 1990-2016." *International Cash Conference 2017.* Frankfurt, Germany. https://www.econstor.eu/bitstream/10419/162910/1/Judson.pdf retrieved May 2021.

[24] Board of Governors of the Federal Reserve System (US), "Currency in Circulation [CURRCIR]," retrieved from *FRED, Federal Reserve Bank of St. Louis*;
https://fred.stlouisfed.org/series/CURRCIR, February 2021.

[25] Board of Governors of the Federal Reserve System (US), "M1 Money Stock [M1]," retrieved from *FRED, Federal Reserve Bank of St. Louis*;
https://fred.stlouisfed.org/series/M1, February 2021. After subtracting the Monetary Base retrieved from the same site.

[26] FRED Federal Reserve of St Louis economic data. *Inflation, consumer prices for the United States*. https://fred.stlouisfed.org/series/FPCPITOTLZGUSA retrieved November 2020.

[27] Wikipedia. *Crisis of the third Century*. https://en.wikipedia.org/wiki/Crisis_of_the_Third_Century#Economic_impact retrieved November 2020.

[28] Wikipedia. *Hyperinflation in the Weimar Republic*. https://en.wikipedia.org/wiki/Hyperinflation_in_the_Weimar_Republic retrieved November 2020.

[29] Wikipedia. *Hyperinflation in Zimbabwe* https://en.wikipedia.org/wiki/Hyperinflation_in_Zimbabwe retrieved January 2021.

[30] *Inflación de 2018 cerró en 1.698.48%, según la Asamblea Nacional.* 9 January 2019. https://web.archive.org/web/20190110133641/http://efectococuyo.com/principales/inflacion-de-2018-cerro-en-1-698-488-segun-la-asamblea-nacional/ retrieved November 2020.

[31] Wikipedia. *Central bank: History*. https://en.wikipedia.org/wiki/Central_bank#History retrieved February 2021.

[32] https://fred.stlouisfed.org/ retrieved June 2021.

[33] Stanley Diller. 1970. "The Seasonal Variation of Interest Rates". NBER 1970. https://www.nber.org/books/dill70-1 retrieved June 2021.

[34] Federal Reserve Bank of New York. "Treasury Securities Operations." https://www.newyorkfed.org/markets/desk-operations/treasury-securities retrieved January 2021.

[35] Macrotrends. "U.S. Inflation Rate 1960-2021." From World Bank data. https://www.macrotrends.net/countries/USA/united-states/inflation-rate-cpi retrieved February 2021.

[36] Board of Governors of the Federal Reserve System (US), "Effective Federal Funds Rate [FEDFUNDS]," retrieved from *FRED, Federal Reserve Bank of St. Louis*; https://fred.stlouisfed.org/series/FEDFUNDS February 2021.

[37] Michael McCullough. September 8, 2016. "How employers are boosting loyalty by paying employees daily". *Canadian Business.*

[38] Board of Governors of the Federal Reserve System. "Open Market Operations." https://www.federalreserve.gov/monetarypolicy/openmarket.htm retrieved February 2021.

[39] *Tax#History*, Wikipedia. https://en.wikipedia.org/wiki/Tax#History retrieved December 2020.

[40] Wikipedia. *Taxation as Slavery*. https://en.wikipedia.org/wiki/Taxation_as_slavery retrieved December 2020.

[41] Richard G. Wilkinson and Kate Pickett. 2009. *The Spirit Level: Why More Equal Societies Almost Always Do Better*. Bloomsbury Press.

See also Wikipedia. *The Spirit Level (book)*. Section *Critical response*. https://en.wikipedia.org/wiki/The_Spirit_Level_(book)#Critical_response retrieved June 2021.

[42] Dr. Thomas Carl Rustici. *Economics and Public Policy Problems. Economics 309*. George Mason University. https://mason.gmu.edu/~trustici/ECON309/Economics%20309.pdf retrieved June 2021.

[43] Elena Holodny. August 2016. *The US is a big outlier when it comes to income inequality*. The Insider. https://www.insider.com/goldman-sachs-chart-shows-us-stands-out-income-inequality-2016-8 retrieved December 2020.

[44] Wikipedia. *Original position*. https://en.wikipedia.org/wiki/Original_position retrieved January 2021.

[45] CIA statistics. *The World Factbook*. https://www.cia.gov/library/publications/the-world-factbook/fields/print_2259.html retrieved November 2020.

[46] Fernando Martin. February 2017. "Why Does Economic Growth Keep Slowing Down?" *Federal Reserve Bank of St. Louis*. https://www.stlouisfed.org/on-the-economy/2017/february/why-economic-growth-slowing-down retrieved January 2021.

[47] U.S. Bureau of Economic Analysis, "Gross Domestic Product [GDP]", retrieved from *FRED, Federal Reserve Bank of St. Louis*; https://fred.stlouisfed.org/series/GDP retrieved February 2021.

[48] Wikipedia. *Irrational exuberance*. https://en.wikipedia.org/wiki/Irrational_exuberance retrieved February 2021.

[49] Wikipedia. *Great Recession*. https://en.wikipedia.org/wiki/Great_Recession retrieved February 2021.

[50] Wikipedia. *1973 oil crisis*. https://en.wikipedia.org/wiki/1973_oil_crisis retrieved June 2021.

[51] Wikipedia. *Phillips curve*. https://en.wikipedia.org/wiki/Phillips_curve retrieved February 2021.

[52] Milton Friedman. 1968. "The Role of Monetary Policy". American Economic Review. 58 (1): 1–17. JSTOR 1831652.

Edmund S. Phelps. 1968. "Money-Wage Dynamics and Labor Market Equilibrium". Journal of Political Economy. 76 (S4): 678–711. doi:10.1086/259438.

Edmund S. Phelps. 1967. "Phillips Curves, Expectations of Inflation and Optimal Unemployment over Time". Economica. 34 (135): 254–281. doi:10.2307/2552025. JSTOR 2552025.

[53] Mark Joób. June 2014. *The Sovereign Money Initiative in Switzerland*. World Economics Association Newsletter. 4 (3) pp 6–7.

[54] Claire Cain Miller, December, 2016. "The Long-Term Jobs Killer Is Not China. It's Automation", *The New York Times, The Upshot* https://www.nytimes.com/2016/12/21/upshot/the-long-term-jobs-killer-is-not-china-its-automation.html retrieved December 2020.

[55] Kimberly Amadeo. October 2020. "US Debt to China, How Much, Reasons Why, and What If China Sells". *The Balance.* https://www.thebalance.com/u-s-debt-to-china-how-much-does-it-own-3306355 retrieved February 2021.

[56] FRED Economics Data, St. Louis Fed. *M1 Money Multiplier.* https://fred.stlouisfed.org/series/MULT retrieved December 2020.

[57] "How has growth changed over time?" *Bank of England.* https://www.bankofengland.co.uk/knowledgebank/how-has-growth-changed-over-time retrieved January 2021. Based on data from J. Bradford De Long. 1998. "Estimates of World GDP, One Million B.C. – Present" https://delong.typepad.com/print/20061012_LRWGDP.pdf retrieved January 2021.

[58] Daniel Kahneman and Angus Deaton. August 2010. "High income improves evaluation of life but not emotional well-being." *Center for Health and Well-being, Princeton University.* https://www.princeton.edu/~deaton/downloads/deaton_kahneman_high_income_improves_evaluation_August2010.pdf retrieved January 2021.

[59] Matthew A. Killingswortha. "Experienced well-being rises with income, even above $75,000 per year." *The Wharton School, Philadelphia.* https://www.pnas.org/content/pnas/118/4/e2016976118.full.pdf retrieved February 2021.

[60] James Ellsmoor. July 2019. "New Zealand Ditches GDP For Happiness And Wellbeing". *Forbes.* https://www.forbes.com/sites/jamesellsmoor/2019/07/11/new-zealand-ditches-gdp-for-happiness-and-wellbeing/?sh=294e0d6f1942 retrieved January 2021.

[61] Annie Kelly. December 2012 "Gross national happiness in Bhutan: the big idea from a tiny state that could change the world." *The Guardian.* https://www.theguardian.com/world/2012/dec/01/bhutan-wealth-happiness-counts

[62] Thomas Piketty. 2013. *Capital in the Twenty-First Century.* English translation 2014.

[63] Data Source: World Wealth and Income Database (2018). Visualization thanks to OurWorldInData.org. Licensed under CC-BY-SA by the author Max Rosner. https://ourworldindata.org/income-inequality retrieved December 2020.

[64] Brian Keeley. 2015. *OECD Insights*, and particularly Chapter 3, *Why is income inequality rising?* OECD Publishing, Paris. https://www.oecd-ilibrary.org/social-issues-migration-health/income-inequality/why-is-income-inequality-rising_9789264246010-5-en retrieved November 2020.

[66] See in particular Hans Rosling, 2007, TED talk: *The best stats you've ever seen.* https://www.youtube.com/watch?v=hVimVzgtD6w&t=375s retrieved December 2020.

[65] Source: Global Economic Inequality. Our World In Data

[67] PK. "Average, Median, Top 1%, and all United States Net Worth Percentiles in 2020". *DQYDJ.* https://dqydj.com/average-median-top-net-worth-percentiles/ retrieved January 2021. Data comes from the Federal Reserve's 2019 SCF, released in September, 2020. Calculation is based on the total net wealth of the bottom 32 or 39 percentiles multiplied by 32% or 39% of the number of U.S. households, 122.8 million.

[68] Wikipedia. *List of countries by total wealth.* https://en.wikipedia.org/wiki/List_of_countries_by_total_wealth retrieved December 2020.

[69] The Giving Pledge. https://givingpledge.org/ retrieved December 2020.

[70] Thomas Piketty. *Capital in the Twenty-First Century.* 2013, English translation 2014.

[71] *Bowley's Law,* Wikipedia. https://en.wikipedia.org/wiki/Bowley%27s_law. retrieved June 2021.

[72] *Share of Labour Compensation in GDP at Current National Prices for United States,* Fred Economic Research, The Federal Reserve. https://fred.stlouisfed.org/series/LABSHPUSA156NRUG retrieved June 2021.

[73] "Rich Americans back inheritance tax". February 14, 2001. BBC http://news.bbc.co.uk/1/hi/world/americas/1170874.stm retrieved December 2020.

[74] OECD Tax Policy Studies. May 2021. *Inheritance Taxation in OECD Countries.* OECD. https://www.oecd.org/tax/tax-policy/inheritance-taxation-in-oecd-countries-e2879a7d-en.htm retrieved May 2021.

[75] BBC. *G7: Rich nations back deal to tax multinationals.* June 2021. https://www.bbc.com/news/world-57368247 retrieved June 2021.

[76] OECD. April 2020. *ODA: Aid by DAC members increases in 2019 with more aid to the poorest countries* https://www.oecd.org/dac/financing-sustainable-development/development-finance-data/ODA-2019-detailed-summary.pdf retrieved December 2020.

[77] Bill & Melinda Gates Foundation. https://www.gatesfoundation.org/ retrieved January 2021.

[78] See e.g. https://www.effectivealtruism.org/ retrieved January 2021.

[79] See e.g. https://www.givewell.org/ retrieved January 2021.

[80] *Staff Working Paper No. 845, Eight centuries of global real interest rates, R-G, and the 'suprasecular' decline*, 1311–2018, Paul Schmelzing, Bank of England https://www.bankofengland.co.uk/-/media/boe/files/working-paper/2020/eight-centuries-of-global-real-interest-rates-r-g-and-the-suprasecular-decline-1311-2018.pdf retrieved June 2021.

[81] U.S. Department of the Treasury. *Daily Treasury Real Yield Curve Rate.* https://www.treasury.gov/resource-center/data-chart-center/interest-rates/Pages/TextView.aspx?data=realyield retrieved December 2020.

[82] *Record-Low 0.0000000091 percent Yield on Yen Bond Shows BOJ Effect*, Bloomberg, October 16, 2019. https://www.bloomberg.com/news/articles/2019-10-16/record-low-0-0000000091-yield-on-japan-bond-shows-boj-effect retrieved June 2021.

[83] *Siemens just borrowed billions. Its corporate bonds had the lowest yields ever*, CNN, 30 August 2019 https://edition.cnn.com/2019/08/30/investing/siemens-corporate-bond/index.html retrieved October 2020.

[84] Kate Duguid, August 2020. Google owner Alphabet issues record $10 billion bond at lowest-ever price. *Reuters Technology News.* https://www.reuters.com/article/us-alphabet-bonds-idUSKCN24Z2PC retrieved December 2020.

[85] Emmie Martin. Aug 2019. "Danish bank offers mortgages with negative 0.5% interest rates—here's why that's not necessarily a good thing." *CNBC.* https://www.cnbc.com/2019/08/12/danish-bank-is-offering-10-year-mortgages-with-negative-interest-rates.html retrieved December 2020.

[86] Francesco Canepa. May 2020. "Germans paid to borrow as negative rates reach consumers". Reuters Business News.

https://uk.reuters.com/article/us-germany-banks-rates/germans-paid-to-borrow-as-negative-rates-reach-consumers-idUKKBN22W2BG retrieved December 2020.

[87] Wikipedia. *Stanford marshmallow experiment.* https://en.wikipedia.org/wiki/Stanford_marshmallow_experiment retrieved December 2020. See also some fun videos on Youtube. *The Marshmallow Test | Igniter Media | Church Video.* https://www.youtube.com/watch?v=QX_oy9614HQ retrieved December 2020.

[88] At the time of writing the real yield on 30 year U.S. Treasury Inflation-Protected Bonds was negative. https://www.treasury.gov/resource-center/data-chart-center/interest-rates/Pages/TextView.aspx?data=realyield retrieved June 2021.

[89] Fixed Income Investor https://www.fixedincomeinvestor.co.uk/x/bondtable.html?groupid=3530 retrieved December 2020. Note that -2.3% per year compounded over 30 years is approximately -50%.

[90] N. Gregory Mankiw. Dec. 4, 2020. "The Puzzle of Low Interest Rates". *The New York Times.* https://www.nytimes.com/2020/12/04/business/low-interest-rates-puzzle.html retrieved December 2020.

[91] Tyler Cowen. *The Great Stagnation: How America Ate All the Low-Hanging Fruit of Modern History, Got Sick, and Will (Eventually) Feel Better.* Dutton Adult. January 2011.

[92] Wikipedia. *Inferno (Dante): Fourth Circle (Greed).* https://en.wikipedia.org/wiki/Inferno_(Dante)#Fourth_Circle_(Greed) retrieved January 2020.

[93] Gustave Doré's illustration to Dante's Inferno https://en.wikipedia.org/wiki/Inferno_(Dante)#/media/File:Gustave_Dor%C3%A9_-_Dante_Alighieri_-_Inferno_-_Plate_22_(Canto_VII_-_Hoarders_and_Wasters).jpg retrieved January 2021.

[94] The World Bank. *Poverty.* https://www.worldbank.org/en/topic/poverty/overview retrieved January 2021.

[95] Olaf Storbeck and Martin Arnold. January 2020. "German savers shrug off negative interest rate fears"

Financial Times. https://www.ft.com/content/ac44f7a0-2d6c-11ea-bc77-65e4aa615551 retrieved December 2020.

[96] Dominika Kolcunova and Tomas Havranek. February 2018. "Estimating the Effective Lower Bound for the Czech National Bank's Policy Rate". Munich Personal RePEc Archive, Czech National Bank, Charles University, Prague. https://mpra.ub.uni-muenchen.de/84725/1/MPRA_paper_84725.pdf retrieved December 2020.

[97] Richard Partington. December 2020. "Bank of England criticised for losing track of £50bn of banknotes." *The Guardian*. https://www.theguardian.com/business/2020/dec/04/bank-of-england-criticised-for-losing-track-of-50bn-of-banknotes retrieved December 2020.

[98] Wikipedia. *Liquidity trap*. https://en.wikipedia.org/wiki/Liquidity_trap retrieved February 2021.

[99] Wikipedia. *Helicopter money*. https://en.wikipedia.org/wiki/Helicopter_money retrieved December 2020.

[100] Fixed Income Investor. https://www.fixedincomeinvestor.co.uk/x/bondchart.html?id=3493&stash=F674FB48&groupid=3530 retrieved December 2020.

[101] S&P Japan Sovereign Inflation-Linked Bond Index https://www.spglobal.com/spdji/en/indices/fixed-income/sp-japan-sovereign-inflation-linked-bond-index/#overview retrieved December 2020.

[102] Limit for cash payments in EU https://peter-ftp.co.uk/aviation/misc-euroga/2018-Limit_for_cash_payments_in_EU.pdf retrieved June 2021.

[103] Data Lab. "How is the federal government funding relief efforts for Covid-19?" https://datalab.usaspending.gov/federal-covid-funding/ retrieved January 2021. Added the Biden stimulus: Tami Luhby, Katie Lobosco. "Here's what's in Biden's $1.9 trillion economic rescue package". CNN. https://edition.cnn.com/2021/01/14/politics/biden-economic-rescue-package-coronavirus-stimulus/index.html retrieved March 2021.

[104] Ziyad Cassim, Borko Handjiski, Jörg Schubert, and Yassir Zouaoui. June 2020. "The $10 trillion rescue: How governments can deliver impact". *McKinsey*. https://www.mckinsey.com/~/media/McKinsey/Industries/Public%20Sector/Our%20Insights/The%2010%20trillion%20dollar%20rescue%20How%20governments%20can%20deliver%20impact/The-10-trillion-dollar-rescue-How-governments-can-deliver-impact-vF.pdf retrieved January 2021.

[105] Board of Governors of the Federal Reserve System (US), Monetary Base; "Total [BOGMBASE]," retrieved from *FRED, Federal Reserve Bank of St. Louis*; https://fred.stlouisfed.org/series/BOGMBASE January 2021.

[106] U.S. Department of the Treasury. "Fiscal Service, Federal Debt: Total Public Debt [GFDEBTN]," retrieved from *FRED, Federal Reserve Bank of St. Louis*; https://fred.stlouisfed.org/series/GFDEBTN January 2021.

[107] Neil Bhutta et al. September 2020. "Changes in U.S. Family Finances from 2016 to 2019: Evidence from the Survey of Consumer Finances." *Federal Reserve Bulletin*. See in particular Table 2, in 2019 median net worth for those in the 25-49.9th percentile is $57,300. Others have estimated that 44% have a net worth below $85,000. https://www.federalreserve.gov/publications/files/scf20.pdf retrieved January 2021. See also https://dqydj.com/average-median-top-net-worth-percentiles/ retrieved January 2021.

[108] This is typically done in a roundabout way by borrowing with a bond and then buying the bond back for cash, but the effect is the same.

[109] Josh Zumbrun. May 2016. "The Rise of Knowledge Workers Is Accelerating Despite the Threat of Automation." The Wall Street Journal. https://blogs.wsj.com/economics/2016/05/04/the-rise-of-knowledge-workers-is-accelerating-despite-the-threat-of-automation/ retrieved January 2021.

[110] U.S. Office of Management and Budget and Federal Reserve Bank of St. Louis, Federal Debt: Total Public Debt as Percent of Gross Domestic Product [GFDEGDQ188S], retrieved from FRED, Federal Reserve Bank of St. Louis; https://fred.stlouisfed.org/series/GFDEGDQ188S, June 2021.

[111] More accurately the sum of the infinite geometric series for a discount rate of d is $(1-d)/d$ but for small d this is close to $1/d$. It would also be more accurate to discount the first year's profits by half a year, but again for our purposes the difference is small.

[112] Zvi Schreiber. "Stock markets are undervalued (when considering bond yields)". Medium. https://medium.com/fortune-for-future/stock-markets-are-undervalued-when-considering-bond-yields-f7832c39f5a1 retrieved January 2021. $PETRY_{30}$ is defined to be the NPV of a 30 year annuity of $1 discounted by a rate equal to the current yield of 15 year TIPS bonds.

[113] Board of Governors of the Federal Reserve System (U.S.), "Monetary Base; Total [BOGMBASE]," retrieved from FRED, Federal Reserve Bank of St. Louis; https://fred.stlouisfed.org/series/BOGMBASE retrieved June 2021.

[114] Board of Governors of the Federal Reserve System (U.S.), "M1 Money Stock [M1]," retrieved from FRED, Federal Reserve Bank of St. Louis; https://fred.stlouisfed.org/series/M1 retrieved June 2021.

[115] Federal Reserve Bank of St. Louis, "Velocity of M1 Money Stock [M1V]," retrieved from FRED, Federal Reserve Bank of St. Louis; https://fred.stlouisfed.org/series/M1V retrieved June 2021.

[116] Why Is Inflation So Low? By Juan M. Sánchez , Hee Sung Kim, Federal Reserve of St. Louis, February 2, 2018. https://www.stlouisfed.org/publications/regional-economist/first-quarter-2018/why-inflation-so-low retrieved June 2021.

[117] For example, Nasdaq trading volumes are up 50% 2020 vs. 2019 while share prices are on average up about 40% so that the amount of money circulating in NASDAQ trading is about double. "Nasdaq 2020/2019 Monthly Volumes." NASDAQ Investor Relations: Volume Statistics: Monthly Volumes. https://ir.nasdaq.com/financials/volume-statistics retrieved January 2021.

[118] Barry Collins. January 2021. "Man Threw $300m Bitcoin Hard Disk In Bin: 7 Years On, He Wants It Back". Forbes. https://www.forbes.com/sites/barrycollins/2021/01/14/man-threw-300m-bitcoin-hard-disk-in-bin-7-years-on-he-wants-it-back/ retrieved January 2020.

[119] Zvi Schreiber. 2020. "k-Root-n: An Efficient Algorithm for Avoiding Short-term Double-Spending Alongside Distributed Ledger Technologies such as Blockchain." Information 11, no. 2:90. https://doi.org/10.3390/info11020090 retrieved January 2021.

[120] Wikipedia. Tulip Mania. https://en.wikipedia.org/wiki/Tulip_mania retrieved January 2021.

[121] Daniel Kahneman. 2011. *Thinking, Fast and Slow*. Farrar, Straus and Giroux. See also Cass R. Sunstein and Richard Thaler. December 7, 2016. *The Two Friends Who Changed How We Think About How We Think.* The New Yorker. https://www.newyorker.com/books/page-turner/the-two-friends-who-changed-how-we-think-about-how-we-think retrieved June 2021.

[122] Bryan Caplan. 2007. *Myth of the Rational Voter: Why Democracies Choose Bad Policies*. Princeton University Press.

[123] Wikipedia. *Rust Belt.* https://en.wikipedia.org/wiki/Rust_Belt retrieved January 2021.

[124] Robert R. Redfield, M.D., CDC Director. November 2018. "CDC Director's Media Statement on U.S. Life Expectancy." https://www.cdc.gov/media/releases/2018/s1129-US-life-expectancy.html retrieved February 2021.

[125] Irving Fisher. 1928. *The Money Illusion*. New York: Adelphi Company

[126] Wikipedia. *Money illusion.* https://en.wikipedia.org/wiki/Money_illusion retrieved December 2020.

[127] Phytoplankton type. 2010. *NASA Earth Observatory.* Public domain. https://commons.wikimedia.org/wiki/File:Phytoplankton_types.jpg retrieved December 2020.

[128] Leslie Hook. February 2019. "Surge in US economists' support for carbon tax to tackle emissions.

Democrats." *Financial Times.* https://www.ft.com/content/fa0815fe-3299-11e9-bd3a-8b2a211d90d5 retrieved January 2021.

[129] Wikipedia. *Carbon Tax.* https://en.wikipedia.org/wiki/Carbon_tax retrieved December 2020.

[130] David Coady, Ian Parry, Nghia-Piotr Le, Baoping Shang. May 2019. "Global Fossil Fuel Subsidies Remain Large: An Update Based on Country-Level Estimates." International Monetary Fund (IMF). https://www.imf.org/en/Publications/WP/Issues/2019/05/02/Global-Fossil-Fuel-Subsidies-Remain-Large-An-Update-Based-on-Country-Level-Estimates-46509 retrieved December 2020.

[131] UNESCO. 2019. "Global Education Monitoring Report (GEM)." https://gem-report-2019.unesco.org/chapter/finance/ retrieved December 2020.

[132] Anders Ydstedt, Elke Asen, Samuel Jonsson. September 2020. "Looking Back on 30 Years of Carbon Taxes in Sweden." *Tax Foundation.* https://taxfoundation.org/sweden-carbon-tax-revenue-greenhouse-gas-emissions/#:~:text=Economic%20Development,percent%20between%201990%20and%202019 retrieved January 2021.

[133] $132 times 36.8 billion tons of global CO_2 emissions is $4.8 trillion.

[134] Arthur Neslen. March, 2015. "Subsidies to industries that cause deforestation worth 100 times more than aid to prevent it." *The Guardian.* https://www.theguardian.com/environment/2015/mar/31/subsidies-to-industries-that-cause-deforestation-worth-100-times-more-than-aid-to-prevent-it retrieved December 2020.

[135] Will McFarland, Shelagh Whitley and Gabrielle Kissinger. March 2015. "Subsidies to key commodities driving forest loss: Implications for private climate finance." *ODI Working Paper*. https://www.odi.org/sites/odi.org.uk/files/odi-assets/publications-opinion-files/9577.pdf retrieved December 2020.

[136] "Emissions Gap Report 2020". *United Nations Environment Programme (UNEP)*. https://www.unenvironment.org/emissions-gap-report-2020 retrieved December 2020.

[137] FRED Economic Data. Federal Reserve of St. Louis. *Federal Debt: Total Public Debt as Percent of Gross Domestic Product*. https://fred.stlouisfed.org/series/GFDEGDQ188S retrieved December 2020.

[138] Minneapolis Fed President Neel Kashkari said this fairly explicitly on a recent Bloomberg Markets OddLots podcast: "If you look at our inflation target it was officially adopted in 2012 at two percent. We basically undershot two percent the entire time. We blew it. And so let's not raise rates this time until we actually get inflation sustainably back at our target."

[139] Wikipedia. *Modern Monetary Theory*. https://en.wikipedia.org/wiki/Modern_Monetary_Theory retrieved December 2020.

[140] Carl Benedikt Frey and Michael A. Osborne. September, 2013. "The future of employment: how susceptible are jobs to computerisation". https://www.oxfordmartin.ox.ac.uk/downloads/academic/The_Future_of_Employment.pdf retrieved December 2020.

[141] Nick Bostrom. July 2014. *Superintelligence: Paths, Dangers, Strategies*. https://en.wikipedia.org/wiki/Superintelligence:_Paths,_Dangers,_Strategies retrieved January 2021.

[142] Stuart J. Russell. October 2019. *Human Compatible*. Viking Press. https://en.wikipedia.org/wiki/Human_Compatible retrieved January 2021.

[143] Wikipedia. *2016 Swiss referendums: Basic income referendum*. https://en.wikipedia.org/wiki/2016_Swiss_referendums#Basic_income_referendum retrieved December 2020.